Language and Literary Structure

G000057136

How does a literary text get to have literary form, and what is the relation between literary form and linguistic form? This theoretical study of linguistic structure in literature focuses on verse and narrative from a linguistic perspective. Nigel Fabb provides a simple and realistic linguistic explanation of poetic form in English from 1500–1900, drawing on the English and American verse and oral narrative traditions, as well as contemporary criticism. In recent years literary theory has paid relatively little attention to form; this book argues that form is interesting. Fabb offers a new linguistic approach to how metre and rhythm work in poetry based on pragmatic theory, providing a pragmatic explanation of formal ambiguity and indeterminacy and their aesthetic effects. He also uses linguistics to examine the experience of poetry. *Language and Literary Structure* will be welcomed by students and researchers in linguistics, literary theory and stylistics.

NIGEL FABB is Professor of Literary Linguistics at the University of Strathclyde. He is the author of *Linguistics and Literature: Language in the Verbal Arts of the World* (1997), co-author of *Ways of Reading: Advanced Reading Skills for Students of English Literature* (2nd edn, 2000), and of four other books. He is also the author of the articles on linguistics and literature in the *International Encyclopedia of the Social and Behavioral Sciences* and the *Blackwell Handbook of Linguistics*.

Index of poets cited

Language and Literary Structure

The Linguistic Analysis of Form in Verse and Narrative

Nigel Fabb

CAMBRIDGE
UNIVERSITY PRESS

PUBLISHED BY THE PRESS SYNDICATE OF THE UNIVERSITY OF CAMBRIDGE
The Pitt Building, Trumpington Street, Cambridge, United Kingdom

CAMBRIDGE UNIVERSITY PRESS
The Edinburgh Building, Cambridge CB2 2RU, UK
40 West 20th Street, New York, NY 10011-4211, USA
477 Williamstown Road, Port Melbourne, VIC 3207, Australia
Ruiz de Alarcón 13, 28014 Madrid, Spain
Dock House, The Waterfront, Cape Town 8001, South Africa

http://www.cambridge.org

© Nigel Fabb 2002

First published 2002

Printed in the United Kingdom at the University Press, Cambridge

Typeface Times 10/12 pt.   *System* LATEX 2_ε [TB]

A catalogue record for this book is available from the British Library

ISBN 0 521 79294 0 hardback
ISBN 0 521 79698 9 paperback

For Janet

Contents

Acknowledgements

My first debt is to Morris Halle, who commented on parts of the typescript and introduced me to the theory outlined in chapter 1. I also wish to thank Alan Fabb, Janet Fabb, Barbara MacMahon, Anneke Neijt and particularly Margaret Fabb for their careful reading of parts of the manuscript.

For advice and help relating to the research project more generally I also thank Derek Attridge, Michael Broe, Curt Rice, Dell Hymes, John Smith and Deirdre Wilson. I acknowledge the use of T. V. F. Brogan's useful and (by Internet) freely available bibliography (Brogan 1981, 1999).

Material from this book was presented and benefited from audience comments at a course at the University of Tromsø, at the Toronto conference 'Formal Approaches to Poetry and Recent Developments in Generative Metrics', and the Linguistics Association of Great Britain and the Linguistic Society of America, and talks at the Universities of Durham, Edinburgh, Glasgow, Leeds, Manchester and Strathclyde.

I wrote this book during a year's research leave funded by the Arts and Humanities Research Board and by the University of Strathclyde. I thank my colleagues for their support during this period.

I thank Routledge (Taylor and Francis group) for permission to reproduce 'Drake's Cannon Ball' from Kathleen Briggs, *A Dictionary of British Folk Tales in the English Language* and Kathleen Briggs and Ruth L. Tongue, *Folktales of England.*

Note on texts used

Spelling and punctuation follow that in the edition used for each text, which is often taken from an anthology. Dating of texts is intended to give an approximate sense of when the texts were written, and is usually publication date, except where publication is long after writing.

Abbreviations

A letter before a number indicates one of the following anthologies (and page number).

F   Fowler, Alastair (ed.) 1991, *The New Oxford Book of Seventeenth Century Verse*. Oxford University Press.

J   Jones, Emrys (ed.) 1991, *The New Oxford Book of Sixteenth Century Verse*. Oxford University Press.

K   Karlin, Daniel (ed.) 1997, *The Penguin Book of Victorian Verse*. Harmondsworth: Penguin.

L   Lonsdale, Roger (ed.) 1987, *The New Oxford Book of Eighteenth Century Verse*. Oxford University Press.

S   Spengemann, William C, with Roberts, Jessica F. (eds.) 1996, *Nineteenth-Century American Poetry*. Harmondsworth: Penguin.

W   Wright, David (ed.) 1968, *The Penguin Book of English Romantic Verse*. Harmondsworth: Penguin.

In representations of rhythms and metres:

x   unstressed or weakly stressed syllable
/   stressed or strongly stressed syllable
˘   light syllable
—   heavy syllable
:   a word boundary must fall here
Δ   a symbol which is not projected

1   Literary form

1.1   What is literary form?

A text has literary form if certain statements are true of the text. Consider, for example, the following statements about a text:

> It is a sonnet.
>
> It is divided into lines.
>
> The lines are grouped by rhyme into a group of eight lines and a group of six lines.
>
> It is in iambic pentameter.

These statements are all true of the following text:

> Say over again, and yet once over again,
> That thou dost love me. Though the word repeated
> Should seem 'a cuckoo-song', as thou dost treat it.
> Remember, never to the hill or plain,
> Valley and wood, without her cuckoo-strain
> Comes the fresh Spring in all her green completed.
> Belovèd, I, amid the darkness greeted
> By a doubtful spirit-voice in that doubt's pain
> Cry, 'Speak once more – thou lovest!' Who can fear
> Too many stars, though each in heaven shall roll,
> Too many flowers, though each shall crown the year?
> Say thou dost love me, love me, love me – toll
> The silver iterance! – only minding, Dear,
> To love me also in silence with thy soul.

Elizabeth Barrett Browning, *Sonnets from*
the Portuguese, XXI, 1847–50
(Browning 1889:IV, 55)

In this book I ask what it means for these statements to be true of this text. More generally, how does literary form hold of a text? I will propose two different but compatible answers, which distinguish the variable from the invariant aspects of literary form. Both answers come from linguistics but from two different kinds of linguistics: generative metrics will explain the invariant aspects of form and linguistic pragmatics will explain the variable aspects of form.

The fact that there are two fundamentally different kinds of literary form, both of which can hold of a text, is a kind of formal multiplicity. This is just one among many kinds of formal multiplicity which we find wherever we find literary form. In this text another kind of formal multiplicity can be seen in the grouping of lines. The rhyme scheme of ABBAABBA+CDCDCD tells us that the text is grouped as 8+6 but punctuation and meaning tell us that the text is grouped as 6+8. The two divisions are incompatible and yet both hold to some extent of the text; this is possible because both groupings hold as interpretations of the text rather than as observer-independent facts about the text. In this way, literary form is seen to be a kind of meaning, a description of itself which the text communicates to its reader, and has all the complex characteristics associated with meaning: uncertainties, ambiguities and contradictions.

I suggest that we experience the inherent complexities and multiplicities of literary form as aesthetic. In this I follow Shklovsky . . .

The technique of art is to make objects 'unfamiliar', to make forms difficult, to increase the difficulty and length of perception because the process of perception is an aesthetic end in itself and must be prolonged. (Victor Shklovsky, 'Art as Technique', 1917 (Lemon and Reis 1965: 12))

. . . and Gascoigne:

the verse that is to easie is like a tale of a rosted horse (George Gasgoigne (1575:53))

Implied form, explicit form and generated metrical form

One kind of literary form which holds of this poem is 'being a sonnet' or sonnethood. In chapter 3 I show that sonnethood holds of a text with a certain degree of strength; in Browning's poem, sonnethood holds strongly. I propose that sonnethood is a kind of form which holds of a text by implicature; the text implies that it is a sonnet and hence the reader infers that it is a sonnet. This is the only sense in which it is a sonnet: the reader 'holds the text to be a sonnet' and as a result 'sonnethood holds of this text'. This is a kind of *implied form*. I will argue that many kinds of literary form are kinds of implied form. The notion of 'strength' is fundamental to this approach: all thoughts are held with a degree of strength corresponding to the thinker's commitment to their truth; the more strong the thinker's commitment, the more strongly the form holds of the text.

Another kind of form which holds of this text is 'being in lines' or lineation. Instances of this kind of form include 'there are fourteen lines in this text' and 'the first line ends on the word "again"'. These might seem to be facts about the text which exist independently of a reader, but in chapter 5 I will argue that they are all kinds of implied form which hold only by virtue of being inferred. The closest we can get to an observer-independent fact about the text is 'there are fourteen printed words which have no words to the right of them' and 'the word "again" has no words to the right of it'. Like the thoughts which are of implied form, I suggest that these also hold as thoughts about the text rather than just being determinate facts, but I acknowledge their relatively unmediated status by classifying them as *explicit form*.

'Rhyme' is a kind of form which holds of this poem and specifically the rhyme pattern ABBAABBACDCDCD. Is rhyme a kind of implied form or a kind of explicit form? Rhyme holds between syllables which are alike but need not be identical; here there is a rhyme between 'repeated' and 'treat it' which is based on the similarity between the sound sequence [i t ɪ d] and [i t ɪ t]. The fact that similarity is involved rather than identity means that rhyme has to be judged to be present, which suggests that it is a kind of implied form rather than a kind of explicit form. On the basis of inferring rhyme we can also infer that the poem falls into two groups, an eight-line group followed by a six-line group, each with separate rhyme patterns. The grouping of lines is another kind of implied form, the topic of chapter 6. There I show that even where lines are grouped by layout, grouping is still a kind of implied form, based on the explicit evidence drawn from the page. For all these kinds of implied form, one of the reasons for thinking that they are implied is that they can hold weakly of a text, and kinds of implied form can contradict one another. In this poem, the rhyme implies a division of the text into an eight-line unit and a six-line group, but the organisation of meaning, sentence structure and punctuation does not support this division of the text into parts; indeed, a division into a six-line unit followed by an eight-line unit is supported by these kinds of form. Complexities of this kind are found wherever we find literary form. They arise because literary form is implied. They are, I suggest, one source of aesthetic experience; as Thomas Hardy says, 'dissonances, and other irregularities can be produced advisedly, as art, and worked as to give more charm than strict conformities' (Taylor 1988:63).

Kinds of explicit form are all facts about a particular instance of the text, whether spoken or printed, and the kinds of explicit form vary according to whether the text is spoken or printed. I will refer to particular instances of a text as *performances* of it in any medium; the printed text given earlier is a performance of this text. A text can be realised by any number of different performances but if it is made of language then it also has an underlying linguistic representation. The linguistic representation of the text is the abstract representation of the sounds which comprise it (its phonological structure), the words from which it is made (its lexical structure), and the relations between those words (its syntactic structure). While a text may have any number of performances, it will normally have just a single underlying linguistic representation with discrete and determinate characteristics. In some kinds of literary text – most obviously, metrical verse – the underlying linguistic representation of the text seems to be the basis of another kind of literary form, which is the metrical form of the text. Metrical form is built by a set of rules and conditions, based on the underlying form of the text, and it fixes certain aspects of the text, most importantly the number of syllables in the line. In this book I assume generative linguistics (Chomsky 1957, Chomsky and Halle 1968) as a theory of linguistic form, and generative metrics (Halle and Keyser 1971, Halle 2001) as a theory of metrical form. This kind of metrical form of a text is a type of *generated form*; I usually call it the *generated metrical form* of the text, and describe it in the rest of this chapter.

Metricality

Metricality is a complex characteristic, a mixture of explicit, implied and generated form. To examine the explicit and implied metrical forms of a line from the poem, consider a performance in speech of the ninth line.

> Cry, 'Speak once more – thou lovest!' Who can fear

There are many possible ways of saying the line; one way of saying the line can be abstractly represented as a pattern of relatively unstressed syllables marked x, and relatively stressed syllables marked / as follows:

> /   /   x   /   x / x   / x   /
> Cry, 'Speak once more – thou lovest!' Who can fear

This is an abstract representation of an observable fact of a performance of the text. It is an example of what I call explicit form. Form is inherently abstract and general but this is as close to concrete and unique as form gets, expressing a specific characteristic of a specific instance of the text. The text can be spoken in other ways and when it is, it will have different explicit forms. Explicit form holds of a particular performance of the text, not of the text in the abstract.

This explicit form resembles a much more abstract and general version of the rhythm of a line, which could be represented like this:

> x / x / x / x / x /

This is a representation of a conventional metre called 'iambic pentameter', where there are ten syllables, with unstressed syllables in odd positions and stressed syllables in even positions. As a kind of form it is not tied to any specific text or performance (unlike the explicit form), but instead it holds as a kind of ideal or norm, a generalisation over many texts, and one of the things that we might know if we know about English poetry. The above representation is a metrical template for iambic pentameter. The explicit rhythm (a) resembles the metrical template (b); they have the same number of elements and differ in just one.

(a) / / x / x / x / x / explicit rhythm
(b) x / x / x / x / x / metrical template

We say that the performed line is 'in iambic pentameter' because the explicit rhythm (a) approximates fairly closely to the metrical template (b). This relation of resemblance or approximation can be understood as a relation of implication. The explicit form implies the metrical template by resembling it, and because the line implies the form, the form therefore holds of the text. Because the resemblance is not exact, the implicature is correspondingly weak, so that the rhythm of the line implies fairly strongly but not with full strength that it is in iambic pentameter. The relation between the explicit rhythm and the metrical template is tendential or approximate, which fits with the fact that iambic pentameter (as a normative rhythm) holds by being implied.

But there are also some facts about this line which are not tendencies or approximations but are rigid facts of the matter, true of this line and of every iambic pentameter line. The two facts are as follows.

Fact A.
A line has ten projected syllables.

Fact B.
A stressed syllable within a polysyllabic word must be projected syllable 2, 4, 6, 8 or 10 or is the first syllable in the line.

In the rest of this chapter I explain what these facts are (e.g. what a 'projected syllable' is) and show that they are true of Browning's poem. Together they constitute 'iambic pentameter' as a kind of generated metrical form. Thus the poem is 'in iambic pentameter' twice, in two different ways; 'iambic pentameter' holds of the text both as a kind of implied form and as a kind of generated metrical form. This is a kind of formal multiplicity, one of the many kinds of complexity which are characteristic of literary form, and which arise because literary form is a matter of the text's psychological reception and not inherent to the text itself.

1.2   Invariant facts about the iambic pentameter line

Facts A and B are not facts about a performance of the text, and may not hold true of any specific performance. The first line of Browning's text can be performed with ten, eleven or twelve syllables, which goes against fact A. This is because the word 'over' can be pronounced as one or two syllables (I symbolise the one-syllable pronunciation here as 'ov'r'):

> Say over again, and yet once over again,   12
> Say ov'r again, and yet once over again,   11
> Say over again, and yet once ov'r again,   11
> Say ov'r again, and yet once ov'r again,   10

Similarly, 'without' is a polysyllabic word, and while its natural stress is on the second syllable, we can pronounce it any way we like so that nothing prevents us pronouncing it with the first syllable given greatest stress:

> / x x   /   / x   x   / x   /
> Valley and wood, without her cuckoo-strain

If we perform the line like this, then it will have a stressed syllable within a polysyllabic word as its fifth syllable. This goes against fact B. Any text can be performed in a variety of ways, some of which might fit with facts A and B and some of which will not. More generally the fact that there is variation in performance means that if there are fixed facts about iambic pentameter lines, then these must be facts about something other than a performance of the line.

Performances of texts correspond to underlying abstract linguistic forms. The parts of the utterance, or performance, correspond to representations of sound (its phonological representations), of words (its lexical and morphological representations), and of phrases and sentences (its syntactic representations). Linguistic representations are more abstract than their instantiations as actual bits of speech or writing, and can also be less fully specified. This is true of both syllabification and stress. In an utterance, the word 'over' can be pronounced as one or two syllables, but there is an abstract level of representation for the word (its lexical entry, where the word is stored in memory) where the word always has two syllables. A syllable may be present or absent in performance but it is always present in the lexical entry. This means that for a given line of poetry we can construct a completely stable and invariant representation of the line which has a specific number of syllables; whether these syllables are all pronounced or not is irrelevant (if we see the linguistic representation as prior to performance then the pronunciation 'hasn't happened yet'). Only once we have a stable number of syllables can we begin to say how many syllables there are in the line of text.

The same applies to stress. Stress is a relational characteristic: rather than being an isolated phonetic fact of the syllable, the stress of a syllable is relative to the syllables which surround it. If we look just at words in isolation, then syllables within a polysyllable will have stress, and one syllable will have greatest stress. But monosyllables will not have stress at all in isolation, because there is nothing for the stress to be relative to. It is only once we put monosyllables into sequence that some are more stressed than others. This difference between polysyllables and monosyllables means that we can construct a representation of the sentence in which syllables in polysyllables have stress but syllables in monosyllables do not. There is a second difference between polysyllables and monosyllables, which is that how monosyllables are stressed is to a much greater degree a matter of performance than the stressing of specific syllables in polysyllables (which tend to be invariant). Here are four different ways of performing one of the lines from the poem, which illustrates that stress on monosyllables varies from performance to performance:

/   x /   / x / x / x   / x
Comes the fresh Spring in all her green completed.

/   x x   / x x x /   x   / x
Comes the fresh Spring in all her green completed.

/   x x   / x / x /   x   / x
Comes the fresh Spring in all her green completed.

x   / x   / x / x /   x   / x
Comes the fresh Spring in all her green completed.

The fact that monosyllables are not fixed in their relative stress has long been recognised, along with its significance for metrical form. Thus King James VI of Scotland says of monosyllables that 'the maist pairt of thame are indifferent, and may be in short or lang place, as ye like' (1584:215). Similarly John Rice says that '*Accent*, properly speaking, and considered as distinct from *Emphasis*, hath nothing to do with *Monosyllables*' (1765:89).

Thus we can only begin to state invariant facts about the iambic pentameter line if we state them in terms of an abstract linguistic representation of the line, rather than by reference to any of the actual performances of the line.

1.3   There are ten metrified syllables in the iambic pentameter line

An abstract linguistic representation of all the lines in Browning's poem gives a count of between ten and twelve syllables in the line. I indicate each syllable with an x below the line, and put the count in the left-hand margin.

Say over again, and yet once over again,   1
12   x x x x x   x   x x   x x   x x

That thou dost love me. Though the word repeated   2
11   x   x   x   x   x   x   x x   x x x

Should seem 'a cuckoo song', as thou dost treat it.   3
11   x   x   x x x   x   x   x   x   x   x

Remember, never to the hill or plain,   4
10   x x   x   x x   x   x x x   x

Valley and wood, without her cuckoo-strain   5
10   x x x   x   x x   x   x x   x

Comes the fresh Spring in all her green completed.   6
11   x   x x   x   x x   x   x   x   x x

Belovèd, I, amid the darkness greeted   7
11   x x x   x x x   x x   x   x x

By a doubtful spirit-voice in that doubt's pain   8
11   x x x   x   x x   x   x x   x   x

Cry, 'Speak once more – thou lovest!' Who can fear   9
10   x   x   x   x   x   x x   x   x   x

Too many stars, though each in heaven shall roll,   10
11   x   x x x   x   x   x x x   x   x

Too many flowers, though each shall crown the year?   11
11   x   x x x x   x   x   x   x   x x

Say thou dost love me, love me, love me – toll   12
10   x   x x x   x x   x x   x   x

The silver iterance! – only minding, Dear,   13
11   x x   x x x x   x   x   x   x   x

To love me also in silence with thy soul.   14
11   x x   x x   x x   x x   x   x x

In this representation of the lines, the syllables vary in number from ten to twelve. I will now present a set of rules which when applied are able to transform this into a metrical representation in which there are exactly ten syllables in every line. These are the projection and non-projection rules.

This is the projection rule (the non-projection rules state limited exceptions to it):

Projection rule
Project a syllable as an asterisk.

This means writing an asterisk beneath each syllable. For line 4, it has the following result:

Remember, never to the hill or plain,
*   *   *   * *   *   * * *   *

The asterisks are counted. Here there are ten asterisks.

The first non-projection rule (which is sometimes called 'extrametricality') is:

Non-projection rule (a)
Do not project a syllable at the (right-hand) end of the line which is unstressed or weak in stress and which comes after a strongly stressed syllable.

If we apply this to the poem then lines 2, 3, 6 and 7 will each have their rightmost syllable not projected and hence not counted, which will bring them to ten syllables each. Here for example is the metrical representation of line 2. Syllables which are projected have ∗ beneath them, and syllables which are not projected are marked for convenience by putting Δ beneath them.

```
            That thou dost love me. Though the word repeated   2
(a)   10     ∗   ∗   ∗   ∗     ∗   ∗     ∗  ∗   ∗ ∗ Δ
```

The number of syllables is now 10, indicated in the left margin, where I have also indicated that non-projection rule (a) has applied to the line.

We can apply another non-projection rule (which is sometimes called 'synaloepha').

Non-projection rule (b)
Optionally: do not project a syllable which ends on a vowel, when that syllable precedes a syllable which begins on a vowel.

This rule looks for certain sequences of syllables and whenever it finds such a sequence it can choose not to project the first syllable. Consider for example line 8.

```
            By a doubtful spirit-voice in that doubt's pain   8
11     x x  x    x   x x  x   x  x    x         x
```

Here there is a syllable ending in a vowel ('by') which precedes a syllable beginning in a vowel ('a'). If the rule chooses not to project the first syllable, this will be the metrical representation, with ten projected syllables.

```
            By  a doubtful spirit-voice in that doubt's pain   8
(b)   10     Δ ∗  ∗    ∗   ∗∗  ∗   ∗   ∗    ∗        ∗
```

If the rule does choose to project the first syllable, this will be the metrical representation, with eleven projected syllables.

```
            By a doubtful spirit-voice in that doubt's pain   8
11     ∗ ∗  ∗    ∗   ∗∗  ∗   ∗   ∗    ∗        ∗
```

I suggest that optional rules like (b) apply where necessary in order to bring the number of syllables to the right number, here applying to bring the number of syllables to ten.

We also need a third rule which applies to syllables based on certain sounds (i.e. sonorants) which they contain:

Non-projection rule (c)
Optionally: do not project a syllable which has as its nucleus one of the following sonorant consonants: [l], [r], [m] or [n], or which has as its nucleus the weak vowel [ə] followed by one of these sounds.

This rule applies in line 1 to 'over' [oʊvər] which has its second syllable twice omitted from the count. It applies in line 10 to 'heaven' [hɛvən] which has its second syllable omitted from the count. It applies in line 11 to 'flowers' [flaʊwəɹz] which has its second syllable omitted from the count. It applies in line 13 to 'iterance' [ɪtəɹəns] which has its second syllable omitted from the count. In all cases, these applications bring the number of syllables to ten. This is the first line:

```
                 Say over again, and yet once over again,   1
      c,c   10    *  * Δ * *   *    * *    * Δ  * *
```

Again, the rule applies optionally. In principle it could apply also in line 4, to 'remember' and to 'never'. If it did, it would bring the number of syllables to eight:

```
                 Remember, never to the hill or plain,   4
      c,c   8     *  *   Δ  * Δ *  * * *   *
```

This shows that the non-projection rule must be allowed to apply optionally. In line 4 we do not want it to apply; if it fails to apply there will be the required ten syllables.

We now have three rules, of which (b) and (c) apply optionally. These rules can be applied to the text to derive the following metrical representation of the text in which all lines have ten syllables. The left-hand margin indicates which rule has applied.

```
                 Say over again, and yet once over again,        1
      c,c   10    *  * Δ * *   *    * *   * Δ   * *

                 That thou dost love me. Though the word repeated  2
      a    10     *   *   *   *    *    *     * *   * * Δ

                 Should seem 'a cuckoo song', as thou dost treat it.  3
      a    10     *    *    * * *   *    *    *   *   * Δ

                 Remember, never to the hill or plain,            4
           10     *  *   *   * * *  * * *   *

                 Valley and wood, without her cuckoo-strain       5
           10     * * *    *    * *   * * *    *
```

		Comes the fresh Spring in all her green completed.	6
a	10	* * * * * * * * * *Δ	

		Belovèd, I, amid the darkness greeted	7
a	10	* * * * * * * * * * Δ	

		By a doubtful spirit-voice in that doubt's pain	8
b	10	Δ* * * ** * * * * *	

		Cry, 'Speak once more – thou lovest!' Who can fear	9
	10	* * * * * ** * * *	

		Too many stars, though each in heaven shall roll,	10
c	10	* ** * * * ** Δ * *	

		Too many flowers, though each shall crown the year?	11
c	10	* ** * Δ * * * * *	

		Say thou dost love me, love me, love me – toll	12
	10	* * * * ** ** * *	

		The silver iterance! – only minding, Dear,	13
c	10	* * * *Δ* * * * * *	

		To love me also in silence with thy soul.	14
b	10	* * ** Δ* ** * *	

Most syllables project and a few (belonging to specific subclasses) do not. This has nothing to do with pronunciation: the syllables which are not projected can be pronounced or not pronounced. Instead, it is a fact about the abstract metrical representation of this poem that 'a line has ten syllables.' This is fact A (p. 5).

1.4   The placement of stressed syllables in polysyllabic words

In iambic pentameter (and other strict metres), there is strict control over the placement of the syllable carrying greatest stress in a polysyllable. In contrast, stressed monosyllables are not strictly controlled. This difference correlates with a difference in the predictability of the stress: within a polysyllabic word we can always predict as a fact about the underlying representation of the word which syllable has greatest stress, while stress on a monosyllable is not as predictable (it depends on its context in the utterance). The fact that polysyllables are fixed in place is a fact which has been recognised since the earliest metrical theory. George Gascoigne recognises that polysyllabic stress is invariant, saying for example that 'this word *Treasure* hath the graue accent vpon the first sillable' (1575:49). He understands the implication for metre:

> Yoùr méanìng Í vndérstànd bý yoùr éye.
> ... The fault of the latter verse is that this worde *vnderstand* is therein so placed as the graue accent falleth upon *der*, and therby maketh *der* in this worde *vnderstand* to be

eleuated; which is contrarie to the naturall or vsual pronunciation, for we say *vndèrstánd*, and not *vndérstànd*.

In contrast he says of monosyllables that 'woordes of one syllable will more easily fall to be shorte or long as occasion requireth'.

I show where the stressed syllables in polysyllables are in the Browning text; they are double-underlined:

		Say over again, and yet once over again,	1
c,c	10	* * Δ * *　*　* *　* Δ　* *	
		That thou dost love me. Though the word repeated	2
a	10	*　*　*　*　*　*　* *　* * Δ	
		Should seem 'a cuckoo song', as thou dost treat it.	3
a	10	*　*　* * * *　*　*　*　* Δ	
		Remember, never to the hill or plain,	4
	10	* *　*　* * * *　* *　*	
		Valley and wood, without her cuckoo-strain	5
	10	* * *　*　* *　*　*　*　*	
		Comes the fresh Spring in all her green completed.	6
a	10	*　* *　* * *　*　*　* Δ	
		Belovèd, I, amid the darkness greeted	7
a	10	* * * * * *　* *　*　* Δ	
		By a doubtful spirit-voice in that doubt's pain	8
b	10	Δ * *　*　* *　*　* *　*	
		Cry, 'Speak once more – thou lovest!' Who can fear	9
	10	*　* *　*　* * *　* * *	
		Too many stars, though each in heaven shall roll,	10
c	10	* * * *　*　*　* * Δ　* *	
		Too many flowers, though each shall crown the year?	11
c	10	* * * * Δ　*　*　*　*　*　*	
		Say thou dost love me, love me, love me – toll	12
	10	*　* * *　* *　* *　* *	
		The silver iterance! – only minding, Dear,	13
c	10	* * * *Δ*　* * * *　*	
		To love me also in silence with thy soul.	14
b	10	* *　* * Δ * * *　*　* *	

The stressed syllables in polysyllables appear only in certain positions: the first position or one of the even-numbered positions. This is shown in the left-hand column of Table 1.1:

Table 1.1 *Placement of stressed syllables in polysyllables*

line	if the line is counted as ten syllables (i.e. excluding non-projected syllables)	if the line is counted as between ten and twelve syllables (i.e. counting all syllables)
1	2, 4, 8, 10	2, 5, 9, 12
2	10	10
3	4	4
4	2, 4	2, 4
5	1, 6, 8	1, 6, 8
6	10	10
7	2, 6, 8, 10	2, 6, 8, 10
8	2, 4	3, 5
9	6	6
10	2, 8	2, 8
11	2, 4	2, 4
12	–	–
13	2, 4, 6, 8	2, 4, 7, 9
14	4, 6	4, 7

I have included the right-hand column to show that the polysyllables are placed regularly only if they are placed relative to the ten projected syllables, not relative to all syllables in the line. This means that first we must build a representation of the line as having ten syllables each, and then we must state the distribution of polysyllables relative to this count.

In the rest of this chapter I first show how the projected syllables are counted. Then I show how, relative to the count, the stressed syllables in polysyllables are placed.

1.5   How to count up to ten

It is true of almost all iambic pentameter lines that they have ten projected syllables. That is, we can do to almost every line of iambic pentameter what we did to the Browning poem, with the same results. More generally, a fact about all metrical verse is that the line, when viewed in a certain way, has a fixed length. There are very few invariant facts about literary form, but this is one of them. Because it is an invariant fact, I propose that it is dealt with by a special mechanism involving some specialised kind of 'metrical cognition' as one of the types of linguistic cognition.

In generative linguistics, linguistic cognition is explained by writing rules. I will take a generative approach, part of the generative metrics tradition, specifically the theory formulated by Halle and Keyser (1999) and Halle (2001). This means that I will write rules which for an iambic pentameter line count exactly ten projected syllables. Our metrical representation represents the line as a series of asterisks, so we can count these (i.e. ignoring the triangles). One rule which gets the right effect is:

Start at the left end of the line of asterisks and count up to ten asterisks, then stop. This must be the end of the line of asterisks.

While this is probably the simplest way of counting up to ten, I will show that it is not the actual way in which the line is counted up to ten. Instead, the line is counted by counting no more than two or three asterisks at a time, and counting several times over.

What follows is a set of rules. The first step is to take a line with its syllables projected as a line of asterisks; I call the line of asterisks 'gridline 0'.

> Remember, never to the hill or plain,
> * * * * * * * * * *   gridline 0

The next step is to begin the count by counting just two at a time.

Rule A. Insert a right bracket at the right-hand edge of the gridline, skip two asterisks, insert a right bracket, and repeat until the rule can no longer be applied.

The rule is an 'iterative' rule (it repeats across the line until it gets to the end of the line); below are the first couple of iterations and the last iteration. I have added < in the right margin to indicate that the brackets are inserted from the right-hand side.

> first iteration:
> Remember, never to the hill or plain,
> * * * * * * * * *) gridline 0 <
> second iteration
> Remember, never to the hill or plain,
> * * * * * * *)* *) gridline 0 <
> final iteration
> Remember, never to the hill or plain,
>)* *) * *)* *) * *)* *) gridline 0 <

It might seem odd to be inserting the brackets from the right-hand side of the line since this would be the last part of the line to be spoken. But this is not a spoken form of the line, not a performance; instead it is an abstract representation of the line with a right-hand side and a left-hand side and with no particular priority put on left over right. There is a reason for inserting right brackets and inserting them from the right-hand side; I explain it on p. 23.

By putting brackets into the line, we have created feet. A *foot* is a sequence of asterisks beginning in a left bracket or ending in a right bracket. This formalism is due to Idsardi (1992); see also Halle and Idsardi (1995). Idsardi's crucial simplification is to have a foot defined by one bracket at either end of the foot, rather than by an opening and a closing bracket at each end of the foot. This incidentally means that feet are not 'constituents', in the sense that feet cannot be contained inside other feet, cannot overlap and so on.

Thus there are five feet in this line. Note that even if we were to leave out the leftmost bracket there would still be five feet – a foot only needs one bracket to be defined, so the leftmost pair of asterisks are defined as in a foot by the bracket which follows them

$$) * *) * *) * *) * *) * *)$$ five feet
$$* *) * *) * *) * *) * *)$$ five feet

If however we were to leave out the rightmost bracket there would be four feet; the rightmost pair of asterisks here are not in a foot because they are not to the right of a left bracket or to the left of a right bracket.

$$* *) * *) * *) * *) * *$$ four feet

Feet can be ternary or binary (and exceptionally unary). The feet we have just built at gridline 0 are binary feet.

Now we apply a new rule. Each foot is represented by an asterisk on another gridline, which will enable us to count feet. We represent feet by projecting one asterisk from each foot. The asterisk in the foot which is chosen to project is called the *head*. In this metre, the rightmost asterisk projects. I explain why on p. 18.

Rule B. Project the rightmost asterisk in each foot to gridline 1.

This is the result:

Remember, never to the hill or plain,
$$) * *) * *)* *) * *)* *)$$ gridline 0
$$* * * * *$$ gridline 1

We can summarise the rules seen so far by table 1.2:

Table 1.2 *Rules for the first gridline in iambic pentameter*

	bracket	foot size	direction	head
Line 0	)	binary	R>L	right

These kinds of rule are the basic kinds of rule in all metres. Now we use the same kinds of rule (but with some changes) to build more structure.

The next step is to put brackets into gridline 1. This time I will insert them by a rule skipping three asterisks at a time, and will add a condition that the leftmost foot must fall short: it will contain two asterisks. At this level of structure it actually makes relatively little difference how the rules are written, so long as there are five gridline 0 feet. The rule is:

Rule C. Insert a right bracket at the right-hand edge of the gridline, skip three asterisks, insert a right bracket, and repeat until the rule can no longer be applied. The left-hand foot must contain two asterisks.

This gives us the following structure:

```
        Remember, never to the hill or plain,
        )*   *)   *   *)*   *)   *   *)*      *  )    gridline 0
             *        *)   *       *         *  )    gridline 1 <
```

We project heads right again, by rule D (which similar to rule B):

Rule D. Project the rightmost asterisk in each foot to gridline 2.

This gives us the following structure:

```
        Remember, never to the hill or plain,
        ) *   *)   *   *)*   * )   *   *)*      *  )    gridline 0
              *        *)   *        *         *  )    gridline 1
                       *                       *       gridline 2
```

Now we insert brackets again by rule E which is the same as rule A:

Rule E. Insert a right bracket at the right-hand edge of the gridline, skip two asterisks, insert a right bracket, and repeat until the rule can no longer be applied.

Which gives us:

```
        Remember, never to the hill or plain,
        )*   *)   *   *)*   * )   *   *)*      *  )    gridline 0
             *        *)   *        *         *  )    gridline 1
         )                *                   *  )    gridline 2 <
```

And project a head, by rule F which is similar to rules B and D:

Rule D. Project the rightmost asterisk in each foot to gridline 3.

This gives us a complete grid because there is nothing left to count. This is a complete scansion of the line.

```
        Remember, never to the hill or plain,
        )*   *)   *   *)*   * )   *   *)*      *  )    gridline 0
             *        *)   *        *         *  )    gridline 1
         )                *                   *  )    gridline 2
                                              *       gridline 3
```

This is a summary of the rules:

Table 1.3 *Grid-building rules for iambic pentameter*

	bracket	foot size	direction	head	final foot built
line 0	)	binary	R>L	right	
line 1	)	ternary	R>L	right	binary
line 2	)	binary	R>L	right	
1	2	3	4	5	6

Column by column, these tell us (1) which gridline is involved, (2) whether a right or left bracket is inserted, (3) whether the rule skips two or three asterisks at a time, (4) which direction the rule goes in, whether from left to right or right to left across the gridline, (5) which asterisk in the foot is the head, rightmost or leftmost. Column (6) states exceptions, with the final foot constructed permitted to fall short.

If there are ten asterisks on gridline 0, these rules will successfully construct a scansion of the line. If there are more or fewer than ten, the rules will not be able to build a grid for the line. Thus these rules can count ten syllables. In the next section, we see that there is evidence that the line is indeed counted by building a grid.

1.6   The placement of polysyllables

The placement of polysyllables in the iambic pentameter line is another fully regular fact: their stressed syllables can only appear in some positions (1, 2, 4, 6, 8, 10) and are unable to appear in others. Because of its regularity, this, like the counting of the line, will need to be formulated as a rule. I suggest we separate out two cases:

Regularity (i). A stressed syllable in a polysyllabic word can appear in the first (leftmost) position.

Regularity (ii). Otherwise, a stressed syllable in a polysyllabic word can appear only in an even-numbered position.

Now we see the advantage of building a grid to count the line. The grid is built in a way which differentiates structurally between even and odd syllables. An even-numbered syllable is a syllable which projects to gridline 1, while an odd-numbered syllable does not. This means that we can reformulate regularity (ii) as:

A stressed syllable in a polysyllabic word must project to gridline 1.

This is the line we scanned, with the stressed syllables in polysyllables underlined:

```
Remember, never to the hill or plain,
)*   *)  *   *)*  *)  *  *)*    *)   gridline 0
      *        *)   *     *      *)   gridline 1
   )          *                  *)   gridline 2
                                 *    gridline 3
```

In this scansion it is true that a stressed syllable in a polysyllabic word (the
second syllable in 'remember' and the first syllable in 'never') projects to
gridline 1. Note that the syllable 'to' also projects to gridline 1 but it is not a
stressed syllable in a polysyllabic word and is not even likely to be stressed
if performed (though this is a performance choice). In effect the rule means:
Any syllable CAN project to gridline 1 but a stressed syllable in a polysyllabic
word MUST project to gridline 1. Note again that these conditions do not say
anything at all about how the line is performed. They relate to the underlying,
abstract linguistic form of the line. In this way we can see that the control
over polysyllables is dependent on the way that the line is counted. This is a
fundamental point: the counting out of the line builds structure which can then
be exploited by other aspects of the metre such as the placement of stressed
syllables.

We need a way of allowing a stressed syllable in a polysyllable also to appear
in first (leftmost) position even though this is not a position which projects to
gridline 1. I adapt Halle and Keyser's (1971:169) notion of stress maximum,
which redefines the relevant syllable so as to exclude line-initial syllables from
consideration.

Definition (iambic pentameter)
    A stressed syllable in a polysyllabic word is a *stress maximum* if it is preceded in a
    line by a syllable of lesser stress.
Condition (iambic pentameter)
    A stress maximum must project to gridline 1.

This means that if we take line 5, we have three syllables which are stressed
syllables in polysyllabic words (underlined) but only two are stress maxima
(the first syllable in 'valley' is not). Only the two stress maxima must project
to gridline 1.

```
Valley and wood, without her cuckoo-strain
)*   *)  *    *)     *  *)   *  *)  *    *)   0
      *        *)       *       *        *)   1
   )          *                          *)   2
                                         *    3
```

If we now look at the scansions for the whole poem, we can see that the condition holds true throughout.

Say over again, and yet once over again,
```
)*   *  Δ)* *)   *     *)*     *)Δ * *)              0
        *)        *)        *        *      *)         1
)                 *                          *)         2
                                             *          3
```

That thou dost love me. Though the word repeated
```
)  *    *)  *    *)    *    *)      *  *)   * *) Δ    0
        *)        *)        *)           *      *)       1
)                 *                             *)       2
                                               *         3
```

Should seem 'a cuckoo song', as thou dost treat it.
```
)  *       *)    *  *) *   *)    *    *)  *    *)  Δ   0
        *)        *)    *        *       *)       1
)                 *                       *)       2
                                          *        3
```

Remember, never to the hill or plain,
```
)*   *)   *    *)*  *)  * *)*    *)                0
        *)        *)   *    *      *)               1
)                 *                 *)               2
                                    *                3
```

Valley and wood, without her cuckoo-strain
```
)*   *) *     *)    * *)   *  *) *    *)           0
        *)        *)        *      *      *)         1
)                 *                          *)       2
                                             *        3
```

Comes the fresh Spring in all her green completed.
```
)*          *) *      *) * *)  *   *)   *   *)Δ    0
        *)        *)    *        *        *)       1
)                 *                       *)       2
                                          *        3
```

Belovèd, I, amid the darkness greeted
```
)* *)*   *)* *)   * *)   *       *) Δ             0
        *    *)  *      *         *)               1
)        *                        *)               2
                                   *                3
```

By a doubtful spirit-voice in that doubt's pain
```
)Δ *  *)    *     *)* *)  * *)   *        *)      0
        *         *)  *       *         *)         1
)                 *                          *)     2
                                             *      3
```

Cry, 'Speak once more – thou lovest!' Who can fear

```
) *    *) *     *)     *  *)*        *) *  *)    0
       *       *)         *        *   *)    1
)              *                       *)    2
                                        *    3
```

Too many stars, though each in heaven shall roll,

```
) *  *)*  *)    *    *)    *  *) Δ   *  *)    0
     *    *)        *        *        *)      1
)         *                           *)      2
                                       *      3
```

Too many flowers, though each shall crown the year?

```
) *   *)*  *)Δ     *    *)    *   *)   *  *)   0
      *    *)          *          *      *)    1
)          *                             *)    2
                                          *    3
```

Say thou dost love me, love me, love me – toll

```
) *    *) *   *)   * *)   * *)   *  *)    0
       *      *)   *      *      *)       1
)             *                  *)       2
                                 *        3
```

The silver iterance! – only minding, Dear,

```
) * *)* *)Δ*     *) *  *) *     *)    0
    *   *)    *    *       *)         1
)       *                  *)         2
                           *          3
```

To love me also in silence with thy soul.

```
)* *)    **) Δ* *)*     *)   * *)    0
    *     *)   *    *      *)         1
)         *               *)         2
                          *          3
```

This is the generated metrical form of this poem. It is constructed by generative metrical rules, consisting of projection rules, grid-building rules and the stress maximum condition. The generated metrical form of a poem captures the invariant aspects of its form. It does not capture all aspects of its metrical or rhythmic form, including aspects of the way the line is performed; these are explained further in chapter 4.

1.7   Rules for other strict English metres

Metrical rules for iambic lines of different lengths

Iambic pentameter lines have ten projected syllables. Other common types of iambic line have six, eight or twelve syllables. These types of metre can be built by small changes to the metrical rules given so far. The changes all involve the iterative bracket-insertion rules for gridline 1. Other rules are the same; in particular, the rule for placement of stress maxima is the same.

Edmund Spenser ends his stanzas in *The Faerie Queen* with an iambic hexameter line, a line with twelve projected syllables. We can generate the grid for this line by changing the iambic pentameter rule for gridline 1:

Table 1.4 *Iambic pentameter rule:*

	bracket	foot size	direction	head	final foot built
Line 1	)	ternary	R>L	right	binary

Table 1.5 *Iambic hexameter rule:*

	bracket	foot size	direction	head	final foot built
Line 1	)	ternary	R>L	right	

This gives us a set of rules as follows, and a grid as shown.

Table 1.6 *Iambic hexameter*

	bracket	foot size	direction	head	final foot built
line 0	)	binary	R>L	right	
line 1	)	ternary	R>L	right	
line 2	)	binary	R>L	right	

```
     Of huge Sea monsters, such as liuing sense dismayd
)*   *)    *    *)   *    *)   *  *)*   *)     *   *)    0<
)    *          *         *)        *     *          *)    1<
)                         *                         *)    2<
                                                    *     3
```

Edmund Spenser, The Faerie Queene, 1590 (J:251)

To get iambic tetrameter (eight projected syllables to the line) we again make an alteration at gridline 1, to build binary rather than ternary feet:

Table 1.7 *Iambic hexameter rule:*

	bracket	foot size	direction	head
Line 1	)	ternary	R>L	right

Table 1.8 *Iambic tetrameter rule:*

Line 1	)	binary	R>L	right

This gives us a grid and scansion as follows:

Table 1.9 *Iambic tetrameter*

	bracket	foot size	direction	head	final foot built
line 0	)	binary	R>L	right	
line 1	)	binary	R>L	right	
line 2	)	binary	R>L	right	

```
Love guards the roses of thy lips
)*      *)      * *)* *)   * *)    0 <
)       *       *)   *     *)     1 <
)               *         *)      2 <
                          *       3
```

Thomas Lodge, 'Love Guards . . .', 1593 (J:434)

To get iambic trimeter (six projected syllables to the line), we build ternary feet at gridline 1 (like hexameter) and (unlike hexameter) have no gridline 2 rule:

Table 1.10 *Iambic trimeter*

	bracket	foot size	direction	head	final foot built
line 0	)	binary	R>L	right	
line 1	)	ternary	R>L	right	

```
Man doth usurp all space
   *  *)  * *)  *    *)    0
)      *     *      *)    1
                    *     2
```

Henry Sutton, 'Man', 1886 (K:423)

All lengths of line can be built in this manner.

Metrical rules for iambic lines with odd numbers of syllables

A fairly common kind of metrical line in English has an odd number of syllables and can begin and end on a stressed syllable. The most common form is the seven-syllable line, and I will call this metre 'sevens'.

The sharp law that steers our life
     *   *   *   *   *   *   *
Was the sacrifising knife.
     *   * * ***   *

Robert Davenport, 'A Sacrifice', early seventeenth century (F:344)

These lines can be analysed as iambic tetrameter lines with the leftmost foot unary. The line is said to be 'headless' if it is missing its initial syllable, as here. These are the rules:

Table 1.11 *Iambic tetrameter, headless*

	bracket	foot size	direction	head	final foot built
line 0	)	binary	R>L	right	unary
line 1	)	binary	R>L	right	
line 2	)	binary	R>L	right	

Since feet are constructed from right to left the final foot built will be the foot at the left edge (i.e. in another sense the beginning) of the line.

The sharp law that steers our life
  *) *   *)   *   *)   *   *)   0 <
) *   *)   *   *)   1 <
)   *   *)   2 <
                      *   3

Was the sacrifising knife.
  *) * *) **)*   *)   0 <
) *   *) *   *)   1 <
)   *   *)   2 <
               *   3

The fact that iambic lines can lose their initial syllable is the strongest reason for concluding that right brackets should be inserted from right to left. This means that the final foot constructed will be the leftmost, at the beginning of the line, and so this foot is permitted to fall short. Other possibilities – inserting left brackets or from left to right – would not achieve this.

Trochaic metres

In a trochaic metre, the stress maxima are in odd-numbered rather than even-numbered positions, and the line characteristically ends on an unstressed syllable. The following rules will, for example, generate trochaic tetrameter:

Table 1.12 *Trochaic tetrameter*

	bracket	foot size	direction	head	final foot built
line 0	(	binary	L>R	left	optionally unary
line 1	(	binary	L>R	right	
line 2	(	binary	L>R	right	

Note some fundamental differences from the rules seen so far: left brackets are inserted and they are inserted from left to right. The reason for this is that in a trochaic metre it is the rightmost foot which can fall short. This is illustrated by the second line below. Both lines have four feet at gridline 0; the second line has a rightmost foot containing just one asterisk (i.e. unary).

In the dark brown wood beyond us,
```
(*   *(*    *   (*    *(*   *   (    0 >
(*    *         (*         *     (    1 >
(          *              *     (    2 >
                           *         3
```

Where the night lies dusk and deep;
```
(   *    *(*   *   (*   *(   *        0 >
(   *    *         (*        *   (    1 >
(          *                 *   (    2 >
                             *       3
```

Mary Howitt, 'The Dor-Hawk', 1838 (K:47)

Note furthermore that it is the left-hand asterisk in a gridline 0 foot which projects. This means that odd-numbered asterisks project to gridline 1. If we assume the same requirement as for iambic metres, that the stress maximum must project to gridline 1, then this fits with projecting the left asterisk in the foot to gridline 1, as any stress maxima are in odd-numbered positions. The following line illustrates this, as well as showing that in principle any syllable can project to gridline 1 and that some syllables are not counted; both are just as in iambic metres.

The great traveller, the great boaster,
```
(   *   *   (*Δ*   (*   *   (*   *(   0
(   *        *     (*       *    (    1
(               *               *    (    2
                           *         3
```

Henry Wadsworth Longfellow, *Hiawatha*, 1855 (S:66)

Anapaestic metre

In an anapaestic metre, any stress maxima are placed three syllables apart or multiples of three syllables apart. This suggests that gridline 0 feet are ternary, with brackets inserted after every three syllables (rather than every two syllables as before). Anapaestic lines can also fall short at the beginning of the line (like iambic metres) which suggests that they involve the insertion of right brackets from right to left. The following are the rules:

Table 1.13 *Anapaestic tetrameter*

	bracket	foot size	direction	head	final foot built
line 0	)	ternary	R>L	right	optionally binary or unary
line 1	)	binary	R>L	right	
line 2	)	binary	R>L	right	

These rules give us the option of having a full ternary foot at the left edge of gridline 0 as in the first of these lines, or a binary foot as in the second. These are the two most common variants (often within a single poem); it is also possible to find anapaestic lines with a unary initial foot.

```
There comes Poe, with his raven, like Barnaby Rudge,
)*    *      *)   *   *  *)*   *   *) * *  *)     0 <
)            *        *)         *       *)      1 <
)                     *                  *)      2 <
                                          *      3
Three fifths of him genius and two fifths sheer fudge,
    *  *)  *   *   *)Δ*  *   *) *      *  *)     0 <
)      *        *)         *          *)         1 <
)              *                       *)         2 <
                                        *        3
```

James Russell Lowell, 'A Fable for Critics', 1848 (S:155)

As for the iambic and trochaic metres, the stress maximum rule applies. This requires any stressed syllables in polysyllabic words to project to gridline 1. Other syllables can also project to gridline 1. Again it is worth repeating that this is not a matter of performance or meaning, but of how the words are placed in the line, based on their syllable structure. Thus consider the following line, as scanned by the rules:

```
She paid English or Dutch or French down on the nail,
 *  *  *)  *  *   *)   *   *      *)  *   *  *)   0 <
       *         *)               *       *)     1 <
                 *)                        *)     2 <
                 *                         *      3
```

Matthew Prior, 'Jinny the Just', 1708 (L:51)

'English' has as its first syllable a stress maximum which must project to grid-line 1. In contrast the lexical monosyllables (hence not stress maxima) 'Dutch' and 'French' are distributed indifferently as regards the grid, with the first projecting to gridline 1 and the second not projecting; instead the weak mono-syllable 'down' projects to gridline 1. The line might be performed with stress on 'French' and not on 'down'; this is irrelevant to the construction of the grid.

Dactylic metres

Dactylic metre differs from anapaestic metre in the same way that trochaic differs from iambic; the leftmost asterisk in the gridline 0 foot projects as the head.

Table 1.14 *Dactylic tetrameter*

	bracket	foot size	direction	head	final foot built
line 0	(	ternary	L>R	left	binary or unary
line 1	(	binary	L>R	right	
line 2	(	binary	L>R	right	

This gives us, for example, this grid for the following line:

```
I must tramp on through the winter night dreary,
(* *   *   (*   *    *(* *  *   (* *    0 >
(*         *        (*       *  (   1 >
(          *                 *  (   2 >
                             *      3
```

Christina Rossetti, 'Crying My Little One ...', 1872 (K:521)

As usual, any stress maxima must project to gridline 1, but asterisks on gridline 1 need not project from stress maxima.

1.8   Rules for the loose metres

Loose iambic metre

A loose metre is a metre in which lines differ in the number of projected syl-lables. All metres allow the number of syllables to vary, but control this by preventing some syllables from projecting, so that each line has the same num-ber of projected syllables.

Consider the following lines in strict iambic tetrameter:

> So dreams, which overflowing be,   5
> *   *   * * * *   *
>
> Departing leave half things, which we   6
> * * *   *   *   *   *   *
>
> For their imperfectness can call   7
> *   *   *   * *   *   *   *
>
> But joys in the fin, or in the scale.   8
> *   *   Δ   *   *   * *   *   *

William Cartwright, 'A Dream Broke', 1651 (F:490)

There are twenty-four lines in this poem, all scannable as eight syllables to the line, but line 8 is a problem. We must choose not to count the syllable projecting from 'in' in the first half of the line (but count it in the second). This requires a new rule to exclude a syllable from the count (i.e. not to project it) if it is a grammatical monosyllable preceding another grammatical monosyllable; here the grammatical words in question are a preposition preceding an article. (I will call this rule (d), adding it to rules (a), (b), and (c) from pp. 9–10.)

Non-projection rule (d)
Optionally: do not project a syllable which is a grammatical monosyllable preceding another grammatical monosyllable (i.e. a preposition, article, pronoun, auxiliary verb, modal verb, conjunction etc.).

Later in the same poem this rule is silently accommodated by respelling 'it was' as ''Twas', where the two monosyllables are projected as just one monosyllable:

> 'Twas made an ease, no punishment   18
> Δ   *   *   *   *   * * *   *

As an occasional principle, this is fairly widespread in English poetry. However, sometimes poems seem to make such extensive use of it as to suggest that something else might be going on, as in this stanza:

> Thine eyes glowed in the glare
> Of the moon's dying light;
> As a fen-fire's beam on a sluggish stream
> Gleams dimly, so the moon shone there,
> And it yellowed the strings of thy raven hair,
> That shook in the wind of night.

Percy Bysshe Shelley, 'On Harriet Shelley', 1816 (W:243)

The third line here could be made metrical by choosing not to project two prepositions:

> As a fen-fire's beam on a sluggish stream
>)Δ * *) *   *)   Δ * *) *   *)

But in the fifth line we would have to choose not to project the preposition, and a conjunction, and '-owed' in 'yellowed':

> And it yellowed the strings of thy raven hair,
>)Δ   * *) Δ   * *)   Δ   * *)*   *)

There are two reasons for thinking that this stanza cannot be handled just by extending the rules excluding syllables from the count. First, there are so many excluded syllables in the stanza that we would seem to have a different metre. Second, in order to make the projection solution work we need to keep adding to the kinds of syllable which are not projected, so that we weaken the overall account.

Instead of treating these lines as in a strict iambic metre, I will treat them as in a completely different metre, called a *loose* iambic metre. This metre is also sometimes called 'iambic-anapaestic metre' because it seems to mix iambic and anapaestic feet, or 'Christabel metre' after the poem of the same name in this metre by Coleridge, or 'dol'nik' (which is Tarlinskaja's name for it, based on its similarity to the Russian metre with this name). The account I present here is based on Halle and Keyser (1999).

The first step is to redefine for this metre what a stress maximum is:

Definition (loose iambic metre)
A stress maximum is

> (a) A stressed syllable in a polysyllabic word; or
> (b) a lexical monosyllable (noun, verb, adjective, adverb) followed by two grammatical monosyllables (preposition, article, pronoun, auxiliary verb, modal verb, conjunction etc.).

Normally, stress maxima are matched to the grid (they project to gridline 1) once the grid has been built. But in a loose iambic metre, the stress maximum has a different role: it influences how the grid is constructed. The first step in all scansions is to project the syllables as a line of asterisks. In this metre, all syllables project (there are no non-projection rules):

> And it yellowed the strings of thy raven hair,
> *   * * *   *   *   * * * *   *   0

Now, before applying the iterative bracketing rules which insert brackets across the line, we do something different. We identify stress maxima and add a bracket to the right of any asterisk projecting from a stress maximum; this is the rule:

Insert a right bracket to the right of a gridline 0 asterisk projecting from a stress maximum.

In this line there are three stress maxima; by (a) the stressed syllable in the polysyllables 'yellowed' and 'raven', and by (b) the lexical monosyllable 'strings'

which is followed by two grammatical words ('of thy'). This gives us the following structure, which is a sequence of asterisks and brackets. (I distinguish
the brackets inserted by this rule by making them square.)

And it yellowed the strings of thy raven hair,
*   * *] *   *   *]   * * *]*   *   0

The next step is to build the grid by the usual types of rule, inserting brackets
and projecting heads. But because there are already brackets in the line, this
affects how the first iterative bracketing rule now works. The rule which inserts
brackets across the line in this metre is of a kind we have seen before, creating
binary feet from right to left.

Insert a left bracket after every sequence of two asterisks, from right to left across the line.

Moving from right to left, the rule inserts brackets into the line as follows. I have
numbered the asterisks under the line, from right to left, for ease of reference.

And it yellowed the strings of thy raven hair,
*   (* *] *   (*   *]   * (* *](* *   0
11   10 9 8   7   6   5 4 3 2 1

From right to left, the first sequence of two asterisks is 1 and 2. The next sequence is 3 and 4. But 5 and 6 are not a sequence of two asterisks, because there
is a right bracket in the way inserted by the special rule. The next sequence of
two asterisks is thus asterisks 6 and 7, and so the left bracket is inserted there.
Similarly, the next sequence of two asterisks after this is 9 and 10. Thus the
right brackets inserted first by the special rule get in the way of the iterative bracketing rule. The consequence of this is that there are asterisks within
the line which are not contained in a foot: this applies to asterisks 5, 8 and 11.
This metre will in principle allow one extra asterisk to the left of every binary
foot. Thus there are limits on how many extra syllables there can be.

The rest of the rules operate as usual, and build a grid for the line as follows.
I summarise the iterative rules below.

And it yellowed the strings of thy raven hair,
*   (* *) *   (*   *)   * (* *)(* *   0 <
)   *   *)   *   *)   1 <
)   *)   *)   2 <
                                      *   3

Table 1.15 *Loose iambic tetrameter*

	bracket	foot size	direction	head
line 0	(	binary	R>L	right
line 1	)	binary	R>L	right
line 2	)	binary	R>L	right

The effect of the combination of two types of rule and two orientations of bracket means that there can be projected syllables which are not in feet, line-internally. This is why the line varies in number of syllables; these positions between feet are spare positions, which can optionally be filled with an extra syllable. In this line this gives the impression of having three anapaestic feet and an iambic foot, but in fact in this scansion there are four iambic feet with the first three preceded by an unfooted syllable.

A loose trochaic metre: imitation 'quantitative dactylic hexameter'

To conclude this chapter, I look at a different kind of metre, used intermittently in English. This is a quantitative metre, a metre which controls syllables in terms of the weight of the syllable. The metre in question is called 'dactylic hexameter' and was used by Homer and Virgil; here it is being imitated by Arthur Hugh Clough:

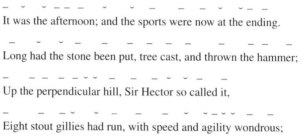

It was the afternoon; and the sports were now at the ending.

Long had the stone been put, tree cast, and thrown the hammer;

Up the perpendicular hill, Sir Hector so called it,

Eight stout gillies had run, with speed and agility wondrous;

Arthur Hugh Clough, 'The Bothie of Tober-Na-Vuolich',
1848 (Mulhauser, 1974:44)

In a note on the poem Clough says, 'The reader is warned to expect every kind of irregularity in these modern hexameters: spondaic lines, so called, are almost the rule' (Mulhauser 1974:592). Some critics (e.g. Mulhauser in his introduction) have suggested that this is basically a loose accentual metre and not quantitative at all; however, I will pursue an approach following Clough's own views that his verse is quantitative with some additional control of stress.

Quantity, so far as, in our forward-rushing, consonant-crushing, Anglo-savage enunciation – long and short can in any kind be detected, quantity attended to in the first place and care also bestowed, in the second, to have the natural accents very frequently laid upon syllables which the metrical reading depresses. (Arthur Hugh Clough, 'Letters of Parepidemus', 1853 (Clough 1869:I, 399))

I have indicated above syllables the syllable weights which I think Clough intends for each syllable. We might formalise Clough's practices with these rules:

A syllable can be counted as heavy or as light if it is a grammatical monosyllable (i.e. preposition, article, pronoun etc.).

Otherwise,
A syllable is always counted as heavy if

(a) it contains a long vowel; or
(b) a vowel followed by two consonants; or
(c) it is the syllable carrying main stress in a polysyllabic word.

Post-vocalic [r] must be pronounced (to get 'were now' as heavy-heavy and 'afternoon' as heavy-heavy-heavy), but perhaps not fully consistently (so that 'Hector' is heavy-light). The permission to count the main stressed syllable in a polysyllable as heavy (even if it is phonetically light) means that 'gillies' projects as -ᵛ, and 'agility' projects as ᵛ-ᵛᵛ. Note that the presence of the (c) condition implies that this is really a stress-based metre like the other English metres with some extra conditions added controlling syllable weight. The special rule for grammatical monosyllables is required because 'and' is light in 'and the' and heavy in 'and thrown'; 'the' is light in 'the stone' and heavy in 'the hammer'. The complexity of the rules by which syllables are defined as heavy or as light perhaps explains why this metre is difficult to scan in English. This in turn may explain why quantitative metres are generally disfavoured in English verse and are generally seen critically as 'failed experiments'.

The lines vary in length between thirteen and seventeen syllables (in this example there are lines of thirteen, fourteen and fifteen syllables). This variation cannot be handled by saying that syllables fail to project. Instead it can be treated as a loose metre. The first step is to insert special brackets:

Insert a right bracket after a light syllable if it is followed by another light syllable.

This gets, for the first line:

```
 _    ᵛ     ᵛ  _  _  _      ᵛ       ᵛ     _      _   _  ᵛ    ᵛ  _   _
It was the afternoon; and the sports were now at the ending.
 *   *]   * * * *    *]    *    *      *    *  *]   * * *        0
```

Now we apply the following rules (note that these are basically the rules for trochaic hexameter):

Table 1.16 *Clough's 'quantitative dactylic hexameter*

	bracket	foot size	direction	head	final foot built
line 0	(	binary	R>L	left	
line 1	(	ternary	R>L	right	
line 2	(	binary	R>L	right	

For the first line the result will be:

```
  ‿  ‿ _ _ _    ‿   ‿    _   _ _  ‿ _ _
It was the afternoon; and the sports were now at the ending.
(*   *]  *(* * (*    *]   * (*   *  (*  *] *(*   *(      0 <
(*      *   *          (*        *     * (        1 <
(          *                          *  (        2 <
                                      *           3
```

Note that syllables fall between feet. This is why the line varies in the number of metrified syllables. The grids for the other lines are:

```
_   ‿  ‿ _   _   _  _ _ _  _    _ _  _
Long had the stone been put, tree cast, and thrown the hammer;
(*    *]  * (*   *  (*  * (*  *   (*    * (*   *(     0 <
(*         *     *    (*     *    *   (  1 <
(                 *                  *  (  2 <
                                   *     3
```

```
_   _ _ _ _‿‿  _  _  _ ‿ ‿ _   _
Up the perpendicular hill, Sir Hector so called it,
(*    * (*  * (* *]* (*   *  (* *] * (*    *(     0 <
(*     *   *    (*     *    *   (  1 <
(         *                *   (  2 <
                          *     3
```

```
_   _  _ ‿ ‿  _  _   _ ‿ ‿ ‿_‿‿ _ _
Eight stout gillies had run, with speed and agility wondrous;
( *     * (* *]  * (*    * (*  * ] *(**]*(*    *(   0 <
( *       *     *    (*    *   *   (  1 <
(             *                *   (  2 <
                             *      3 <
```

Clough's imitation of the classical dactylic hexameter is fairly accurate. Three of his four lines end on a sequence –‿‿–; in the classical metre, the line must end on this rhythmic sequence. Though there is freedom in the line, the ending is metrically fairly strict; I return to this kind of phenomenon (which turns up in many metres) in chapter 5, section 4. In the classical metre, there is never a word boundary in the middle of the line; that is, the fourth foot never begins at the beginning of a word. Because English has so many monosyllables, it is difficult to do this systematically, but Clough's substitute appears to be that he ensures that there is never a comma at the beginning of the fourth foot (instead there is usually a comma midway through the third or fourth feet).

1.9   Generative metrics

This chapter has outlined a theory of metrical form which belongs to the group of theories called 'generative metrics'. The version of generative metrics used in this chapter is based on Halle and Keyser (1999) and Halle (2001), and is explored fully in Fabb and Halle (forthcoming); I call this the 'bracketed grid' theory of generative metrics.

Generative metrics has its origins in Halle and Keyser (1966, 1971), and the present theory is quite close to this original formulation in that it takes the counting out of the line to be the fundamental problem for metrical rules. The present theory is also influenced by adaptations to generative metrics made by Kiparsky (1975, 1977), Hayes (1983, 1988, 1989), Neijt (1993), Hanson and Kiparsky (1996), Youmans (1988, 1989) and other work. Kiparsky and Youmans (1989) is a useful anthology, and for a summary see Rice (1996), and also Fabb (1997). There is currently a competing way of looking at metrical form in Optimality Theory, a theory of phonology which approaches sound structure in a fundamentally different way from the phonology assumed by Halle and Keyser. This Optimality-Theoretic account of metrics is illustrated for example by Golston (1998), Fitzgerald (1998), Hayes and MacEachern (1998), Hayes (2000). Optimality Theory differs from the present theory in several crucial ways. The approach outlined here assumes that rules are ordered, and thus that the metrical grid is built step-by-step from the line; furthermore, rules cannot be broken, which means that only certain aspects of metricality can be handled by the theory. Optimality Theory dispenses with ordering of rules, and instead takes a holistic and simultaneous approach to the text, and furthermore an approach which allows rules to be broken. One of the potential advantages of Optimality Theory is that it aims to capture tendencies as well as fixed and rigid facts about the metre. In the present book I use generative metrics to capture just the rigid facts. The tendencies are explained by a completely different theoretical approach, using pragmatics, in chapter 3.

2   Generated metrical form

This chapter explores in more detail some of the topics introduced in chapter 1.

2.1   Trochaic inversion

Line-initial trochaic inversion involving polysyllables

Normally the stressed syllable in a polysyllable must appear in an even-numbered metrical position but it can also be in the first position. This is called 'trochaic inversion' (because the iambic foot x / appears to have been replaced by a trochee / x). Attridge (1982:233) says of line-initial trochaic inversion that it is an alternative enshrined by convention. I have made it part of the metrical rules.

To illustrate how systematically trochaic inversion is found in iambic pentameter verse, consider the following sonnet by Robert Browning. The sonnet has thirty-two polysyllables. I have underlined the stressed syllables in all cases. In twenty-six of the polysyllables, the syllable with strongest stress is line-internal and is always projected to gridline 1. In six of the polysyllables, the syllable with strongest stress is line-initial (i.e. trochaic inversion). There are no other possibilities. This is the scansion, with stressed syllables in polysyllables underlined.

The Names

```
Shakespeare! – to such name's sounding, what succeeds
) *      *)      *  *)   *      *)   *      *) *  *)      0
          *           *           *        *      *       1

Fitly as silence? Falter forth the spell, –
) * *)* *) *      *)* *)     * *)              0
     *   *       *   *      *                  1

Act follows word, the speaker knows full well,
)*   *) *      *)    *  *) *   *)   *    *)      0
     *        *        *       *        *        1

Nor tampers with its magic more than needs.
) *   *) *    *) *   *)* *)    * *)              0
       *        *       *   *       *            1
```

Two names there are: That which the Hebrew reads
) * *)   * *)   *   *)   * *) *   *)   0
    *   *   *   *   *   1

With his soul only; if from lips it fell,
)*   *) *   *) * *)   *   *) * *)   0
   *   *   *   *   *   1

Echo, back thundered by earth, heaven and hell,
)* *) *   *) *   *)*   *) Δ *   *)   0
   *   *   *   *   *   1

Would own 'Thou did'st create us!' Naught impedes
)   *   *)   *   *)   **) *   *)   *   *)   0
    *   *   *   *   *   1

We voice the other name, man's most of might,
)   *   *)   ** *) *   *)   *   *) *   *)   0
    *   *   *   *   *   1

Awesomely, lovingly: let awe and love
)*   *)   * *)*   *) * *)   *   *)   0
    *   *   *   *   *   1

Mutely await their working, leave to sight
)   *   *)* *)   *   *) *   *)   * * *)   0
    *   *   *   *   *   1

All of the issue as – below – above –
)* *)   * *)* *)   **)   * *)   0
   *   *   *   *   *   1

Shakespeare's creation rises: one remove,
)   *   *)   **)* *)* *)   * *)   0
    *   *   *   *   *   1

Though dread – this finite from that infinite.
)   *   *)   * *)*   *)   * *) * *)   0
    *   *   *   *   *   1

Robert Browning, 'The Names', 1884 (Pettigrew 1981:II, 964)

A conscious differentiation between line-internal and line-initial placement of polysyllables is revealed in sixteenth-century revisions to Sir Thomas Wyatt's poetry (discussed by Thompson 1961:18). In his manuscripts Wyatt appears not to have used the stress maximum rule; he places polysyllables somewhat indifferently throughout the line. Thus the following is a line by Wyatt in which 'fortune' with its first syllable stressed is in mid-line position but does not project to gridline 1.

The power of them to whome fortune hath lent
)*   *) Δ *   *)   *   *)   * *)   *   *)
   *   *   *   *   *

Sir Thomas Wyatt, 'Myne Owne John Poyntz ... ', 1536 (Thompson 1961:18)

Thompson discusses but rejects the possibility that Wyatt stresses 'fortune' with initial stress; in other poems such as 'With Serving Still . . .' Wyatt places 'fortune' so that its first syllable projects to gridline 1. Wyatt's manuscript poems were revised for publication by Richard Tottel in his *Miscellany*, and Tottel does seem to have assumed the stress maximum rule, and uses it as a guide to revision of the texts. Thus he moves 'fortune' so that its first syllable projects to gridline 1:

> The power of them: whom fortune here hath lent
>)* *) Δ *   *)   *   *) *   *)   *   *)
>   *   *   *   *   *

as revised by Richard Tottel, 1557 (Thompson 1961:18)

However, and this is the crucial point, Tottel leaves in place all thirty-one of the line-initial trochaic inversions, suggesting that there already existed a distinction between line-internal and line-initial stressed syllables in polysyllables.

Trochaic inversion is explicitly allowed as a possible variation in traditional accounts of metre. Thus Campion (1602:338) refers to 'a *Trochy*, which neuer enters into our Iambick verse but in the first place'. Watts (1721:74) says that in English metre, accent falls on positions 2, 4, 6, 8, 10, 12, and that 'it adds a Beauty and Grace to the Poetry, sometimes to indulge such a Variety, and especially in the first and second Syllables of the Line', which is trochaic inversion, citing (my annotations and grid):

> Angels invisible to sense,
>)* *) * *)**) * *)
>   *   *   *   *

> Spreading their Pinions for a Shield,
>)   * *)   *   *)Δ* *) *   *)
>   *   *   *   *

Webster (1789:293) permits trochees to substitute for iambs at the beginning of the line, saying 'Writers have generally supposed that our heroic verse consists of five feet, all pure Iambics, except the first foot, which they allow may be a Trochee.' Tellingly, when Bysshe (1705) quotes exemplary iambic pentameter lines, some have (unremarked on) trochaic inversion at the beginning of the line.

The special status of trochaic inversion can be seen in poetic practice, where poets make overt use of it. It is not uncommon to have a word in a trochaic inversion repeated later in the line in an even position.

> Being on being wrecked, and world on world,
>)* *) *   *) *   *)   *   *) *   *)
>   *   *   *   *   *

Alexander Pope, *An Essay on Man*, 1733 (L:237)

Horror on horror! see! behind his grates
) * *) *   *) *   *)   * *)   *   *)
      *   *   *   *   *

Andrew Brice, Freedom ... , 1730 (L:223)

Spirit to Spirit, Ghost to Ghost.
) **) *   *)*   *)   *   *)   0
      *   *   *   *   1

Alfred Lord Tennyson, In Memoriam, XCIII, 1850 (K:183)

The conscious use of trochaic inversion can also be seen when poets use trochaic inversion in an important line, either the first or last line in the poem or a line which demarcates a subsection. Trochaic inversion in the first line is common; for example Milton begins many sonnets with stress-initial names such as Fairfax, Cromwell, Lawrence, Cyriack, while both Wordsworth and Edwin Muir begin sonnets with the stress-initial name Milton. Herrick's poem 'To His Dying Brother ... ' has its only clear trochaic inversion in the final line. This is the final line of another poem, and the only trochaic inversion in the poem:

Gather ye rosebuds while ye may
) * *) * *)   *   *)   *   *)   0
      *   *   *   *   1

Robert Herrick, 'To the Virgins to Make Much of Time', 1648 (F:264)

Herrick's 'On Poetry his Pillar' has one trochaic inversion at the beginning of the first line, and another trochaic inversion at the beginning of the final stanza. William Ernest Henley's 'At Queensferry' (1897, Fuller 2000:241) is a sonnet with line-initial trochaic inversions at the beginning of line 5 (second quatrain) and line 9 (sestet).

A particularly subtle use of trochaic inversion on polysyllables can be seen in Gray's 'The Progress of Poesy. A Pindaric Ode' (1757) a poem in iambic metre but variable length lines. The first six sections of the poem are structured as in Figure 2.1 below, which shows the division of the poem by classical divisions into a pair of metrically identical sections, the strophe and antistrophe, followed by a metrically different epode section.

The arrows indicate the only four lines with trochaic inversions on polysyllables, which are:

Headlong, impetuous, see it pour:	11
Parent of sweet and solemn-breathing airs,	14
Labour and penury, the racks of pain,	43
Glory pursue, and generous shame	64

These lines are in mirror-image order. Line 11 is second-to-last line in its stanza and line 14 is the second in its stanza. Line 43 is the second in its stanza and line 64 is the second-to-last in its stanza. Thus strophe inverts antistrophe in each

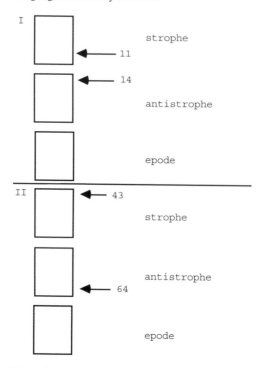

Figure 2.1 Trochaic inversions and ode structure in 'The Progress of Poesy'

part, and the strophe – antistrophe pattern of part I inverts the pattern of part II. The original Greek odes were danced to, and it is possible that Gray intended to symbolise the mirror-image movements of the dancers as they switched between parts of the ode, which Congreve calls 'the Contraversion of the *Chorus*; the Singers, in performing that, turning from the Left Hand to the Right, contrary always to their Motion in the *Strophé*' (1706, Hodges 1964:214). This involves specifically the trochaic inversions on polysyllables. Patterns of stress involving monosyllables are irrelevant to this aspect of the poem.

'Trochaic inversion' involving monosyllables

In performance, the following line is likely to begin with a rhythm /xx/, which is similar to that seen in trochaic inversion:

Deign on the passing world to turn thine eyes,
) *   *)   * *) *   *)   * *)   *   *)   0
       *   *   *   *   *   1

Samuel Johnson, 'The Vanity of Human Wishes', 1749 (L:319)

'Inversions' involving monosyllables are ignored by our metrical rules because our rules do not constrain the distribution of monosyllables. Nevertheless, there is clearly some surface similarity to line-initial trochaic inversions with polysyllables which are built into the rules (via the definition of stress maximum). Furthermore, when grammatical monosyllables like 'on' (or very commonly 'the' or 'a') project to gridline 1 as here, it is most likely to be at the beginning of the line, thus showing the same kind of initial looseness as we see in polysyllabic trochaic inversion (Fabb 2001). Thus in the first eighteen lines of Arnold's 'Sohrab and Rustum' the word 'the' is in second position seven times, giving the effect of 'monosyllabic trochaic inversion'. I return to this broad similarity in chapter 5, section 4.

Our metrical rules distinguish the two types of 'trochaic inversion', monosyllabic and polysyllabic, and we can find some justification for this distinction in poetic practice. Thus in Johnson's 368-line 'Vanity of Human Wishes' there are many lines like this, with monosyllabic 'trochaic inversions' but not a single polysyllabic 'trochaic inversion'. Similarly, we saw that Gray in his Pindaric Ode controls the distribution of lines with polysyllabic trochaic inversions, but he does not control lines with monosyllabic trochaic inversions.

Line-internal polysyllables which appear to 'invert'

Trochaic inversion is basically a line-initial phenomenon. There are some lines in which we appear to get 'trochaic inversion' within the line. Consider for example the following line.

> Love, more than honey; nothing more sweet than love:
>
> Phineas Fletcher, 'To Thomalin', 1633 (F:190)

In this poem, the word 'nothing' is used nineteen times with its first syllable in a head position, and seven times with its first syllable at the beginning of the line (i.e. trochaic inversion), all of which suggests that in this poem the first syllable of the word has greater stress. This line is the only exception to the pattern because 'nothing' has its first syllable in a non-head position in the middle of the line. We might reanalyse the line so that 'nothing' is treated here as a phrase, 'no thing', which therefore falls outside the control of the metrical rules. But this is to miss something about the line-internal division, which is that there is also a case of line-internal 'extrametricality' here in the word 'honey', as the following scansion shows:

```
Love, more than honey; nothing more sweet than love:
  *     *)    *    * Δ ) * *)    *     *)    *  *)      0
        *         *         *           *       *        1
```

Normally an unstressed syllable will fail to project only at the end of a line, and a stressed syllable in a polysyllable will fail to project to gridline 1 only at the beginning of a line. Putting these two facts together, we might conclude that this is actually treated as two distinct short lines, joined at the semicolon. This would permit the stressed syllable in 'nothing' not to count as a stress maximum. Tarlinskaja claims (1976:148) that 'Inversions in mid-line [involving polysyllables] usually occur after the syntactic boundary between speech segments.' (For further discussion see Kiparsky 1975, Hayes 1989:223).

Variable placement of stress or line-internal trochaic inversion?

For most polysyllabic words we can specify exactly which syllable has greatest stress; this is determined by phonological rules of English unrelated to the metrical rules and is a fact about the word which does not vary in performance. But there are some complications. Consider the following lines:

```
        Work without hope draws nectar in a sieve,
        )*      *) *    *)     *    *) * *) * *)      0
                *       *            *     *   *       1

        And hope without an object cannot live.
        )*      *)    * *) * *) *    *) * *)        0
                *        *    *   *      *   *        1
```
S.T. Coleridge, 'Work Without Hope' (Fuller 2000:117)

'Without' is a polysyllable, and so should have one syllable more strongly stressed. But whichever syllable is stressed, in one of these lines it will not project to gridline 1. There are two possible solutions. First, the word may perhaps be reanalysed as a compound of two monosyllables, 'with' and 'out', and thus escape definition as containing a stress maximum. Second, we might consider changing the definition of stress maximum to exclude grammatical polysyllables.

More interestingly, names seem sometimes to have variable stress. Halle and Keyser (1971:104) comment on this in Middle English verse; it is seen for example in Chaucer's *Troilus and Criseyde* where the name 'Criseyde' can apparently have any of its three syllables treated as the stress maximum. I suggest that this is a possibility for the name 'Hero' in Marlowe's *Hero and Leander*. Throughout the poem, the name 'Hero' is treated as though it has initial stress. But there are two lines in which this is a problem:

```
        At Sestos, Hero dwelt; Hero the fair,      (1:5)
        )*    *) *     *)*    *)     * *) * *)      0
              *       *      *      *     *          1
```

So Hero's ruddy cheek Hero betrayed   (2:323)
)*   *)*   *) *   *)   **) * *)   0
      *   *   *   *   *   *   1

Christopher Marlowe, Hero and Leander, 1598 (Orgel 1971:17,40)

In each of these lines, the second use of 'Hero' fails to project its initial syllable to gridline 1. One possibility is that the line is split into two, and that 'Hero' is thus at the beginning of a short line in both cases; this is more plausible for line 1:5 than for line 2:323, however. The alternative possibility is that 'Hero' is flexible in its stress, or perhaps that Marlowe exploits a marginal possibility, which is to restress this word because it is a name. Marlowe's practice is clearly deliberate here; we can see this both because these are two of only three lines in the poem which have 'Hero' twice in the line, and these are also the first and the last lines which say her name. Interestingly, in his continuation of Marlowe's poem, Henry Petowe copies Marlowe's strategy (though this time exploiting trochaic inversion) which again illustrates how deliberate and noticeable it is.

Hero wants comfort, Hero needs must die   (line 418)
) * *) *   *) *   *)* *)   *   *)   0
     *   *   *   *   *   1

Henry Petowe, The Second Part of Hero and Leander ..., 1598 (Orgel 1971:104)

Summary

In this section I have argued that there is a distinction between trochaic inversion of a polysyllable at the beginning of the line and other kinds of 'trochaic inversion' line-internally or involving monosyllables. This distinction is made part of the generative metrical rules, which permit polysyllabic trochaic inversion at the beginning of a line and rule it out elsewhere, and which ignore monosyllabic trochaic inversion altogether. The distinction is also reflected in poetic practice, where the different kinds of 'trochaic inversion' are deployed in different ways.

2.2   Projection and non-projection

How many syllables there are in a line depends on which representation of the line is being counted. In chapter 1, I proposed that there is a metrical representation of the line, constructed by taking a linguistic representation of the line and selectively projecting syllables from it. As a general rule, all syllables project to gridline 0, but there are classes of syllable where projection to gridline 0 is either prevented or is optional; these classes are defined by the non-projection rules (we saw four in chapter 1).

Non-projection is not the same as non-pronunciation

The projection of syllables to form a metrical representation is in principle unconnected to the pronunciation of syllables.

> The assignment of syllables to positions is, of course, strictly metrical. It does not imply that the syllables assigned to a single position should be slurred or elided when the verse is recited. The correspondence rules are not instructions for poetry recitations. They are, rather, abstract principles of verse construction whose effect on the sound of the recited verse is indirect. (Halle and Keyser (1971:171))

The same word can be used with different projections by the same poet; this shows at a minimum that the choice to project does not depend on quirks of the poet's pronunciation. Consider for example the word 'heaven'. The second syllable falls into the class of optionally projecting syllables (because it is based on [n]). There is explicit discussion of the word in the late sixteenth-century correspondence between Harvey and Spenser (Harvey thinks that the word is pronounced as one syllable but mistakenly scanned as two because of the way it is spelled). Both projections of the word can be seen in this line, where first it projects as one and then as two asterisks:

> Yet, all heaven's gifts being heaven's due
> * * * Δ * *Δ * * *
>> Ben Jonson, 'Epigram XXII: On my First Daughter', 1616 (F:125)

The following pairs of lines show that the same poet can sometimes project 'heaven' as one syllable and sometimes as two.

> Looking to heaven; for earth she did disdayne,
> * * * * Δ * *   * * * *
>> Edmund Spenser, *The Faerie Queene*, 1590, I.iv.10

> That every breath of heaven shaked it:
> * *Δ* * * * * * * *
>> Edmund Spenser, *The Faerie Queene*, 1590, I.iv.5

> Set me in earthe, in heaven, or yet in hell,
> * ** *   * * Δ * ** *
>> Earl of Surrey, 'Set Me Wheras the Sonne . . . ' (Jones 1964:2)

> Heaven and earth disturbed in nothing
> * * * *   * * * * * *
>> Earl of Surrey, 'Alas, So All Things Nowe . . . ' (Jones 1964:4)

> Heaven the judicious sharp spectator is
> * Δ * * **   *   * ** *
>> Sir Walter Ralegh, 'What Is Our Life?', 1612 (J:390)

In heaven queen she is among the spheres,
*   *   *   *   *** *   *   *

> Sir Walter Ralegh, 'Praised be Diana's Fair ... ', 1593 (J:363)

To him that made heaven, earth, and sea:
* *   *   *   * Δ *   *   *

> Anonymous,'The Passionate Man's Pilgrimage', 1604 (J:462)

From thence to heaven's bribeless hall
*   *   * * *   * *   *

> Anonymous 'The Passionate Man's Pilgrimage', 1604 (J:461)

Something similar can be seen for the non-projection of a vowel before another vowel (synaloepha); in the following lines a word first projects as one syllable and then as two.

What hours, O what black hoūrs we have spent
*   *Δ *   *   *   **   * *   *

> Gerard Manley Hopkins, 'I Wake and Feel ... ', 1885 (Fuller 2000:233)

When Gullion died (who knows not Gullion?)
*   * Δ*   *   *   *   *   * **

> Joseph Hall, *Virgidemiae*, 1597 (J:700)

Is she self truth and errs? now new, now outwore?
*   * *   *   *   *   *   *   Δ *   *

Doth she, and did she, and shall she evermore
*   * *   *   Δ *   *   * * *   *

> John Donne, 'Sonnet XVIII', early seventeenth century (F:119)

There can be a punctuation mark between the two vowels, and still the first syllable does not project, as in the following examples.

By virtue, and virtue by religious fires
*   * Δ   *   * *   * * *   *

> John Donne, 'The Second Anniversary', 1612 (F:114)

For so God help me, I would not miss you there
*   *   *   *   Δ* *   *   *   *   *

> John Donne, 'To the Countess of Bedford', 1633 (F:112)

In the following example, a pause is necessary in speaking in order to make sense of the sentence (i.e. the shift from main to subordinate sentence).

Her father lessons me I at times am hard,
) * *) * *) *   Δ *)* *) *   *)   0
     *   *   *   *   *   1

Augusta Webster, *Mother and Daughter*, VII, 1895 (K:614)

Non-projection of a vowel before another vowel is seen also in the metres of French, Spanish and Italian. Halle and Keyser (1971:141) and Halle (1992) show that in Spanish and French dramatic verse there can even be a mid-line change of speaker between the two syllables and still the first syllable is not projected. These facts all show that projection or non-projection is not a matter of pronunciation but rather holds of the sequence of syllables in the text; that is, it holds of the linguistic representation of the line not of its performance.

Sometimes spelling is used to indicate that a syllable is or is not projected. Thus consider the inflectional suffix '-ed'. There is some reason to think that this is one of a group of word endings with weak vowels which optionally can be non-projected; optional projection of these suffixes is widely exploited in mediaeval English poetry (Duncan 1995:254). In Tottel's printing (1557) of Surrey's *The Aeneid Book Two* we can see variant forms of the same word, showing optional projection. Here Tottel tends to use spelling to differentiate projected and non-projected forms, 'returnd' and 'returned' and 'armd' and 'armed'. (It is possible that the functional/syntactic differences between the two forms of each word are relevant.)

If she by chaunce had ben returned home.   1005
*   *   *   *   *   *   ** *   *

Which erst returnd clad with Achilles spoiles,   349
   *   *   ** Δ *   *   *   ** *   *

A seemly thing to dye armd in the feld.   405
*   *   *   *   *   *   * Δ*   * *

And armed foes in th' entrie of the gate.   625
*   *   *   *   * Δ *   **   * *

Surrey, *The Aeneid, Book Two*, 1557 (Jones 1964)

Prescriptions for performance

While projection and performance are in principle distinct, there is still a question about whether non-projected syllables should or should not be pronounced in performance. Cowley requires non-pronunciation of non-projected syllables:

The *Numbers* are various and irregular, and sometimes (especially some of the long ones) seem harsh and uncouth, if the just measures and cadencies be not observed in the *Pronunciation*. So that almost all their *Sweetness* and *Numerosity* (which is to be found, if I mistake not, in the roughest, if rightly repeated) lies in a manner wholly at the *Mercy* of the *Reader*. (Abraham Cowley, 'Preface to *Poems*', 1656 (Spingarn 1957:II.86))

In contrast, Rice (1765:112) suggests that all syllables are pronounced, so that pentameter lines might have fourteen or twelve syllables as in the following cited lines:

> And many an amorous, many a humorous Lay,
> Which many a Bard had chanted many a Day.

He comments 'The vicious Custom of contracting our Syllables in order to reduce them to the Standard of five accented and five unaccented, would make us read these Verses in the Manner following.'

> And man' an am'r'us, man' a hum'r'us Lay,
> Which man' a Bard had chanted man' a Day.

Webster (1789:297) takes a similar position, suggesting that extra syllables in the line create trisyllabic feet in an otherwise binary sequence, and that this is a poetic effect: 'Poetic lines which abound with these trisyllabic feet, are the most flowing and melodious of any in the language.' Walker (1781:197) attempts a middle way such that the syllables are sounded but not heard.

Rule III. The vowel e, which is often cut off by an apostrophe in the word the, and in syllables before r, as dang'rous, gen'rous, &c. ought to be preserved in the pronunciation, because the syllable it forms is so short as to admit of being sounded with the preceding syllable, so as not to increase the number of syllables to the ear, or at all hurt the harmony.

Also attempting a compromise, but veering more toward the non-pronunciation of the syllables, Hewitt (1891) says that 'syllables are dropped or softened':

> That máde | great Jóve | to húm | ble him tó | her hánd

here *-ble him to* are pronounced almost like *-blim to*

> Place bárrels | of pítch | upón | the fát | al stáke

here *barrels* is pronounced almost like *barls*.

Thus there are various views about how non-projected syllables should be pronounced. For our purposes, all this suggests is that the choice to project or not to project relates to the linguistic representation instead of the performance of the line. Projection is a way of ensuring that the line fits the metrical grid which is built from the linguistic representation. Independently of this, there is also a choice to pronounce or not to pronounce.

Generalisations about projection and non-projection

While non-projection is optional, we can make some overall generalisations. Tarlinskaja (1976) says that words used attributively are more likely to have non-projected syllables than words used non-attributively, and that imported foreign words are less likely to lose vowels than native words. Her most interesting generalisation is that non-projection is avoided at the end of a line, where all possible syllables tend to project. This is a point made first by King James VI (1584:216), who cites these lines:

> Sen patience I man haue perforce,
> *   **Δ   *   *   *   * *
>
> I liue in hope with patience.
> * *   *   *   *   ***

He says that 'patience' is a disyllable at the beginning of a line and a trisyllable at the end. The following examples show this same pattern.

> Created evil, for evil onely good,
> *** *Δ   * * **   * *
>
> John Milton, *Paradise Lost*, 2:623, 1667 (Darbishire 1952:I,42)

> Him plunder! He ne'er swore our Covenant.
> *   *   *   * *Δ   *   *   * * *
>
> Give me a thousand Covenants, I'll subscrive
> *   ** * *   *Δ *   *   *   *
>
> William Drummond, 'Against the King . . . ', 1711 (F:220)

> That e'er did wag a tail or ever bark.
> * *Δ *   * * * * * ** *
>
> Emanuel Collins, 'The Fatal Dream', 1762 (L:500)

The fact that all syllables tend to project at the end of the line might be interpreted as a case of 'final strictness', as discussed in chapter 5, section 4, and might be one of the ways in which projection rules provide evidence for line boundaries.

How to deal with optionality

The fact that some classes of syllables are optionally projected has long been acknowledged:

This poeticall licence is a shrewde fellow, and couereth many faults in a verse; it maketh wordes longer, shorter, of mo sillables, of fewer, newer, older, truer, falser; and, to conclude, it turketh all things at pleasure, for example *ydone* for *done*, *adowne* for *downe*, *orecome*, for *ouercome*, *tane* for *taken*, *power* for *powr*, *heauen* for *heaun* . . . (George Gascoigne (1575:53))

Watts (1721:77) uses the phrase 'favouring the metre' to describe a choice between options which best fits the global metrical pattern. Thus he cites two different projections for 'glittering', where the number of syllables which project
is chosen in order to make the line metrical (I add grids):

```
All glittering in Arms he stood.
)*    *)* *)  * *)     * *)        0
      *  *    *        *           1

All glittering in his Arms he stood.
)*    *)Δ*  *)  * *)    * *)       0
      *     *   *       *          1
```

For syllable types which are optionally projected, the choice of whether or not
to project is sensitive to the final outcome.

This might be a problem for our metrical theory, with its ordering of one
process before another. In our theory, syllables are first projected and then the
grid is built, but the discussion in this section has shown that which syllables are
projected cannot be decided until we have built the grid, which is an ordering
paradox. Fitzgerald (1998) cites this as evidence that metrical processes are
not ordered. But there is an alternative possibility which is compatible with
ordered rules and allows scansions to be abandoned and started again. In this
approach, a decision is made on which syllables to project and then the grid is
constructed from the projected syllables. If the grid fails, the process starts again
by projecting different syllables. This would suggest that the optionality of non-
projection rules presents a practical problem for the author or reader/listener
in scanning the lines, and thus makes those lines more complex when they
include syllables which are candidates for non-projection. This is Halle and
Keyser's (1971:142) view, now reformulated; they suggest for example that
the possibility of non-projection of a vowel before another vowel increases the
complexity of the line, because the number of syllables is more difficult to
discern. In this book I claim that literary form holds of a text in ways which are
inherently complex; the problem of non-projection would then be another kind
of complexity, and possibly a complexity experienced as aesthetic.

Summary

My argument in this book is that literary form holds of a text in ways which
are inherently complex, and that this complexity is experienced as aesthetic.
In this section we have seen that non-projection of syllables in the metrical
representation is a source of two kinds of complexity. One kind of complexity
is in the relation between the various representations of the line. The number of
syllables may vary between the linguistic representation of the line, the metrical

representation of the line, and the performance of the line. Thus multiple representations of the same text differ from one another; this may be an instance of the 'metrical tension' which is often claimed as a fundamental aesthetic effect of metrical verse. A second kind of complexity is the fact that the text does not fully determine which syllables need to be projected in order to scan the line, or which syllables should be pronounced. This indeterminacy may also perhaps be an instance of a complexity which may be experienced as aesthetic. The fact that there are relatively few classes of non-projecting syllables means that these complexities are manageable and thus experienced as aesthetic rather than as the disintegration of the text.

2.3   Why counting is fundamental to metre

This theory of generated metrical form proposes that metrical verse is processed by a specialised cognitive system which builds bracketed grids from the line. In this theory, counting is fundamental; the grid is built in order to count a specific number of syllables into the line. Rhythm is secondary; it consists just of the requirement that where there is a stress maximum it must project into the grid so that it projects to gridline 1. This theory claims that in all kinds of metrical verse counting is fundamental and other characteristics of the line are secondary. In some metres, the 'other characteristics' involve not rhythm but something else. In syllable-counting classical Irish metre, the line has a fixed length but does not have a fixed or predictable rhythm; instead, what is predictable for each metre is the length of the final word. In mediaeval Welsh metre, the line again has a fixed length and lacks a fixed rhythm, but as I will show shortly, rhyme is fixed by the metrical rules.

The idea that counting is fundamental to metre makes certain predictions which seem to be true. The first prediction is that there should not be a metre in which the line has a regular rhythm but no specific length. That is, there is no rhythm without counting. There are two apparent exceptions; one is texts whose lines unpredictably vary in length, such as odes, and the other is texts which have a rhythmic beginning or ending to a line whose length varies unpredictably. I discuss the first case in chapter 5; in these texts each line is in itself metrical and thus measured in length, but the metre changes from line to line. One example of the second case is the 'clausula', the metrical ending which is often seen in Cicero's prose sentences (p. 174) which vary in length. Another example cited by Fitzgerald (1998) is Tohono O'odham songs, where the beginning and the end of the line is a trochaic foot but the line varies in length (and is otherwise not footed). I suggest that both examples are best handled by appeal to some explanation outside the generative metrical rules.

Putting counting at the centre of the metre makes another prediction, which is that metrical texts should always be verse texts: that is, divided into lines. In order to count syllables, the count must begin somewhere and must end somewhere; these places where the count begins and ends are the beginning and the end of the line. In a prose text, the count would have to begin at the beginning of the whole text and would then continue to the end of the whole text. Thus we can explain why there is no systematically rhythmical prose, for example a prose text which is throughout in an iambic rhythm but where there is nothing to suggest division into lines. We can explore some of the possibilities by considering a text which in the eighteenth century *was* sometimes considered to be rhythmical prose, or as Walker puts it, 'numerous or harmonious prose' (Walker 1781:210). The text in question is Milton's *Paradise Lost*, which Samuel Johnson called 'verse only to the eye'. Here is a section from *Paradise Lost* which I have rewritten as prose:

Thus saying rose the monarch, and prevented all reply; prudent, lest from his resolution raised others among the chief might offer now (certain to be refused) what erst they feared.

If Johnson and Walker are right, then this should be iambic prose with a continuous rhythm from beginning to end and no hint of line divisions. In fact they are wrong, as can be seen by the use of trochaic inversion in the text. Consider the iambic grid which would be built if this was continuous prose, inserting right brackets every two syllables from the end of the text. I have underlined the stressed syllables in polysyllables. (Read the grid as continuous.)

```
        Thus saying rose the monarch, and prevented all
        )*   *)*    *)    *   *)*    *)    * *) * *)
             *      *       *    *       *     *    *

        reply; prudent, lest from his resolution raised
        * *)  * *)   *    *)   * *)* *)*   *)
           *      *       *    *  *  *

        others among the chief might offer now (certain
        * *) * *)   *    *)   *   *) *  *)   * *)
           *    *        *      *      *       *

        to be refused) what erst they feared.
        * *) * *)      * *)    *   *)    0 <
           *    *         *        *      1
```

Stressed syllables in polysyllables are defined as stress maxima and must project to gridline 1, except at the beginning of a line (where they are not defined as stress maxima). In the scansion above, we can see that three stressed syllables in polysyllables do not project to gridline 1 and this means that they must be at the beginning of a line. They turn out to be ten metrical syllables apart; that is, it is straightforward to work out where the line divisions are in this text. Thus while this has been rewritten as prose it has one of the fundamental characteristics of verse, which is trochaic inversion at the beginning of the line.

The following is Milton's printed lineation in which the trochaic inversions are clearly line-initial.

Thus saying rose

)*   *)*   *)   0
            *   *   1

the monarch, and prevented all reply;

* *)*   *)   * *) * *) * *)   0
   *   *   *   *   *   1

prudent, lest from his resolution raised

* *)   *   *)   * *)* *)*   *)   0
  *   *   * *   *   1

others among the chief might offer now

* *) * *)   *   *)   *   *) * *)   0
  *   *   *   *   *   1

(certain to be refused) what erst they feared.

* *) * *)* *)   * *)   * *)   0
  *   *   *   *   *   1

John Milton, *Paradise Lost*, 2:466–70, 1667 (Darbishire 1952:I.38)

Rhythm always requires lineation. This is because the rhythm of a text is organised on the basis of the counting out of the text, and the text can only be counted out if it is divided into units of a fixed length; that is, divided into lines.

How do poets ensure that there are for example ten syllables in a line? One possibility is that they count on their fingers; poets occasionally claim to do so. Thus Thomas Randolph in 1638, mourning his little finger lost in a fight (Mullick 1974):

> Oft did you scan my verse, where if I miss
> Henceforth I will impute the cause to this.
> A finger's loss (I speak it not in sport)
> Will make a verse a foot too short.

Thomas Randolph, 'Upon the Loss of His Little Finger', 1638 (F:384)

There is a functionalist argument to the same effect by Rarick (1974) who explains the commonness of ten-syllable lines in English verse from the Old English period onwards: 'In a more primitive age than our own, when most things were made by hand, fingers were much nearer the center of consciousness than they are now.' Finger-counting undoubtedly has some explanatory value in some domains (it might partly explain five-base and ten-base counting systems), but for metre, it is not clear why it would hold in some cases and not others. Celtic metres are not based on ten (Irish and Welsh both have seven as a characteristic length of line), while in French the twelve-syllable line has had a dominant place.

We might alternatively suggest that poets (or their readers) count under their breath, but this would suggest that metrical abilities are dependent on poets and readers being numerate, a possibility for which there is certainly no evidence. However, in this regard we might ask whether the characteristic numbers of syllables in a metrical tradition relate to the counting systems of the language. Again there is no evidence for any relation. Thus for example the Australian language Dyirbal has metrical verse with lines of six syllables, eight syllables and eleven syllables (Dixon and Koch 1996). But as a language Dyirbal has number words only for one, two and three; there are no number words for six or eight or eleven, but just a single word translating as 'a good few' for four to fifty or more (Dixon 1972). For these reasons I suggest that we abandon an attempt to relate metricality to explicit counting and instead ask whether counting might be built into the way in which metrical verse is processed, as suggested in the 'metrical grid' theory.

One of the basic claims of the metrical grid theory is that the iterative rules which insert brackets and thus ultimately count the line can insert brackets after every two or every three syllables, but cannot count any higher. Thus the rule cannot count all ten syllables of the iambic pentameter line in one go. One direct piece of evidence for this comes from the fact that when stress maxima are distributed across the line, they are distributed in ways which suggest that gridline 0 feet are either binary or ternary (for example, stress maxima might be two or three syllables apart, but they are not five or seven syllables apart). But there is indirect support from other areas of specialised cognition. Metrical cognition is like linguistic cognition, perhaps a part of linguistic cognition, and in linguistic cognition there is evidence for counting up to two and possibly up to three but no evidence for counting up to four or higher. Most linguistic structure is binary, some possibly ternary, but nothing higher than this. The idea that specialised cognitive processes are restricted to small bases is also argued by Butterworth (1999), who argues that the core of mathematical cognition is restricted to counting up to four or five. In Fabb (1997:95) I argued that because metrical lines apparently involve large numbers they are therefore processed by a cognitive system which is able to count above three and is therefore unlike linguistic cognition. In this section I have suggested a different approach, where counting of large numbers is reduced to repeated counting in small numbers and hence metrical cognition *is* like linguistic cognition.

An example from Welsh

In this section I will consider a metrical tradition in which the lines have a regular syllable count but do not have a regular rhythm. The general view of such syllable counting metres is that the lines are not organised into feet, a view expressed by Rowlands (1979: 203), who says that 'as one would expect, scansion into feet bears no relevance to the prosody of Welsh strict poetry'. In the present theory, counting always involves foot construction. I will show that there is in fact evidence that the line is divided into feet, which comes from the distribution of rhyme.

The metre in question is *englyn penfyr*, as codified by Einion Offeiriad in the fourteenth century, and represented by the following stanza which has a line of ten syllables followed by two seven-syllable lines.

> Ónid ýnad a darlléad – llýfreu,
>   a'i éireu yn wástad,
> Áreith mywn cýfreith ni ád.
>
> *A magistrate who is a reader of books and his words*
> *are appropriate, he would not allow speechifying in a*
> *court.*

cited by Morris-Jones 1980:320

I suggest the following grids, and the following rules:

```
Ónid ýnad a darlléad – llýfreu,
(*   * *(*  *  * ( **    * ( *    0 >
(     *       *         * ( *    1 >
(                       *  * (   2 >
                        *        3

a'i éireu yn wástad,
(*  **(* *    * (*            0 >
(    *       *  * (           1 >
              *              2

Áreith mywn cýfreith ni ád.
(* *    *    (* *   *(*       0 >
(      *         * * (        1 >
                *            2
```

Table 2.1 *Ten-syllable line*

	bracket	foot size	direction	head	final foot built
line 0	(	ternary	L>R	right	unary
line 1	(	ternary	L>R	right	unary
line 2	(	binary	L>R	left	

Table 2.2 *Seven-syllable line*

	bracket	foot size	direction	head	final foot built
line 0	(	ternary	L>R	right	unary
line 1	(	ternary	L>R	right	

The grids are built in order to count ten syllables and seven syllables. We have indirect evidence that the grids are indeed present (and hence that the syllables are organised into feet) which comes from the distribution of rhyme in this metre.

Normally rhyme comes at the end of a line but if we look at the rhyme at the end of the seven-syllable lines (i.e. in '-ad') we find that in the ten-syllable line it is the eighth syllable rather than the tenth syllable which rhymes. In this metre, the seventh or eighth or ninth syllable in the ten-syllable line will always rhyme with the syllable at the end of the line in the seven-syllable lines. Why these syllables? The answer is clear if we look at the grids. These are the syllables in the third gridline 0 foot. In the seven-syllable line, the syllable at the end of the line is the only syllable in the third gridline 0 foot. In the ten-syllable line there are three syllables in this foot, any of which can rhyme. This condition therefore holds:

Rhyme between all three lines involves any syllable in the third gridline 0 foot.

Thus the fact that we get this unusual rhyme pattern, involving any of three syllables in the first line, demonstrates that the line is indeed divided into feet. In Welsh, it is rhyme rather than the distribution of stress which exploits foot structure.

2.4   Periodicity

A periodic sequence is a long sequence made by repeating a short sequence. Thus the unstressed (x) and stressed (/) sequence x/x/x/x/x/x/ is a periodic sequence made by repeating x/. The strict English metres show some tendency towards rhythmic periodicity in performance, though lines are not usually strictly periodic. The grid has a periodic structure because it is built by iterative bracket-insertion and head-projection rules, but this does not directly relate to a performance of a line as having a periodic rhythm. The metrical rules for strict metres govern only stressed syllables in polysyllables, which by itself is not enough to ensure that the whole line is periodic. In chapter 4 I offer an explanation of the tendency towards rhythmic periodicity which does not refer to the generated metre.

The loose metres are not as clearly rhythmically periodic. Thus in the performance of lines in loose iambic metre, the stressed syllables can be adjacent or separated by one or two unstressed syllables. It has sometimes been claimed that lines of this type are (or should be) performed so as to spread out the stressed syllables in time, so that there is a temporal periodicity. However, this is a convention of performance rather than a necessity.

In the present theory, the rhythm of the line is attached by convention to the grid. While the grid is periodic it does not contain rhythmic characteristics. Thus the present theory differs from previous accounts of the English metres, which have structural descriptions which directly represent relative strength and weakness. In Halle and Keyser (1971) this was done by matching the line to a sequence of differentiated metrical positions in a sequence WSWSWSWSWS. In later accounts, a tree structure or grid is built for the line which represents strength and weakness relative to position in the tree or grid (e.g. Kiparsky 1977, Hayes 1983). In all these accounts, the scansion directly represents relative stress. In these theories, rhythm is taken to be at the heart of metre, rather than counting, and the metrical scansion has a relation of 'fit' with the line rather than having been built across the line from beginning to end. These accounts thus have no explanation of why there is no rhythmic prose, and must also treat syllable counting metres as fundamentally different from rhythmic metres. Thus Halle and Keyser (1971:141) had to differentiate between the WSWSWSWSWS template for iambic pentameter and the template XXXXXX for Spanish syllable-counting verse, while later theories usually ignore syllable-counting verse altogether. These other theories which make periodic rhythm fundamental to the structure of the scansion also cannot account for rhythmic but non-periodic rhythms.

The term 'rhythm' is sometimes used only for periodic sequences. But there are metres in which there is a long sequence of differentiated syllables in which there is no repetition of a shorter sequence; these are metres which are rhythmic without being periodic. The classical Sanskrit metres offer an example of this (Keith 1920). This for example is a line in the twenty-one-syllable *sragdharā* metre (from Coulson 1992). ˘ indicates that the syllable is light, and – that it is heavy; a colon indicates a caesura, an obligatory word boundary. Every line in this metre follows exactly this pattern (with the exception that the twenty-first syllable in the line can be heavy or light).

$$ -\quad -\quad -\,-\quad \breve{}\ -\,-\ :\ \breve{}\ \breve{}\ \breve{}\ \breve{}\breve{}\ \breve{}\ -\ :\quad -\quad \breve{}\ -\ -\ \breve{}\quad -\ - $$

mrabhnair yānāṃ   trayeṇa   trimuniyati-yutā   sragdharā kīrtit eyam

The pattern is non-periodic but still 'rhythmic' in the sense that it is a pattern of phonologically differentiated, heavy and light, syllables. These rhythms can be accounted for, just like the rhythms of English poetry, by conditions which hold of the metrical grid. These metres are best dealt with by dividing them into sub-parts at the caesurae. (I thank John Smith for this suggestion). Here three seven-syllable sub-parts can be given a grid by the following set of rules:

Table 2.3 *Sragdharā*

	bracket	foot size	direction	head	final foot built
line 0	)	ternary	R > L	left	unary
line 1	)	ternary	R > L	right	

This gives the following periodic grid, the same for each part, but with different conditions for each part as shown. There is one general condition which they all share:

 i. The rightmost syllable in each part is heavy. The rightmost syllable in the line is heavy or light.

```
mrabhnair yānāṃ trayena
 _    _    _  _   ˘  _ _
*)   *   * *)    * * *)  0
)  *   *          *    )  1
                  *        2
```

conditions: first part
 ii. a syllable projecting to line 2 is light.
iii. other syllables are heavy.

```
trimuniyatiyutā
 ˘  ˘  ˘  ˘  ˘  ˘  _
*) * * *) * * *)        0
)* *        *    )      1
            *            2
```

conditions: second part
 iv. a syllable projecting to line 2 is light.
  v. other syllables are light.

```
Sragdharā kīrtit eyam
 _    ˘ _  _ ˘ _ _
*)    * * *) * * *)     0
)  *   *     *    )     1
             *           2
```

conditions: third part
 vi. a syllable projecting to line 1 is light, except at the beginning of the line.
vii. other syllables are heavy.

This metre usefully illustrates the arbitrary association between the rhythm of the line and the structure of the grid. All metrical grids have a periodic structure (because of the iterative bracket-insertion rules) but in this case a non-periodic rhythm is attached to it. And it is the light syllables which project the furthest in this grid, even though these might be thought of as phonologically weak. Thus extent of projection does not necessarily indicate phonological strength.

2.5   Summary

In chapters 1 and 2 I have outlined a theory of metrical form. The linguistic representation of the line is the basis for a metrical representation, by selectively projecting syllables as the first line of a grid. Iterative rules take over and build the rest of the grid. Conditions, such as the condition on stress maxima, hold of the grid and its relation to the line. This all operates on the linguistic form of the line, and I assume operates by specialised cognitive processes similar to the phonological processes which structure the sounds of the language. In chapters 3 and 4 I will introduce a different theory of metre, which is compatible with and operates alongside the first. This new theory is based on linguistic pragmatics. It works with performances of metrical verse rather than abstract linguistic representations, and aims to explain aspects of metrical verse which so far remain unexplained.

3   Communicated form

Some kinds of literary form hold systematically of a text; these were the kinds of metrical form examined in chapters 1 and 2. For example, for iambic pentameter lines, there are always ten projected syllables and stress maxima always project to gridline 1; they are instances of invariant form. But many kinds of literary form do not hold fully of the text, and instead are best thought of as holding to a certain extent; these are instances of variable form. In this chapter I show this by looking at 'being a sonnet' as a kind of variable literary form and associated kinds of form such as 'being in lines', 'rhyming' and so on. Because these kinds of form hold to a certain degree rather than holding invariably, they cannot be generated by rule. Instead I suggest that they hold of the text in an entirely different way from the kinds of metrical form discussed in the previous chapters. These variable kinds of form hold of a text only by virtue of being the content of weaker or stronger thoughts about the text. Thus literary form of this kind has no objective existence in the text. This kind of literary form is explained by reference to a theory of thoughts and how thoughts are derived, which is a theory of linguistic pragmatics (specifically, Relevance Theory).

3.1   Being a sonnet

Then haue you Sonnets: some thinke that all Poemes (being short) may be called Sonets, as in deede it is a diminutiue worde deriued of *Sonare*, but yet I can beste allowe to call those Sonnets whiche are of fouretene lynes, euery line conteyning tenne syllables. The firste twelue do ryme in staues of foure lines by crosse meetre, and the last two ryming togither do conclude the whole. (George Gascoigne (1575:55))

George Gascoigne's account of what it means for a text to be a sonnet can be interpreted as follows:

(a) People may disagree about whether a text is a sonnet.
(b) 'Being a sonnet' involves having certain characteristics. These are unconnected to one another (having fourteen lines is not related in principle to having lines of ten syllables). A text is a sonnet if it has all the characteristics.

    (c) The characteristics of the sonnet are: fourteen lines, a specific metre (here, ten syllables to the line), and a specific rhyme scheme (here, ABAB CDCD EFEF GG).

We might also take the following from his account:

    (d) There is a close relation between being a sonnet and being called a sonnet. Gascoigne's discussion of the etymology of 'sonnet' acknowledges the significance of naming.

    (e) Some texts might be better examples of sonnets than others (as Gascoigne says 'I can *beste* allowe . .'). This means that 'sonnethood' can be a matter of degree, perhaps based on how many of the sonnet characteristics a text has.

    (f) Some characteristics are more important than others. Gascoigne first states the requirement for fourteen lines and the metrical requirement (ten syllables), and in the next sentence states the basically 'English' pattern for the rhyme scheme. We might interpret this sequencing as indicating that lineation and metre are considered more important than rhyme.

The opinions extracted in (a-f) more or less hold in all accounts of the sonnet. On (a), disagreement about whether a text is a sonnet, some are more concerned to lay down the law than others, with the more prescriptive approaches exemplified by Oliphant's (1932) rules for sonnet writers, or Fuller's (2000) decision to include only fourteen-line poems in his anthology of sonnets. On (b) and (c), the characteristics of the sonnet, all accounts are likely to begin with the characteristics proposed by Gascoigne (further specifying the metre as iambic pentameter), with an extended range of possible rhyme schemes. Both Spiller (1992) and Fuller further suggest that we should expect an asymmetric division of the sonnet into parts, as exemplified for example by the 8+6 line division of the 'Italian'-style English sonnet. And Spiller adds as characteristics the movement towards a conclusion and the use of the sonnet as a 'stage' on which the 'I' of the poem speaks to his audience. This brings us to (f), the difference in importance between characteristics. Even the rigid approach of Oliphant has ten core rules and fifteen peripheral rules, such that 'A violation of any of the ten rules already listed is sufficient to cause a poem to be esteemed no sonnet; a violation of any or all of the fifteen now to be given will not prevent a poem from being styled a sonnet: they constitute rather a demand for perfection' (1932:136). Fuller speaks of 'the essence of the sonnet' (2000:xxxiii), which he proposes is a sequence of a slightly longer statement (i.e. eight lines) and slightly shorter response (i.e. six lines); texts may lack some characteristics of the sonnet but retain its essence. Thus for Fuller the essence of the sonnet is better kept in variants which shorten the sonnet to $6:4\frac{1}{2}$ lines (which are exemplified by Gerard Manley Hopkins's 'curtal sonnets') than in variants which divide the poem into a sequence of separate stanzas followed by a final couplet.

The notion of more core and more peripheral characteristics means that most would accept (e): some texts are better examples of sonnets than others. Spiller (1992:3–4) says that a text which

infringes one of these parameters [length, metre, proportion] will remind us of a sonnet quite closely; a poem which infringes two will be more difficult to accommodate, but we will probably try to establish some procedure to account for the deformation, and a poem which infringes all three will not be recognisable as a sonnet at all and we will regard it as something else unless there is contextual pressure.

This brings us to (d): being a sonnet means being recognised and named as a sonnet. Jakobson (1960) suggested that the poetic function requires a focus on the message (he means the text itself not its content), by which he means that we become aware of the formal characteristics of the text. This is a focus on literary form, and Bauman (1975) explains this by suggesting that literary production ('verbal art') seeks evaluation by an audience in terms of its exploitation of fairly explicit or overt principles of literary form; thus recognition of form is fundamental to having form. The explicit naming of form seems particularly important for sonnets, which are often titled 'sonnet'.

3.2   The relation between components of literary form: conditionals

'Being a sonnet' is a kind of literary form which is defined in terms of other kinds of literary form: most texts which are sonnets are also 'in iambic pentameter', and most texts which have fourteen lines are sonnets. I propose to represent these relations between kinds of literary form by writing them out as conditional sentences, with an *if . . . then* structure.

(a) If a text is a sonnet then it is in iambic pentameter.
(b) If a text has fourteen lines then it is a sonnet.

These conditionals do not always hold, and this is a key difference between conditionals of this kind and the conditional formulated in chapter 1 which was one of the generative metrical rules for iambic pentameter.

(c) If a syllable is a stress maximum then it must project to gridline 1.

This is one of several important differences which suggest that conditionals as illustrated by (a) and (b) (and which include most conditionals relating to literary form) are different in kind from conditionals (c).

Conditional of the type exemplified by (a) and (b)	Conditional of the type exemplified by (c)
Does not hold as an absolute.	Always holds.

Accessible to introspection: we can know that we know it. Its accessibility is evidenced by the fact that it is often explicitly codified.	Inaccessible to introspection.
Formulated in ordinary language terms, and can in fact be reformulated; the vocabulary in which it is written is not restricted in any particular way.	Formulated in terms specific to the metrical module (e.g. 'stress maximum', 'gridline 1').
An open set; new conditionals can be formulated at any time.	A closed (and small) set.
Invoked as one of a set of conditionals, but its relation with those conditionals is more 'cloud-like' than 'clock-like': it is unordered, varies from other conditionals in 'strength', and can be more or less prominent relative to other conditionals depending on the context.	Invoked as an indispensable, sequentially ordered and interlocking part of a set of rules, e.g. the rules for English iambic pentameter.

In the next section I show that conditionals as exemplified by (a) and (b) can be theorised as part of the account of thought and communication offered by Relevance Theory.

3.3   Relevance Theory and thoughts about literary form

Relevance Theory (Sperber and Wilson 1986, 1995) is a theory of linguistic pragmatics: that is, it seeks to explain how meanings are communicated. Meanings are in part encoded into syntactic structures, and the syntactic rules can derive these aspects of meaning. But this is rarely enough to derive the full meaning of an utterance, which therefore requires a different kind of theory of meaning to be added: the theory of linguistic pragmatics. In this book I draw upon the pragmatic theory of Relevance Theory, though I use it rather loosely. While other theories of pragmatics might here deliver similar overall results, Relevance Theory is well suited to my account of literary form, not least because Relevance Theory has been the basis of some interesting discoveries about literary meaning (Pilkington 2000, Sperber and Wilson 1995:202–43). While my discussion will be fairly non-technical, nevertheless my goal is to begin to make as explicit as possible the processes by which we formulate thoughts about textual form. By making explicit and attempting to formulate psychologically realistic accounts of thoughts about form, we can thereby begin to speculate about the reception of form, including the aesthetic experience of form.

Relevance Theory assumes certain proposals made by Jerry Fodor about what thoughts are. For Fodor, thoughts are propositions, instantiated as sentences in a 'language of thought' (Fodor 1975); in this book I represent thoughts as sentences in English. In other work, Fodor proposes a distinction between modularised and general cognitive processes (Fodor 1983). Some mental processes take place in specialised and encapsulated modules, inaccessible to introspection and operating by module-specific principles. Syntactic and phonological processing are modular in this way, and I suggest that the metrical rules which scan a text by building a grid are also contained in a 'metrical module'. Other mental processes take place in a central undifferentiated area as general cognition. This is where thinking and inference, whether conscious or not, takes place, and thus where we find the propositions which are thoughts.

Modus Ponens

Thinking is the manipulation of thoughts. Sperber and Wilson (1995:93) argue that thinking characteristically operates by the use of rules of inference such as the rule of *modus ponens*, illustrated as follows. Given the two premises A and 'if A then B', B is the conclusion.

The rule of modus ponens

A	premise 1
If A then B	premise 2 (a conditional)
	by *modus ponens*
B	conclusion

An example is:

(1) The text has fourteen lines.
(2) If a text has fourteen lines then it is a sonnet.
        by *modus ponens*
(3) The text is a sonnet.

(In this book, representations of thoughts are always numbered, as here. Numbering is continuous from beginning to end of each chapter. Numbering is for convenience of reference only and does not have theoretical implications.)
Here, the thought (1 = A) that a particular text has fourteen lines is combined with the thought (2 = if A then B) that texts with fourteen lines are sonnets, to derive the new thought (3 = B) that the text in question is a sonnet. This is a characteristic kind of inferencing. A text which warrants the thought (1) in the context (2) thereby implies (3).

This describes the thought process. Shortly I discuss where thoughts come from in terms of a theory of communication. The basic idea will be that thoughts can be deliberately communicated, in which case they are called implicatures. In principle, any of (1), (2) and (3) can be deliberately communicated by the author, and thus can be implicatures. I will be suggesting that form is communicated by being the content of implicatures, as here.

Propositions and propositional attitudes

Thoughts are propositions. In the simplest formulation, thoughts are propositions which represent states and events; thus 'the text has fourteen lines' is a proposition which represents a state of a text. However, thoughts are always *someone's* thoughts, and hence strictly speaking we should always represent a thought not as a simple proposition but as a more complex proposition, such as:

(4) I believe that the text has fourteen lines.

Thoughts with this 'embedded' structure express propositional attitudes.

Strength

Not all texts which have fourteen lines are sonnets, which means that in the abstract we cannot be certain that the conditional (2) is true. We can therefore not be certain that the conclusion (3) is true for the text in question. In order to capture this 'variable certainty' of thoughts, Sperber and Wilson propose that thoughts carry a degree of strength (1995:75). The strength of a thought is the degree to which it is held to be true by the thinker, and thus is a relation between a specific thought and a specific thinker. Strength is probably best understood as a characteristic of the propositional attitude rather than the proposition on its own. Thus the strength with which the thought 'the text has fourteen lines' is held might be represented by one of the following thoughts, with different degrees of strength instantiated by different expressions of attitude.

(5) I believe weakly that the text has fourteen lines.
(6) I believe strongly that the text has fourteen lines.
(7) I know that the text has fourteen lines.

For convenience in the discussion which follows I will rarely represent strength directly, and when I do I will just tag the thought as [strong] or [weak], using the terms categorially to represent what are actually gradient degrees of strength or weakness:

(8) The text has fourteen lines. [strong]
(9) The text has fourteen lines. [weak]

Whether explicitly indicated or not, all thoughts hold with some degree of strength.

The strength of the premises influences the strength of the conclusion. The fact that strength enters into deductions and hence can be increased or decreased is a point of fundamental importance in what follows. The strength of thoughts about form directly correlates with the extent to which specific kinds of form hold of the text.

Consider again the deduction with which we began:

> (1) The text has fourteen lines. [strong]
> (2) If a text has fourteen lines then it is a sonnet. [fairly strong]
> > by *modus ponens*
> (3) The text is a sonnet. [fairly strong]

For a text which very clearly has fourteen lines the strength of the first premise (1) will be strong. The strength of the second premise (2) will be fairly strong (this depends on the thinker, and on the extent to which the thinker thinks that all texts with fourteen lines are necessarily sonnets). Hence the strength of the conclusion (3) inherits the strong to fairly strong combination of the premises to derive a strong to fairly strong conclusion.

The thought (3) will be further strengthened if other applications of *modus ponens* with different premises also derive it as a conclusion. It will also be strengthened if it is a premise in a further deduction which reaches as its conclusion a thought which is for other reasons strongly held. Consider for example a text which is in fourteen lines of iambic pentameter. If we combine (3) with the conditional (10) we derive as a conclusion a statement (11) which is true of the text; thus (3), the thought that the text is a sonnet, is further strengthened. (Note that 'strength' is not identical to 'truth'.)

> (3)   The text is a sonnet.
> (10) If a text is a sonnet then it is in iambic pentameter.
> > by *modus ponens*
> (11) The text is in iambic pentameter.

Literary form is derived inferentially

The account of sonnethood just outlined is the model for almost all kinds of literary form (except for the invariant forms discussed in chapter 1). 'Being a sonnet' holds of a text only because there is a thought 'The text is a sonnet', and holds of the text to the degree that the thought is strong. The form 'being a sonnet' is thus not inherent to the text itself; the relation between the form and the text is that the text provides evidence for the form. The literary form of a text can be understood as holding in the relationship between the reader and the text, and thus the literary form of the text will vary between different readers of the same text. Literary form is thus very similar to meaning; in fact, literary form is a kind of meaning, because it is the content of a thought. Just as the text implies certain meanings, so it implies certain forms. By making literary form a kind of meaning, we can begin to understand how literary form and literary meaning can interact: because they are both derived inferentially, they thus exist in the same cognitive place and this enables them to interact.

Where thoughts come from

Where do thoughts come from? Some already exist as the thinker's knowledge, which is a collection of thoughts. Thoughts which already exist differ in accessibility, which affects the likelihood of any particular thought being invoked in thinking. Thoughts change in their accessibility, and connections between thoughts mean that the increased accessibility of one thought increases the accessibility of others: once we have thoughts about sonnets, other thoughts about sonnets will become more accessible. Thus once we undertake the first deduction above (relating lineation to sonnethood), it is more likely that we will undertake the second deduction above (relating metre to sonnethood).

Thoughts can also be newly formulated, and this includes conditionals. *Modus ponens* combines a premise A with a premise conditional 'If A then B', to derive a conclusion B. But these premises might be formulated anew as a way of deriving a conclusion which is already known to be true; if we know a text is a sonnet, then we can formulate new premises to derive this as a conclusion. For example, if we read various sonnets by Milton we might note that there is a tendency for them to begin with someone's name. For each text, this observation can be formulated as a thought (12):

(12) This text has a name as its first word.

We already have the thought (3):

(3) This text is a sonnet.

And so we could formulate a conditional (13), which holds relatively weakly in that it is likely to be supported by relatively few observations.

(13) If a text is a sonnet then it has a name as its first word.

The formulation of this conditional is achieved by building backwards from (12) as a conclusion and (3) as a premise, and formulating another premise (13) to derive the conclusion by *modus ponens*.

(3) This text is a sonnet.
(13) If a text is a sonnet then it has a name as its first word.
             by *modus ponens*
(12) This text has a name as its first word.

Here it is the conditional (13) which is the new thought. In this way, new generalisations arise – and so new kinds of literary form come into existence. The conditional would probably be held very weakly because it is formulated anew on the basis of reading a few texts; it does not exist in general knowledge, and the likelihood of its being stored in general knowledge will relate to its strength and the extent to which it is used in other deductions. Furthermore, while the conclusion would seem to be directly derived from the text, it should be recognised that there are a very large number (perhaps an infinite number) of thoughts which could be fairly directly derived from the text; the fact that this particular conclusion is formulated is because it can play a role in an inferential process. Thus *modus ponens* influences what formal features we notice in a text.

We might, for example, have a slightly different thought about the text; instead of (3) we might formulate (14) as a thought:

(14) This text is a Miltonic sonnet.

Then by the process derived earlier we would formulate a different conditional:

(15) If a text is a Miltonic sonnet then it has a name as its first word.

This conditional holds weakly. But as a thought it has some potential use. When we read Wordsworth's or Muir's sonnets which begin 'Milton...' the conditional (15) might be invoked along with the deduction which involves it and this might activate other expectations about Miltonic sonnet form for these texts.

The literary form of a text is the content of a thought about the text. The text provides evidence for the thought about literary form in the form of a premise such as 'this text is called a sonnet'. But this premise must be combined with a conditional such as 'if this text is called a sonnet then it is a sonnet'. Conditionals of this kind do not come directly from the text, but there is also no reason to think that there is a store of conditionals which are accessed in interpretation. Rather, these conditionals can be invented anew in the interpretive process, gaining their strength from their compatibility with what the thinker knows (e.g. their knowledge of sonnets). An important claim in Relevance Theory is that 'context is not given in advance', with 'context' including conditionals which are used in inferencing. In this view it is incorrect to think of the reader or listener as drawing solely on a pre-existing encyclopedia of background knowledge which he or she draws upon in making deductions; while there is pre-existing background knowledge, the reader or listener also adds to that background knowledge and indeed reshapes the pre-existing background knowledge in the process of making inferences.

Explicatures

This brings us to the question of how we get thoughts from external stimuli, such as poems. A piece of speech or writing can be decoded into a set of logical forms by the systems of syntax and phonology; this is the mapping between sound and meaning which can be accomplished by the rules of generative phonology and syntax. 'Sound' and 'meaning' are best understood here as abstracted or idealised; it is not sound itself which is mapped to meaning but a psychological representation of sound. Similarly, the meaning which is derived by the syntax as a set of logical forms is not (yet) the meaning of the utterance. One reason for this is that logical forms are not necessarily full propositions. They characteristically need to be enriched or developed into full propositions which can then be manipulated as premises in inferencing.

For example if I hear an utterance 'she didn't bring the book here', the syntactic processes will deliver a logical form which contains information about its meaning: that someone brought some book to some place. But the logical form by itself will not tell us who 'she' is or which book is being spoken of or which precise location 'here' is. The fact of these variables means that the logical form is not yet fully propositional: it is neither true nor false. But in most conversational contexts, the hearer will be able to fill in all three variables, thus producing a full proposition. The process of filling in the variables is what Sperber and Wilson (1995:182) call the development of an explicature from the logical form. Their term 'explicature' expresses the fact that it is an explicit meaning of the utterance, as opposed to the implicit meanings which are derived by inferencing (e.g. by *modus ponens*). Explicatures are thus those thoughts which are most directly developed from the text itself.

If a text is titled 'sonnet' then we can get a logical form from this title which can be developed to derive the explicature 'This text is called a sonnet.' This is a rare case where we get a thought about form by developing a logical form derived from the text: the formal features of a text are not usually included in the content of logical forms. Nevertheless, there are formal characteristics of a text which would seem to be more like explicatures than implicatures, because they are in some sense directly present in the text. Consider for example the fact that for most sonnets as printed on a page, in the body of the text there are exactly fourteen words which have no words to their right on the page. This is a determinate characteristic of the text, an explicit fact about the text's form. I suggest that we extend the notion of explicature so that it includes propositions which are developed directly from determinate characteristics of the text. Thus the thought (16) is an explicature of the text, in this expanded sense.

> (16) This text has fourteen words which have no words to their right on the page.

This in turn will provide evidence (via *modus ponens* and the appropriate conditional) for the inference that there are fourteen lines.

(16) This text has fourteen words which have no words to their right on the page.
(17) If this text has fourteen words which have no words to their right on the page then it has fourteen lines.
by *modus ponens*
(18) This text has fourteen lines.

In chapter 5 I show that 'having lines' or 'having fourteen lines' are indeed implicatures of the text, kinds of variable form which can hold to a certain degree.

We can do something similar with rhyme. Consider the first four lines of the sonnet by E. B. Browning:

Say over again, and yet once over again,
That thou dost love me. Though the word repeated
Should seem 'a cuckoo-song', as thou dost treat it.
Remember, never to the hill or plain,

The fact that rhyme holds between 'again' and 'plain' and between 'repeated' and 'treat it' is best considered an inference. The strength to which it holds as a thought depends on the degree of similarity between the sounds involved; sounds which are not identical (as in the rhymes in lines 2 and 3) can nevertheless be judged as rhymes because they deviate from each other in ways held to be legitimate, and also fit into a pattern both expected for the text and justified by the rest of the text. But there are explicatures which can be drawn from the text and which are the basis for the deductions which lead to these inferences. Thus the actual sounds with which the line ends can be represented in thoughts which are descriptions of explicit form:

(19) Line 2 ends in the sounds [ɪd].
(20) Line 3 ends in the sounds [ɪt].

From these explicatures, we can develop the thought that the lines rhyme.

In this section I have extended Sperber and Wilson's notion of explicature from explicit meaning to explicit form. They take an explicature to be specifically a development from a logical form; I suggest extending this so that an explicature can also be a newly formulated proposition about the explicit form of the text as suggested above. It is possible to enumerate the explicatures which are developed from logical forms because there are a fixed number of logical forms derivable from a text and a fixed set of ways in which they can be developed (Sperber and Wilson 1995:175). In contrast, explicatures like (16, 19 or 20) which can be developed from the text itself are probably not enumerable; there may be an infinite number of direct observations to be made about any text, depending on how one looks at it. Nevertheless, the core notion of 'explicitness' holds for both the meanings which Sperber and Wilson call explicatures and the descriptions of forms which I propose also to call explicatures.

Weak implicature and aesthetic experience

A text offers evidence for inferences about its literary form, but any individual piece of evidence will usually only weakly imply a conclusion about the form of the text, and must be combined with other evidence in order to lead to fairly strong conclusions of literary form. Consider for example the relationship between a pause and the end of a line. We might formulate the following conditional:

> (21) If a word is followed by a pause then it is at the end of a line.

Pauses are used as evidence for line-endings, but there are inevitably pauses throughout the text, and at each of these pauses this conditional will come into play, thereby leading to the conclusion that these too are line-endings. For example in the Elizabeth Barrett Browning poem quoted at the beginning of this book there are about twenty-four pauses (taking punctuation as a guide); this conditional will lead to conclusions that there are twenty-four lines, ending at these pauses. For fourteen of these line-boundaries there will be evidence from other sources (such as metre and rhyme and layout) to strengthen the conclusions that these are line boundaries; the remaining ten implied line boundaries are implied so weakly that they are not in the end held to be line boundaries.

This weakness of implicature thus has two characteristic effects. First it means that there will be a large number of weak implicatures of form arising from any text. Many of the implicatures are unsupported by any other kind of evidence and so remain very weak. Following Sperber and Wilson (1995) I suggest that this is experienced as aesthetic.

Let us give the name *poetic effect* to the peculiar effect of an utterance which achieves most of its relevance through a wide array of weak implicatures. (Sperber and Wilson (1995:222))

Sperber and Wilson's aim is to explain why certain kinds of meaning, including metaphor and kinds of evocation, are experienced as 'poetic' (or in our terms 'aesthetic'). I have argued that literary form always involves a wide array of weak implicatures, and this explains why literary form might be experienced as aesthetic. This is a situation where just being in a certain cognitive state (entertaining a wide array of weak implicatures) counts as having aesthetic experience.

Contradictions and complexity are not always experienced as aesthetic; sometimes they are experienced as annoying or upsetting, and sometimes as problems which must be solved (as in scientific enquiry). Thus clearly more must be said about various kinds of experience of complexity and specifically aesthetic experience. Perhaps an 'aesthetic set' or willingness to entertain complexity without attempting to resolve it is the reader's contribution to his or her own aesthetic experience.

3.4   Conflicting conclusions

> *A Sonnet to Opium; Celebrating its Virtues. Written at the Side of Julia, when the Author was Inspired with a Dose of Laudanum, more than Sufficient for two moderate Turks*
>
> Soul-soothing drug! your virtues let me laud,
>   Which can with sov'reign sway
> Force lawless passion into harmless play!
>   Oft have I owned your pow'r
>   In many a moody hour,
> When grief with viper-tooth my heart hath gnawed.
>   Still friendly to the plaintive muse,
>   You can a balm infuse.
>   If, sick with hopeless love,
>   Too tenderly I mourn,
> You can the shaft of anguish quick remove;
> Or make desire's destructive flame less fiercely burn:
> Guardian you are of Julia's innocence,
> When madd'ning rapture goads to vice my throbbing sense.
>
> Anonymous ('Orestes'), 1796 (L:818)

This text gives evidence for the following thought (22), which combines with a conditional (23) to derive the conclusion (24) that the text is a sonnet:

> (22) This text has fourteen lines.
> (23) If a text has fourteen lines then it is a sonnet.
>   by *modus ponens*
> (24) This text is a sonnet.

And similarly the text gives evidence for thought (25) which combines with a conditional (26) to derive the same conclusion (27) that the text is a sonnet.

> (25) This text is called a sonnet.
> (26) If a text is called a sonnet then it is a sonnet.
>   by *modus ponens*
> (27) This text is a sonnet.

However, the use of these thoughts about sonnets makes other thoughts about sonnets more active, and these include the following conditional:

> (28) If a text is a sonnet then it is in iambic pentameter.

We can combine this with premise (29), a thought already strongly evidenced by the other inferential processes, and derive as a conclusion (30).

> (28) If a text is a sonnet then it is in iambic pentameter.
> (29) This text is a sonnet.
>   by *modus ponens*
> (30) This text is in iambic pentameter.

But the text (which is in a variable length iambic metre) also provides strong evidence for this thought (31):

> (31) This text is not in iambic pentameter.

Now we have a collection of thoughts about the same text which are not fully compatible with one another. Either the text both is and is not in iambic pentameter, or the text both is and is not a sonnet. We have a choice between two contradictions.

There are three fundamentally different strategies, any of which can be used to resolve an incompatibility between thoughts about form, and which represent what we might call 'categorial', 'tendential' and 'ambiguity' strategies for recognising literary form.

In the 'categorial' strategy, the text either is or is not a sonnet; thus we can resolve this incompatibility by acknowledging that the strength of the conclusions that 'this text is a sonnet' are not sufficient to prove the point, given the metre, and so this thought must be abandoned: it is not a sonnet. This is Oliphant's (1932) position; his attempt to lay down the law has a strategic purpose in guiding sonnet-writing practice but carries no general weight or authority.

In the 'tendential' strategy, the text can be more or less sonnet-like; this is captured here by saying that the thought 'this text is a sonnet' holds to a certain degree of the text but is weakened by the failure of the inference relating to metre. This strategy exploits the weakness of implicature, which I suggested earlier is also a way of experiencing implied form as aesthetic.

In the 'ambiguity' strategy the text is at the same time both a sonnet and not a sonnet; both thoughts hold fairly strongly, with the competition between them thus unresolvable. Following Empson (1953), I suggest that this ambiguity is experienced as aesthetic. As Robert Venturi puts it, our aesthetic experience is premised on 'both-and' rather than 'either-or', and thus is an experience of ambiguity and paradox (Venturi 1977:48).

3.5   Interpretive use and approximation to a pattern

If we stay with this same sonnet, and consider its rhyme scheme, we might derive an inference (32).

> (32) The text has a rhyme scheme ABBC CADD EFEF GG.

Part of a reader's knowledge of sonnets is a knowledge that certain rhyme schemes are found in sonnets. For example we may know a conditional (33):

> (33) If a text has a rhyme scheme ABAB CDCD EFEF GG then it is a sonnet.

If the text warrants a premise (34) then the conclusion is that the text is a sonnet:

> (33) If a text has a rhyme scheme ABAB CDCD EFEF GG then it is a sonnet.
> (34) This text has a rhyme scheme ABAB CDCD EFEF GG.
> by *modus ponens*
> (35) This text is a sonnet.

But this particular text warrants the premise (32) rather than (34); I compare them below:

> (32) This text has a rhyme scheme ABBC CADD EFEF GG.
> (34) This text has a rhyme scheme ABAB CDCD EFEF GG.

While (32) is not identical to (34) it clearly resembles it (the last six lines have exactly the same pattern), and we need to find a way of capturing the fact that if a rhyme scheme resembles a sonnet rhyme scheme then this contributes (weakly) to the evidence that the text is a sonnet.

The mechanism for doing this comes from Sperber and Wilson's (1995:229) notion of interpretive use, and the possibility of a deduction from one thought to another by an interpretive relation between them. An interpretive relation holds between a proposition and another proposition which it resembles in some way; one proposition is an interpretation of the other. In the Elizabeth Barrett Browning poem cited earlier there is the following line:

> Cry, 'Speak once more – thou lovest!' Who can fear

Here the section 'Speak once more – thou lovest' is a piece of writing which interpretively resembles (i.e. can be interpreted as resembling) a spoken utterance. Mimicry of this kind is one of the simplest kinds of interpretive use.

Another simple kind of interpretive use is the representation of speech. The Browning poem has:

> Say over again, and yet once over again,
> That thou dost love me.

Here the author of the poem represents another speaker, who is asked to say something like this:

> I love you.

Here there is an interpretive resemblance between 'That thou dost love me' and 'I love you'. The resemblance comes from the fact that while their forms are different, they have the same meanings once the referents (the lover and the beloved) are established. As a rather different example of interpretive use, consider a metaphor, taken from the sonnet by 'Orestes' quoted earlier.

> grief with viper-tooth my heart hath gnawed

This utterance interpretively resembles the following utterance:

> I grieve.

We say that there is an interpretive resemblance between the two utterances because the conclusions which can be derived from the first utterance are shared with the conclusions which can be derived from the other: they share a set of implicatures and thus resemble one another. The advantage of the poetic line in comparison to 'I grieve' is that there are other implicatures which can be derived from it which cannot be derived from the short paraphrase.

Sperber and Wilson suggest that interpretive use is fundamental to the success of communication, and the possibility of communicating a meaning by stating it approximately or roughly. I propose to apply 'interpretive use' to the characteristic kinds of approximation seen in literary form. Rhyme schemes illustrate this, where a thought like (32) resembles a thought like (34).

> (32) This text has a rhyme scheme ABBC CADD EFEF GG.
> (34) This text has a rhyme scheme ABAB CDCD EFEF GG.

I suggest that we take (32) to constitute evidence of (34) by resemblance. Thus (32) implies (34). The closeness of resemblance will affect the strength of the final outcome; here the resemblance is not exact and so the conclusion is somewhat weak.

> (32) This text has a rhyme scheme ABBC CADD EFEF GG. [strong]
>   by resemblance
> (34) This text has a rhyme scheme ABAB CDCD EFEF GG. [weak]

Now we have the basis for a further implicature, though weakened by the fact that one of the basic premises is weak.

(34) This text has a rhyme scheme ABAB CDCD EFEF GG. [weak]
(36) If a text has a rhyme scheme ABAB CDCD EFEF GG then it is a sonnet. [strong]
                          by *modus ponens*
(37) This text is a sonnet. [weak]

Interpretive use (resemblance) can be a powerful tool for understanding literary form, to explain why texts can approximate roughly to a pattern rather than exactly conforming to the pattern. Here it explains approximation to a rhyme scheme; shortly I will use it to account for texts which approximate to fourteen lines (by having fifteen or thirteen or twelve lines). In chapter 4 I will use it to explain approximation to rhythmic patterns, thereby explaining kinds of form unexplained by the generative rules of chapter 1. Smith (1968:98) puts mimicry at the centre of verbal art when she describes a poem not as an utterance but as the imitation of an utterance: 'poems resemble nonliterary utterances and imitate their structures'. She shows that poems imitate speech genres, such that knowledge of the speech genre can enable inferences to be drawn about the poem such as how it will end. Smith's imitation is our interpretive use. Empson also has a notion which approximates to interpretive use, as an instance of his first type of ambiguity. He says that 'The demands of metre allow the poet to say something which is not normal colloquial English, so that the reader thinks of the various colloquial forms which are near to it, and puts them together; weighting their probabilities in proportion to their nearness' (Empson 1953). Thus for Empson the actual wording of the text implies other wordings by being interpretations of them.

The notion of interpretive use can also account for 'deviance' of literary language away from the norms of the language. In some cases, we can understand innovative (or archaic) linguistic forms as involving direct intervention into the encapsulated sound-structure, word-structure and sentence-structure systems. For example, Kiparsky (1972) argues that poets can use a slightly different phonology from the phonology of the language around them, while Austin (1984) claims that Shelley's deviant word orders come from violations of specific syntactic rules. But it is also possible to see deviant linguistic forms not as direct manipulations of the systems which produce them but as imitations and approximations to non-literary language. Joyce's portmanteau words in *Finnegans Wake* are not derived from English or any other language by specific linguistic processes; instead they are new words which relate to the familiar words by imitation and allusion (MacMahon 1995). In these kinds of text, the words of the text do not themselves have linguistic form but they resemble and hence imply words which do have linguistic form.

3.6   Weak sonnets

I now look at the various conditionals which are involved in assessing whether a text is a sonnet. I will look specifically at sonnets where inferential processes run into problems (usually contradictions), to examine how sonnethood nevertheless can be argued to hold. We might call these weak sonnets, because the thought 'this text is a sonnet' is never at full strength, varying from slightly weak in texts which are just short of exemplary sonnets to very weak in texts which exhibit just a trace of sonnethood. The possibility of conditionals failing comes from the fact that these conditionals exist within the pragmatics, and not within a modularised rule system such as is found in the syntax or phonology. If sonnets were derived by generative rules we would not expect weak sonnets to exist.

Fourteen lines

(38) If a text has fourteen lines then it is a sonnet.

Fuller says of his anthology 'I have not included "sonnets" in other numbers of lines, since one can soon reach the absurdity of concluding that something like Tennyson's "The Kraken" (fifteen lines) is "really" a sonnet' (Fuller 2000:xxxiii). Fuller holds conditional (38) to be inviolable. But conditionals have no universal characteristics, and while one reader may hold (38) to be inviolable, another may not. I now consider 'The Kraken' from a perspective which allows (38) to hold with less than full strength.

The Kraken

> Below the thunders of the upper deep;
> Far, far beneath in the abysmal sea,
> His ancient, dreamless, uninvaded sleep
> The Kraken sleepeth: faintest sunlights flee
> About his shadowy sides: above him swell
> Huge sponges of millenial growth and height;
> And far away into the sickly light,
> From many a wondrous grot and secret cell
> Unnumber'd and enormous polypi
> Winnow with giant arms the slumbering green.
> There hath he lain for ages and will lie
> Battening upon huge seaworms in his sleep,
> Until the latter fire shall heat the deep;
> Then once by man and angels to be seen,
> In roaring he shall rise and on the surface die.

Alfred, Lord Tennyson, 1830 (Ricks 1969:246)

This text is not called a sonnet, it has fifteen lines, its rhyme pattern does not exactly fit a sonnet rhyme pattern, and while it is in iambic pentameter (compatible with its being a sonnet) so are many non-sonnet texts. In order to get some usable premises which might derive the conclusion that the text is a sonnet, we must derive them by resemblance between propositions. Thus the explicature (39) resembles (40) and so weakly implies it; this in turn means that the conclusion 'the text is a sonnet' is weakly implied.

> (39) The text has fifteen lines. [strong]
> (40) The text has fourteen lines. [weak]

Note incidentally that the poem also looks on the page as though it might be a sonnet (it is what Hollander calls a 'poem-shaped poem' (1975:272)); it requires actual counting of the lines to be sure that it has fifteen rather than fourteen lines. Thus the thought (41) is a strong thought derived as an explicature from the text, this being a description of form gained by direct observation.

> (41) This text is roughly as deep as it is wide. [strong]

We can take this as a conclusion, formulate a conditional (43) and combine it with the thought (42) which thereby inherits some strength from the strength of the conclusion.

> (42) This text is a sonnet.
> (43) If a text is a sonnet it is roughly as deep as it is wide.
>   by *modus ponens*
> (41) This text is roughly as deep as it is wide.

As regards the rhyme scheme, (44) can be formulated, which resembles the standard pattern in (45) by closely resembling it in the first two thirds of the text, and thus weakly implies it.

> (44) The text has a rhyme scheme ABAB CDDC EFE GG FE [strong]
>   by resemblance
> (45) The text has a rhyme scheme ABAB CDCD EFEF GG [weak]

Again, by invoking a suitable conditional, sonnethood is weakly implied. The fact that the poem is in iambic pentameter now provides some strengthening of the sonnethood of the text.

Thus sonnethood is weakly implied for this text, which gives rise to two questions. First, what is the function of implying sonnethood for this text, and second, why is sonnethood only weakly rather than strongly implied for this text? The answer comes from Sperber and Wilson's proposal that weak implicature is capable of being experienced as a type of aesthetic experience. This type of aesthetic experience is triggered by textual uncertainty, complexity and indeterminacy, and in this case specifically by formal (generic) uncertainty and indeterminacy. The complexity of the text comes partly from its generic uncertainty. But the possibility that the text is a sonnet can lead us inferentially into further complexities. One of the conditionals involving sonnethood is:

> (46) If a text is a sonnet then the text's meaning is resolved at the end.

This conditional can be invoked as part of an interpretive procedure, taking 'the text is a sonnet' as the other premise, and thus leading to the conclusion that the sonnet ends by resolving a problem. Another conditional is relevant here:

> (47) If a death is mentioned at the end of a text then the text's meaning is resolved at the end.

This conditional can be derived from various sources (such as general metaphorical associations between death and ending), and is strengthened to the degree that texts manifest it (see Smith 1968). Note that like any conditional, this need not exist as a thought in advance of the interpretive procedures; it can be formulated for the first time and assigned some degree of strength, as part of an interpretation.

By (46), sonnethood is retroactively strengthened if the text is resolved at the end. By (47) the mention of death at the end of the text derives the proposition that the text is resolved at the end, thus, indirectly strengthening the thought that the text is a sonnet. But there is a complication, which is that in terms of the actual development of meanings in this particular text we expect the Kraken to emerge as a terrifying threat instead of emerging and dying; this can be read as an anticlimactic ending. An inferential process which derives this result will thus be in conflict with the inferential processes based on generic expectations about how sonnets end. Thus by reading the text as a sonnet we get a kind of contradiction, which I suggest is a source of aesthetic experience.

The contradiction is further strengthened by the rhyme structure of the text. The initial rhyme structure of the text resembles the representation of sonnet rhyme in (45), which ends in a couplet on lines 13 and 14. In this poem there is a couplet on lines 12 and 13 with line 13 ending on the same word as line 1. There would be some justification for reading these two characteristics as evidence that this is the end of the poem (we could invoke or invent a weak conditional 'if a line ends in the same word as the first line of the poem then the line in question is the final line of the poem'; such a conditional would find some limited support in poetic practice). Thus we weakly conclude that the poem ends on line 13 but then there are two more lines, separated off as though they are a couplet, not rhyming as a couplet, and with an anticlimactic structure. As no more lines follow, there is strong evidence that line 15 is the end of the poem, but as an ending this competes with the weakly evidenced but still implied ending at line 13; thus there is some uncertainty about whether we should treat lines 14 and 15 as a kind of post-textual coda (of a kind sometimes seen in sonnets, as I shortly show).

As our next example of a non-fourteen line weak sonnet, consider now the following poem of twelve lines, rhyming ABAB CDCD BABA.

A Wreath

A wreathed garland of deserved praise,
Of praise deserved, unto thee I give,
I give to thee, who knowest all my ways,
My crooked winding ways, wherein I live,
Wherein I die, not live: for life is straight,
Straight as a line, and ever tends to thee,
To thee, who art more far above deceit
Than deceit seems above simplicity.
Give me simplicity, that I may live,
So live and like, that I may know thy ways,
Know them and practise them: then shall I give
For this poor wreath, give thee a crown of praise.

George Herbert, 1633 (F:334)

The poem's rhyme scheme is (48), and this interpretively resembles the rhyme scheme (49), which is a premise that can be combined with conditional (50) to derive the conclusion that the text is an English sonnet.

(48) The text has a rhyme scheme ABAB CDCD BABA.
(49) The text has a rhyme scheme ABAB CDCD EFEF GG.
(50) If a text has a rhyme scheme ABAB CDCD EFEF GG then it is an 'English' sonnet.

Because the premise (49) is based on interpretive resemblance to the explicature (48) rather than being an explicature itself, the conclusion is thus weakened. Another formal characteristic of the poem is that every line ends in a word which is repeated in the next line, except line 10. This gives rise to the following implicature:

(51) The last two lines are a separate unit.

This proposition can combine with a (fairly weak) conditional (52), to derive the conclusion that the text is an 'English' sonnet.

(52) If the last two lines are a separate unit then the text is an 'English' sonnet.

Thus the poem warrants the interpretation that it is an 'English' sonnet, in two individually weak ways which because they have the same conclusion thereby strengthen the conclusion. Note however that the two routes by which this conclusion is reached are incompatible with each other, even though they lead to the same conclusion: the rhyme scheme suggests four quatrains, and the repetition/ non-repetition of final words suggests a final couplet, so that by a kind of double exposure we get a fourteen-line 'English' sonnet from a twelve-line text.

A different way of getting a twelve-line text to imply sonnethood is seen in Shakespeare's sonnet 126. In the 1609 quarto publication of Shakespeare's sonnets, there are twelve lines of text followed by two pairs of curved parentheses in italic, bracketing empty lines. Lennard (1991:41) suggests that there are simultaneous effects from this formal trick – the sonnethood of the text is weakened, but we can also read the twelve lines as complete, and at the same time can see the empty ending as a contribution to the meaning of the text. The interesting question here is whether we take the poem to have fourteen lines (counting the bracketed spaces as lines) or twelve lines. This does not seem to be immediately resolvable, and incidentally shows that the number of lines is not an explicature but an implicature of the text, in this case with two distinct implicatures both equally strong.

In chapter 5 I further discuss the possibility that lineation is a matter of implicature rather than explicature. This is shown by the anonymous 'Prayer to Hymen', thirteen lines of iambic pentameter in rhyming couplets AA BB CC DD EE X FF. The eleventh line falls out of the couplet scheme, not rhyming with any other line; instead its final word 'use' rhymes with a line-internal word 'refuse' (technically a 'leonine rhyme'):

> But what I did refuse now fain would use   line 11
>
> Anonymous, 'Prayer to Hymen', before 1655 (F:639)

If the line were reanalysed as two lines this would give a full couplet structure and a poem of fourteen lines. There are various ways of determining how many lines there are in a text. One is to count how many words have no words to the right of them (which is an explicature of the text); in this case there are thirteen such words, which implies that there are thirteen lines. But another is to count how many words are involved in rhymes; in this case there are fourteen such words, which implies that there are fourteen lines. Both lineations are thus implied by the text, even though they are incompatible with each other. This is an example of a very widespread formal device of using a line which can alternatively be analysed as two lines. The decision to divide the line into two (which is itself an inferential act relating to lineation) both strengthens one kind of evidence and weakens another kind of evidence for the sonnethood of the poem.

Explicit naming of the poem as 'sonnet'

(53) If a text is explicitly called a sonnet then it is a sonnet.

When the title of the poem tells us that it is a sonnet this would seem to be particularly strong evidence that a text is a sonnet, as it apparently codes the writer's intentions. But the writer's saying that a text is a sonnet is like any communicative act: what is explicitly said need not be what is actually communicated, and there are potential advantages to be gained from saying that a text is a sonnet when there are other reasons to think that it is not. Naming a text 'sonnet' does not determinately make it a sonnet or constitute undeniable proof that it is a sonnet; it is just one kind of evidence which might in fact be contradicted or weakened in combination with other evidence offered by the text such as its metre. This is an important point about form which is worth repeating: even when the form is apparently coded by explicitly naming it as part of the text, the naming can only be taken as evidence for form rather than as actually encoding the form in a determinate manner. This shows that when a text is titled 'sonnet' we should take the explicature to be (54) rather than (55):

> (54) This text is called a sonnet.
> (55) This text is a sonnet.

There is a further complication, which is that the term 'sonnet' was ambiguous in English use at least until the eighteenth century. After the range of forms seen in thirteenth-century Italy (Spiller 1992:3), Petrarch and other Italian son-neteers took 'sonnet' to mean a fourteen-line poem with rhymes structured in octave and sestet (with some allowed variations), and this is the meaning which Gascoigne (1575) takes it to have. But English practice until the seventeenth century appears to have allowed the term to have quite a wide range of meanings; Spiller (1992:94) suggests that the title of Tottel's miscellany, *Songes and sonettes* implies that sonnets were discursive poems defined in part by just not being songs. Reflecting some uncertainty about the term, Campion (1602) chooses to call what we might call sonnets 'quatorzains'. The ambiguity of the term 'sonnet' can in part be seen as a looseness of use, but in part it also reflects the fact that being a sonnet (more than most genres of text) is a combination of distinct features of a text which may be present to a greater or lesser degree.

Consider for example some of the texts called sonnets in Fulke Greville's posthumously published collection *Caelica* (1633), after the major sonnet se-quences of the turn of the century might have been expected to stabilise the meaning of the term. Sonnet 56 is organised as a sequence of ungrouped lines rather than in stanzas, in sevens, organised in nineteen quatrains by ABAB rhyme (and meaning), and ending in a couplet. Thus it resembles a Shakespearean sonnet in its rhyme scheme and its quatrain- and-couplet struc-ture, but not in its length and its metre. Sonnet 87 is in iambic pentameter, consisting of two six-line stanzas rhyming ABABCC; here we have the right metre and the second stanza looks exactly like the last six lines of a Shakespeare sonnet but the division of the text into stanzas and the length are evidence against sonnethood. Sonnet 105 is in four four-line stanzas ABAB and a fifth stanza ABABCC, thus resembling a Shakespearean structure in some ways but not others (overall length and division into stanzas). It would be wrong, I think, to suggest that Greville (or his printer) is ignoring what by then would be an increasingly standardised characterisation of the sonnet; rather he is exploiting the distinctness between the kinds of evidence for the sonnet, promoting now one, now another kind of evidence to produce weak sonnets.

The rhyme scheme

Sub-types of sonnets have distinctive rhyme schemes, with a major distinction between the 'Italian' scheme where the rhyme distinguishes two groups of 8 and 6 lines, and the 'English' scheme where the rhyme scheme distinguishes four groups of 4 + 4 + 4 + 2 lines. The most significant difference is in the last six lines which either hold together as a single unit or are split into 4 + 2.

'Being an Italian sonnet' is a kind of implied form, as is 'being an English sonnet', and so we might expect some sonnets to be ambiguous between the two, with evidence for both (incompatible) conclusions. We can see examples of this in the American poet Jones Very's sonnets. Many of those anthologised in Spengemann (1996) tend to have a rhyme pattern which divides the poem into three quatrains and a couplet: ABAB CDCD EFEF GG, but other aspects of the poems offer evidence for a final sestet. In four of the sonnets ('The Spirit', 'The Serpent', 'The Robe', 'The Slowness of Belief in a Spiritual World') the ninth line begins with 'but'. As a connective, 'but' characteristically marks out sub-segments of a text in English verse (and narratives); in the sonnets it implies the 'turn' after the octave. The following sonnet shows a more complex strategy:

> ### Slavery
>
> Not by the railing tongues of angry men,
> Who have not learned their passions to control;
> Not by the scornful words of press and pen,
> That now ill-omened fly from pole to pole;
> Not by fierce party cries; nor e'en by blood,
> Can this our Country's guilt be washed away;
> In vain for this would flow the crimson flood,
> In vain for this would man his brother slay.
> Not by such means; but by the power of prayer;
> Of faith in God, joined with a sense of sin;
> These, these alone can save us from despair,
> And o'er the mighty wrong a victory win;
> These, these alone can make us free from all
> That doth ourselves, our Country still inthral.

Jones Very, 1851 (S:134)

Here the rhyme scheme divides the poem into quatrains and a couplet, but the punctuation divides the poem into an octave and a sestet, each consisting of one long sentence. Note that 'but' again appears in the first line of the sestet though it is not the first word. The divisions of the text are more complex still; 'Not by' initiates lines 1, 3 and 5, and thus appears to define the octave, but the next appearance is in line 9 where it initiates the sestet; and lines 7 and 8 are the most distinctively 'couplet-like' lines in syntactic structure; instead of ending on a couplet the poem ends on a four-line unit beginning and repeating 'These, these alone'.

Sonnets can thus weaken, or complicate, the evidence for their form while still having a standard rhyme scheme. But sonnets can also dispense with the rhyme scheme altogether. Thus James Russell Lowell's 'Science and Poetry' (1888, S:163) is a fourteen-line poem in iambic pentameter but without rhyme; the evidence for sonnethood here is weak, coming mainly from the number of lines, but weak evidence is still evidence. Then there are the many fourteen-line texts which are in couplets throughout (AA BB CC DD EE FF GG). Not only does the absence of the expected rhyme scheme weaken the evidence for sonnethood, it also removes a potential source of evidence for grouping the lines into quatrains, octave or sestet. However, other kinds of evidence can be used. Thus Jonson's 'Epigram XIV: To William Camden' (1616, F:124) has a major pause after quatrains, and in addition the first quatrain has its first line-final pause at the end of the quatrain, thus drawing attention to pausing as evidence for grouping. Christina Rossetti does something rather similar in 'Sappho' (Jay and Lewis 1996:113) which is fourteen lines of iambic tetrameter in couplets; evidence that it is a sonnet comes from the full stop after fourth, and semi-colon after eighth and twelfth lines, thus isolating the couplet at the end. Another problem which comes from using couplets throughout is that the final couplet is not distinctive. Herrick solves this problem by using specific words at the beginnings of couplets and distinguishing the final one. In his fourteen-line poem 'Delight in Disorder' (1648, F:257) each couplet begins with 'a/an' except the final one which begins 'do', thus bringing out the characteristic sonnet pattern of a distinctive final couplet (though evidence for sonnethood is weakened by the poem's iambic tetrameter). In the following poem, the word 'sing' is used six times and the word 'write' four times; each couplet begins with either 'I sing' or 'I write', in a pattern sing-sing-write, sing-sing-write, write; thus the final couplet is separated off.

The Argument of His Book

I sing of brooks, of blossoms, birds, and bowers,
Of April, May, of June, and July-flowers.
I sing of May-poles, hock-carts, wassails, wakes,
Of bridegrooms, brides, and of their bridal cakes.
I write of youth, of love, and have access

By these to sing of cleanly-wantonness.
I sing of dews, of rains, and piece by piece
Of balm, of oil, of spice, and amber-Greece.
I sing of times trans-shifting; and I write
How roses first came red, and lilies white.
I write of groves, of twilights, and I sing
The court of Mab, and of the fairy king.
I write of hell; I sing (and ever shall)
Of heaven, and hope to have it after all.

Robert Herrick, *Hesperides*, 1648 (F:255)

Thus while rhyme implies a certain grouping, other kinds of evidence can help distinguish sub-groups within a text. This is the topic of chapter 6.

Implied form in 'perfect' sonnets

Even where a sonnet has all the right characteristics – fourteen lines, iambic pentameter and an acceptable rhyme scheme – the text may still increase the evidence for sonnethood, so strengthening already strong evidence for form. Treip (1970:19) says of the punctuation in the 1609 printing of Shakespeare's sonnets that 'it frequently happens that one or both lines of the concluding couplet are also pointed at the caesura, thus creating a slower, more deliberate and suitably final effect.' Furthermore full stops ('periods') are avoided sonnet-internally until the couplet. Thus even though there is already strong evidence for the couplet from rhyme and general expectation, evidence is still added. This suggests that there is no upper limit on the strength of a thought about literary form; we never arrive at a plateau at which we can say that form is finally and fully determined.

But there is another way of interpreting Shakespeare's formal practice, which is to see the piling up of evidence for already-clear formal divisions as having the consequence of breaking a unified text into parts and thus reducing evidence for sonnethood. Spiller (1992:11) argues that the sonnet is generically akin to a collection of proverbs or maxims, particularly in the final couplet. Thus just as a Romantic ode might, when 'magnified', break down into sonnets, so a sonnet might break down into epigrams. Horace Walpole brings this clearly out as a formal possibility in his 'Epitaph on Two Piping Bullfinches...' (1798, L:588), a text in fourteen lines (but rhyming couplets, a weakening of its son-nethood), which separates off the final pair of lines and gives this couplet a title of its own ('On the other Bullfinch, buried in the same place'). Walpole thus simultaneously strengthens the sonnethood of the text as a whole, by separating off the final couplet from the preceding six couplets, while also weakening the sonnethood of the text by cutting it into parts. A single formal practice can thus constitute evidence for two incompatible conclusions.

The sonnet as a distinct text

A sonnet is a distinct text, though often combined with other texts (e.g. in a sonnet sequence). The distinctness of the sonnet is reinforced by the notion that the sonnet expresses a structured thought, from opening to a clearly defined closure. But distinctness, like any other characteristic of a sonnet, can be stronger or weaker. In this section, I consider the possibility that a sonnet might be isolated as a sub-unit within a larger text of a different kind. This is an observation which has been made before; thus Häublein (1978:110) suggests that in Tennyson's *In Memoriam* (in quatrains) 'several of its sections resemble stanzaic poems or sonnets'.

As another example, Oliver Wendell Holmes's 'Prologue' (1861, S:124) is a twenty-eight-line poem in two stanzas, each of which has a rhyme pattern, which suggests that it should be considered a double sonnet. As another fairly clear example consider Shelley's 'Ode to the West Wind', which can be divided into five sub-sections, each consisting of four tercets and a couplet (in ABA BCB CDC DED EE rhymes), fourteen lines ending in a couplet; good evidence for isolating each sub-section as a sonnet (Wilcox 1950). But while the Ode can be seen as a series of sonnets, the sonnets themselves are made from something different again: tercets in *terza rima*. Thus the text is in different genres depending on the size of unit under consideration. Another example of an ode containing potential sonnets is the ten-line stanza used by Keats in some of his odes, with its ABABCDECDE rhyme which Häublein (1978:33) says 'looks like a truncated Italian sonnet'; here the evidence for sonnethood is weaker but still present. Similarly it has been argued that there are sonnet-like fourteen-line sequences in *Paradise Lost*.

Sonnets can emerge in various ways from a different kind of text. Frederick Goddard Tuckerman's 'Rhotruda' (1860, S:337) is a 165-line poem in blank verse separated by blank lines into irregular paragraphs, two of which are of fourteen lines. In this case there is little evidence from internal structure that these are sonnets, but being in fourteen lines is weak evidence, and this is strengthened by the fact that one is the final section of the poem; this placement in a prominent position implies some significance to the form. A more complex example can be found in Richard Crashaw's 'A Letter . . to the Countess of Denbigh . . .' (1652, F:512). This is a ninety-line stichic text in sevens (headless iambic tetrameter) and in rhyming couplets. Though the text in general is in headless iambic tetrameter, there are three couplets of iambic pentameter lines, one of which is at the end of the poem. These couplets can be 'grown backward' into the text to produce potential sonnets ending in the couplets. The first sequence is a new verse paragraph consisting of four lines (beginning 'So') and the couplet; the second sequence immediately follows as a new paragraph and has ten lines followed by the couplet; the final sequence is in two paragraphs, a six line-sequence, a four-line sequence and a couplet. Are these sonnets? In the first, we could identify a quatrain and couplet, a legitimate sonnet ending. In the second, the sequence of ten and two is close to the desired twelve and two. In the last, the pattern of sestet, quatrain and couplet again comes close to sonnet structure. Evidence for sonnethood is weak here, but again the evidence exists. This 'backwards reconstruction' of a sonnet from an identified sonnet ending can be seen also in Herman Melville's 'The March into Virginia' (1866, S:267). This is a variable-line-length iambic text in 36 lines and three variable-length stanzas; the third stanza has the structure of a sestet, with an ABABAB rhyme structure and a sense-division of 4+2. Here the text appears to be transforming into a sonnet at its end, as I argue also for the end of Arnold's 'Dover Beach' in Fabb (2002).

These are examples of 'emergent sectioning', where a form emerges amidst a different form – here a sonnet emerging from blank verse. If 'being in continuous (stichic) blank verse' and 'being a sonnet' were determinate facts of the text, then – since they are incompatible – we would not expect both possibilities to hold at the same time. But if form is implied then it is straightforward to explain how they can co-occur. Here there are two thoughts about the text, both implied by the text, but incompatible with each other; nothing prevents implicatures being mutually incompatible.

3.7   The communication of literary form

In this chapter I have focused on the tendential aspects of 'being a sonnet'. I have proposed that the type of literary form 'being a sonnet' holds of a text as the content of an inference with a certain degree of strength. In this section I consider the advantages of looking at a thought about form not just as an inference but more specifically as an implicature.

An implicature is an implication which is intentionally communicated. Literary texts have authors and are written for an audience, and can thus be seen as instances of communication. A writer writes a poem which stimulates a reader to have thoughts about its meaning and form. The communicator has a set of assumptions (her informative intention) and communication is successful to the extent that her audience holds that she is communicating this set of assumptions. Communication is more or less successful and always takes place at a risk, because the writer can neither directly plant the thoughts in the reader's head nor look into the reader's head to be sure that the thoughts derived are as intended by the communicator. Instead the writer must induce the reader to formulate the thoughts. Thoughts derived from a text are implications; in Relevance Theory, implications which are intentionally communicated are implicatures. The production of implicatures is guided by the principle of relevance:

Every act of ostensive communication communicates the presumption of its own optimal relevance. (Sperber and Wilson (1995:158))

The presumption of optimal relevance is that the thoughts communicated (and other cognitive effects) will repay the cognitive effort put into constructing them, and that the communicator's behaviour (e.g. the text produced) is optimally designed to communicate this set of thoughts.

From a social or cultural perspective, an interesting aspect of communication is the creation of mutuality, the shared sense between communicator and audience (and perhaps between members of an audience) that they know similar things. Sperber and Wilson (1995:218) show that by leaving things implicit a communicator makes manifest that a greater degree of knowledge is assumed to hold. Their example is an exchange in which Peter asks 'Is Jack a good sailor?' and Mary replies 'He's English'; one possible result is that the first speaker will assume that Mary means 'yes' and so must formulate the conditional 'If Jack is English then he is a good sailor.' Peter can assume that Mary has left implicit the conditional in order to imply to him that Mary and Peter both share cultural knowledge and share the knowledge that they share this knowledge (i.e. an effect of mutuality) and that the knowledge they share is that the English are good sailors, thus implying that they implicitly share a sense of national pride. Maria Chona is supposed to have said about Papago (Tohono O'odham) songs, 'the song is so short because we understand so much' (Krupat 1979:47). Here it is not just that shared knowledge makes it possible to make the songs short but also that the performance of the songs reinforces the effect that everyone shares an implicit knowledge, which implies a coherence of culture and community. When it comes to literary form, the fact that literary form is mostly communicated somewhat indirectly (with exceptions such as titling a text 'sonnet') might be interpreted as suggesting that one of the functions of literary form is to increase the effect of mutuality. Bauman (1975) suggests that the performance of verbal art is an appeal for evaluation, such that the formal features of the text must be recognised and evaluated. By making these formal features implicit, the processes of performance and listening or reading thus invoke a greater sense of mutuality; the production of verbal art promotes cultural community precisely by communicating literary form.

Sperber and Wilson characterise their theory specifically as a theory of ostensive-inferential communication. Ostension means making it mutually known that a communication is taking place; it is the drawing of the hearer's or reader's attention. Ostension automatically communicates a presumption of relevance; by drawing the reader's attention the author guarantees that it will be worth the reader's while. The addressee's attention can be explicitly drawn to these parts of a text in some cases; thus Labov and Waletzky (1967) show that when the fundamental turning point of a narrative is almost reached, various strategies are used to draw the addressee's attention. The principle of relevance guarantees that additional attention at this point will be rewarded. We might also take the beginning and ending of a text to be inherently ostensive, suggesting that these parts of a text will repay particular attention (Unger 2001). In the previous section we saw that in both Tuckerman's and Crashaw's texts, one of the sections evidencing sonnethood is at the end of the text. Smith (1968:178) suggests that the meaning of a formal strategy which can in principle imply closure is strengthened by its being at the end of a text (and furthermore that there is more evidence for form in general at the end of the text). Thus it can be argued that by placing these fourteen-line sections at the end of the text, Tuckerman and Crashaw invite increased attention to them, which is rewarded by assuming that these sections have some special status, such as emergent sonnethood.

3.8   Summary

In this chapter I have offered a way of formalising Hollander's (1975:213) suggestion that 'the way we ascribe to any literary work membership in a particular class or genre is by means of an interpretive act', or Smith's (1968:13) suggestion that 'poetic structure is, in a sense, an inference which we draw from the evidence of a series of events'. These informal references to pragmatic terms such as 'interpretation' and 'inference' can be built into a comprehensive pragmatic account of generic identity.

In the course of this chapter I have suggested that other aspects of literary form, such as rhyme scheme and lineation, might be best explained by appeal to the pragmatics. What all these 'pragmatic' kinds of literary form have in common is that they are characteristics of a text which hold to a certain degree rather than absolutely and rigorously. While many texts are unambiguously sonnets and have explicit rhyme schemes and certain lineation, nevertheless all these characteristics are subject in principle to slippage; they are not finally de-terminate characteristics of the text. The pragmatic theory used in this chapter, Relevance Theory, enables us to correlate the degree to which a literary form holds with the strength of the thought about the literary form. Thoughts hold with a certain degree of strength relating to how strongly they are held to be true, and strengths are inherited, readjusted and compared with one another as inter-pretations proceed. Implicatures can also hold with a certain degree of strength relating to how strongly they are held to be intended by the communicator. There are no absolute poles of strength or weakness such that final certainty is reached. Similarly, given the notion of interpretive use, a proposition can more or less closely resemble another proposition; again we have a gradient relation which is useful in understanding tendencies towards conformity to a pattern. Thus the gradient characteristics of many kinds of literary form are captured well in Relevance Theory.

But not all kinds of literary form are variably true of a text. In chapters 1 and 2 I suggested that there are also categorial and determinate kinds of form, as manifested in certain aspects of metrical form. There I proposed that a kind of literary form is generated by a rule system which involves a specialised kind of cognition analogous to linguistic processing. This is compatible in overall terms with the account in this chapter of literary form as the content of thoughts and hence part of general cognition. In the next chapter I show that the account of 'implied form' developed here can be extended to explain the aspects of metricality not yet accounted for.

4 The communication of metre

In chapters 1 and 2 I showed that some aspects of metrical form can be accounted for by generative metrical rules. In this chapter I show that remaining aspects of metrical form can be accounted for by the inferential approach of chapter 3.

4.1 Iambic pentameter revisited

Explanatory gaps

The generative rules for iambic pentameter are a set of projection rules, a set of grid-building rules and a set of conditions defining stress maxima and relating stress maxima to the grid. An iambic pentameter line must project a grid which conforms to these rules and conditions.

Pretty! in amber to observe the forms	*line A*
Of hairs, or straw, or dirt, or grubs, or worms;	*line B*

Alexander Pope, 'Epistle to Arbuthnot', 1735 (L:242)

The lines project these grids:

```
Pretty! in amber to observe the forms
) * *) * *)  *  *)* *)     * *)            0
     *   *)    *   *        *)             1
)         *                 *)             2
                            *              3

Of hairs, or straw, or dirt, or grubs, or worms;
)*  *)  *   *) *  *) *   *)  *   *)        0
    *       *)    *      *       *)        1
)           *                   *)         2
                                *          3
```

Both lines project ten syllables to gridline 0. The condition that stress maxima project to gridline 1 is observed for both of the stress maxima in the first line: the first syllable in 'amber' and the second syllable in 'observe'. (Recall that the first syllable in 'pretty', though stressed, is not a stress maximum because it is at the beginning of the line, and hence need not project to gridline 1.)

One of the tasks of a metrical theory is to explain why a line is composed as it is, given the metre. Here, we can explain why the lines add up to ten syllables each, and why the polysyllabic words are placed as they are. What we cannot explain is why the monosyllabic words are placed as they are. In particular, we have nothing yet to say about the striking regularity in the second line, where 'of' or 'or' is in every odd position and a noun is in every even position.

The first step in explaining the distribution of monosyllables is to note that while in performance any rhythm is in principle possible, some are preferred. While it is possible to stress every grammatical word in the second line, the effect is to suggest that the grammatical words are being given emphatic or contrastive stress:

> /   x   /   x   / x   /   x   /   x
> Of hairs, or straw, or dirt, or grubs, or worms;

The most neutral stressing of the words gives the nouns greater stress than the grammatical words.

> x   /   x   /   x /   x   /   x   /
> Of hairs, or straw, or dirt, or grubs, or worms;

Thus there is some relation between the kind of monosyllable and the level of stress which it might be given. In general, lexical monosyllables (nouns, adjectives, verbs, adverbs) will often have greater stress in performance than grammatical monosyllables (articles, prepositions, pronouns, conjunctions etc.). Tarlinskaja (1976:68) suggests that whether or not a monosyllable is given stress relates to word class. Thus for certain poets in iambic metres a monosyllabic noun is more likely to be in a head position than a monosyllabic verb: in Surrey's poetry for every noun in a non-head position there are twenty-two nouns in head positions, but for every verb in a non-head position there are only nine in head positions. Similarly, in English iambic poetry a definite article is more likely to be in a head position than an indefinite article.

This all means that a poet might organise monosyllables in the line so that a certain pattern of stress might be predicted for the line, or at least a relatively small range of patterns of stress; this is what Pope does in line B. But none of this can be accounted for by generative rules, because in talking of the distribution of monosyllables we are talking of tendencies rather than rigid rules. Thus we need some way of explaining how a performed rhythm might approximate to some desired pattern without having to exactly conform to that pattern. The solution is to use the pragmatic notion of interpretive resemblance introduced in chapter 3.

The communication of iambic pentameter

When the line is performed it has a rhythm. The rhythm is an explicit formal fact of the performance, and can thus be the content of an explicature of the performed line. Thus the most likely performance of line B has an explicature which is a thought (1). As in chapter 3, I number all representations of thoughts.

> (1) Line B has a rhythm x/x/x/x/x/.

This is a translation of a gradient pattern of actual stress into a categorical sequence of strong and weak positions. Thus the explicature is an explicit fact about the performed line when idealised in a particular way. Now, I propose a conditional which represents one of the things we know about iambic pentameter and which can be formulated as follows:

> (2) If a line has a rhythm x/x/x/x/x/ then it is in iambic pentameter.

This gives us the following deduction.

> (1) Line B has a rhythm x/x/x/x/x/. [strong]
> (2) If a line has a rhythm x/x/x/x/x/ then it is in iambic pentameter. [strong]
> by *modus ponens*
> (3) Line B is in iambic pentameter. [strong]

An explicature is always strong, and the conditional (2) is strong, which means that the line strongly implies the conclusion that it is in iambic pentameter.

Consider line A. This can be performed in various ways, which include as three fairly plausible performances:

> / x x /   x x x /   x /
> Pretty! in amber to observe the forms

> / x x /   x /x /   x /
> Pretty! in amber to observe the forms

> x / x /   x /x /   x /
> Pretty! in amber to observe the forms

Each of these performances has an explicature expressing its rhythm, respectively:

> (4) Line A has a rhythm /xx/xxx/x/.
> (5) Line A has a rhythm /xx/x/x/x/.
> (6) Line A has a rhythm x/x/x/x/x/.

Only the third of these explicatures will combine with the conditional (2) to derive the conclusion that the line is in iambic pentameter. One possibility is to use other conditionals, and we might formulate a conditional (7) which incorporates the fact that trochaic inversion is a regular possibility in iambic pentameter:

> (5) Line A has a rhythm /xx/x/x/x/. [strong]
> (7) If a line has a rhythm /xx/x/x/x/ then it is in iambic pentameter. [strong]
>   by *modus ponens*
> (8) Line A is in iambic pentameter. [strong]

In contrast, explicature (4) requires a different kind of explanation. Here the reader's knowledge of iambic pentameter is unlikely to give clear justification for formulating a conditional which says that /xx/xxx/x/ is an iambic pentameter line. We could in principle formulate conditionals for every kind of rhythm actually found in iambic pentameter, including this one, but there is a simpler option open to us. This is to appeal to inference by interpretive resemblance (p. 71). The two patterns resemble one another by each having ten elements, and being identical in positions 3, 4, 5, 7, 8, 9 and 10.

> (4) Line A has a rhythm /xx/xxx/x/. [strong]
>   by resemblance
> (9) Line A has a rhythm x/x/x/x/x/. [weak]

Now we can undertake a deduction:

> (9) Line A has a rhythm x/x/x/x/x/. [weak]
> (10) If a line has a rhythm x/x/x/x/x/ then it is in iambic pentameter. [strong]
>   by *modus ponens*
> (11) Line A is in iambic pentameter. [weak]

This performance of the line thus implies that it is in iambic pentameter, but slightly more weakly than does the performance of line B. Conclusion (11) will be further strengthened by the fact that the surrounding lines also imply this conclusion.

Now we have an explanation of why the rhythm of the line as performed approximates more or less to a regular periodic rhythm. The closer the performed rhythm to a certain pattern (x/x/x/x/x/ or /xx/x/x/x/, both of which are templates for iambic pentameter), the stronger the implicature that the line is in iambic pentameter. This reassignment of the explanation from generative rules to pragmatics can account for a gradient characteristic, which is that lines approximate more or less closely to a pattern. Generative rules in contrast explain only categorial characteristics of the line such as the rigid requirement on placement of polysyllables.

Trochaic inversion

Line A shows trochaic inversion involving a polysyllable, which is permitted by the generative metrical rules. In the previous section I suggested that trochaic inversion should be explicitly allowed as part of a strong conditional (7), such that it constitutes strong evidence for iambic verse.

(7) If a line has a rhythm /xx/x/x/x/ then it is in iambic pentameter.

By building trochaic inversion into a conditional we thus characterise it as a type of form which can be manipulated. In this way we solve a problem we created by our account of trochaic inversion in chapter 1. In that chapter, trochaic inversion on a polysyllable was permitted by making the beginning of the line 'invisible' to the rule defining stress maxima. Because the first syllable cannot be defined as a stress maximum it thus cannot violate the stress maximum condition. But trochaic inversion is clearly not invisible as a poetic practice; as we saw in chapter 2, section 1, trochaic inversion is manipulated very precisely by poets. By formulating trochaic inversion as part of conditional (7), we now allow trochaic inversion to be explicitly recognised as a manipulable kind of form.

There is another major advantage to building trochaic inversion into the conditionals for iambic pentameter, which is that it explains why monosyllables often show line-initial 'irregularity' analogous to trochaic inversion, with a pattern in performance of /xx/ at the beginning of the line (p. 38). This is seen in the following lines, where a sequence of lexical and grammatical monosyllables is arranged so that there is likely to be a rhythmic disruption at the beginning of the line in performance:

```
Sigh no more, ladies, sigh no more,
)*    *) *   *)*   *)  *  *)            0
      *      *    *     *               1
```
William Shakespeare, from *Much Ado About Nothing*, 1600 (J:571)

```
Weep no more, woful Shepherds weep no more,
)*    *) *   *)*   *)*   *)  *  *)   0
      *      *     *     *    *      1
```
John Milton, *Lycidas*, 1638 (Darbishire 1952:II,165)

```
Power above powers, O heavenly Eloquence,
)*    *)*   *)   *  *)  * *)* *)     0
      *     *      *    *   *        1
```
Samuel Daniel, 'Power above Powers', 1599 (J:530)

```
Love, faithful love, recalled thee to my mind –
)*    *) *  *)  * *)    *  *) *  *)   0
      *     *    *      *    *        1
```
William Wordsworth, 'Surprised by Joy ...', 1815 (Hayden 1977:863)

Generative metrical rules cannot explain this because they ignore monosyllables. But condition (7) does explain why monosyllables behave like polysyllables in this regard: this condition does not differentiate between them.

'Natural speech rhythms'

Given the deductions so far, of the three performances of the first line, (6) and (5) imply equally strongly that the line is in iambic pentameter, while (4) more weakly implies that the line is in iambic pentameter. Nevertheless for some, (4) is the preferred performance of the line. Walker (1785:121–4) states as his Rule One: 'In verse every syllable must have the same accent, and every word the same emphasis as in prose.' As regards the stressing of weak grammatical words like 'the', 'of' and 'as' and secondary stresses in polysyllables he says, 'to a good judge of reading scarcely any thing can be conceived more disgusting'. Webster (1789:311) takes a similar view, specifying that verse requires the same accentuation as in normal speech such that 'no stress should be laid on little unimportant words, nor on weak syllables'. And Thomas Sheridan (1781: 135) says 'All the words should be pronounced exactly in the same way as in prose.'

A way of explaining this preference would be to formulate another conditional, which would hold strongly for Walker, Webster, Sheridan and others who prefer irregular but natural sounding performances.

(12) If a line is in iambic pentameter then it sounds like normal speech.

Given the thought 'this line is in iambic pentameter', we derive the conclusion that the line sounds like normal speech.

(13) This line is in iambic pentameter.
(14) If a line is in iambic pentameter then it sounds like normal speech.
                    by *modus ponens*
(15) This line sounds like normal speech.

This conclusion holds more strongly for the performance represented by the 'irregular but natural' (4) than it does for (5) and more strongly for either than it does for 'regular but unnatural' (6), which sounds distinctly unlike normal speech. The more strongly the conclusion holds, the more the premises are strengthened. Thus the thought 'this line is in iambic pentameter' is sufficiently strengthened by the natural rhythm of the line to overcome the problem of the aperiodic rhythm. It is worth asking how we know how closely the line sounds like normal speech. Perhaps this again involves interpretive resemblance between the line and a 'non-metrical' performance of the rhythm of the line, such that the line resembles this performance to a greater or lesser extent.

Terms such as 'normal speech' or 'natural speech' appear problematic. 'Natural' is one of the most complex words in the English language (Williams 1976), so including it as part of a conditional would appear to beg many questions. But the exact formulation of conditionals is a matter of local need in a particular inference rather than global significance; conditionals are not built from a special technical vocabulary. All that is needed is for the thinker to have some way of describing speech rhythms such that (4) corresponds to these better than (6); whether these are described as 'normal' or 'natural' makes no difference to the deduction. Terms in thoughts need not be fully understood by the thinker; the terms can still be used in deductions (Sperber 1985).

Does line B have a 'normal speech rhythm' in its fully periodic performance? In one sense it does, in that the nouns are stressed more strongly than the grammatical words, but perhaps the notion of 'naturalness' here also involves less than full periodicity: ordinary speech does not have a fully periodic rhythm. Thus while the second line strongly implies that it is iambic pentameter by virtue of its periodic rhythm matching the template, it also weakens the evidence for iambic pentameter by its high regularity not corresponding to 'natural speech'. If this is the right approach, it means that no iambic pentameter line implies the metre with full strength: there are conflicting requirements on it of both periodicity and aperiodicity. This is a chronic complexity, a complexity built into the way literary form exists; it is often called 'metrical tension' (I discuss it on p. 132).

There are other routes by which a similar complexity might arise. For example, the following conditional might be held:

> (16) If a line is in iambic pentameter then it will not have exactly the same rhythm as the preceding line.

This means that the lack of full regularity is driven by a need for variation. It will be a source of chronic complexity, because it means that in the sequence of lines, the relation between rhythmic explicature and rhythmic template will always need to vary. There are also alternative ways of getting the lines not to be fully regular without formulating conditionals of this type. It may be that there is a learned rule by which iambic pentameter lines are evaluated, such as one of the following.

(Rule:) A good line of iambic pentameter will not have exactly the same rhythm as the preceding line.

(Rule:) A good line of iambic pentameter sounds like normal speech.

These are not conditionals and do not enter into inferencing. Instead they are rules by which texts are judged. In this approach, lines do not vary in whether they *are* iambic pentameter (i.e. in the strength of the thought that they are iambic pentameter) but in whether they are *good* iambic pentameter. It may be that there is no real difference; perhaps evaluation and categorisation are not clearly differentiated activities when it comes to making deductions about literary texts (as Bauman 1975 implies).

Variation in rhythm is not equally important for all metres. It has often been claimed that iambic pentameter lines are composed so that in performance they will show greater variation. Thus Tarlinskaja (1976:144) suggests that there is greater rhythmic variation in iambic pentameter than in the shorter iambic tetrameter: 'The iambic pentameter has a higher average non-ictic stress [i.e. not projecting to gridline 1] than the iambic tetrameter: 12.9 to 9.4% in Milton, 14.0 to 11.3% in Shelley, 15.1 to 14.3% in Rossetti.' She also suggests that even within iambic pentameter, there are differences between genres in how regular the performances of the lines are (1976:229). This all suggests a degree of complexity and variability which are best captured by a pragmatic approach. We can see the difference between iambic pentameter and other metres even within a single text, as in Robert Browning's 'A Grammarian's Funeral', which alternates iambic pentameter lines with a five-syllable line consisting of a full dactyl followed by a short dactyl /xx/x (possibly loosely mimicking the sapphic metre, p. 126). In fairly speech-natural performances, the rhythms of the iambic pentameter lines vary but the five-syllable lines do not (partly because the five-syllable lines tend to be stuffed with polysyllables).

> Leave we the unlettered plain its herd and crop;
>   Seek we sepulture
> On a tall mountain, citied to the top,
>   Crowded with culture!
> All the peaks soar, but one the rest excels;
>   Clouds overcome it;
> No! yonder sparkle is the citadel's
>   Circling its summit.
>
> Robert Browning, 'A Grammarian's Funeral', 1855 (K:248)

This supports the idea that thoughts about rhythmic variation are best attached specifically to iambic pentameter, perhaps as conditionals involved in the implicature of iambic pentameter.

The previous discussion assumes that there is a conditional relating the metre to 'natural speech rhythms'. This conditional does not seem to hold for all speakers:

For want of this knowledge most people read all verse like the Iambic measure. The following are pure Iambics:

> Above how high progressive life may go!
> Around how wide, how deep extend below!

It is so easy to lay an accent on every second syllable, that any school boy can read this measure with tolerable propriety. But the misfortune is, that when a habit of reading this kind of metre is once formed, persons do not vary their manner to suit other measures. Thus in reciting the following line,

> Load *the* tall *bark*, and launch in*to* the main,

many people would lay the accent on every second syllable; and thus read, our poetry becomes the most monotonous and ridiculous of all poetry in the world. (Noah Webster (1789:311))

Similarly, Sheridan (1781:135) says: 'The usual fault of introducing sing-song notes, or a species of chanting into poetical numbers, is disagreeable to every ear, but that of the chanter himself.' For the described readers, we simply assume that they do not make use of conditional (12). The consequence is that lines can imply the metre with full strength, and indeed for these performers every line implies the metre with full strength. The critics' dislike for this perhaps comes from a valuing of the complexity which exists if conditional (12) is used, thereby introducing an unresolvable conflict into the iambic pentameter line.

Other explicatures

It may be possible to develop an unlimited number of formal explicatures from a single line. This can be shown by looking at explicatures of rhythm. The explicatures used so far all involve just two symbols, x and /, which represent relatively weakly stressed syllables and relatively strongly stressed syllables res-pectively. This two-element categorial representation of stress is an abstraction from the relational patterns which constitute linguistic stress. Other abstractions are possible.

Thus we might represent three rather than two levels of stress in our expli-cature. Explicatures of this kind seem to be appropriate for 'dipodic' English verse in which the iambic feet are alternatingly weaker and stronger. Consider the following stanza:

> 'Er petticoat was yaller an' 'er little cap was green,
> An' 'er name was Supi–yaw–lat – jes' the same as Theebaw's Queen,
> An' I seen her first a–smokin' of a whackin' white cheroot,
> An' a–wastin' Christian kisses on an 'eathen idol's foot:
> > Bloomin' idol made o' mud –
> > Wot they called the Great Gawd Budd –
> > Plucky lot she cared for idols when I kissed'er where she stud!
> > On the road to Mandalay,
> > Where the flyin'–fishes play,
> > An' the dawn comes up like thunder outer China' crost the Bay!

> Rudyard Kipling, 'Mandalay', 1892 (K:754)

Most lines in this text have an odd number of syllables, with the initial syllable lost in three lines (one of which is the first quoted above). One possibility is that the line begins with a short foot (which is lost in three lines) and the other possibility is that the line begins with an extrametrical syllable (which is present in all but three lines). Because the initial syllable is sometimes a strongly stressed syllable in a polysyllable (e.g. 'Bloomin' and 'Plucky') I will assume that the line begins with an initial short foot in all cases except the three lines where this foot is deleted. Thus the generated metre of the text is iambic eight-foot metre.

```
An' I seen her first a–smokin' of a whackin' white cheroot,
 *)  *  *)    *  *)  *    *)*  *)  *   *)  *     *)   *  *)   0
 )*     *)       *        *)     *     *)        *     *)    1
 )      *         *)             *               *)    2
 )                 *                              *)    3
                                                  *     4
```

Weak monosyllables in most iambic verse do not project with any frequency to gridline 1. However, in this poem, weak monosyllables project forty times to gridline 1 (but only once to gridline 2). This gives a pattern where the third, seventh, etc. syllables tend to be given stronger stress in performance than the first, fifth etc., even though these are all head positions. This is a dipodic pattern, sometimes represented as follows, with the symbol / indicating the highest level of stress and the symbol \ indicating a middle level of stress, and, as before, x representing very weak stress or lack of stress.

```
 \   x  /    x  \   x   /x  \ x /   x     \       x /
An' I seen her first a–smokin' of a whackin' white cheroot,
```

Rather than trying to capture this tendency in conditions on the grid (which are not suited to capturing tendencies but only certainties), we can capture it in the implied metre, by developing from the line a more differentiated explicature. Up to now, I have assumed that the rhythmic explicature distinguishes just two levels of stress, x and /:

(17) This line has a rhythm /x/x/x/x/x/x/x/.

But the organisation of the line would suggest that it more strongly supports the following explicature, differentiating three rather than two types of stress.

(18) This line has a rhythm \x/x\x/x\x/x\x/.

Stewart (1924) shows that Pope's 'Universal Prayer', whose couplets are in a very similar generated metre, does not have the same distribution of weak monosyllables. It does not have the rhythmic form in (18). For example, in

Pope's poem there are five prepositions in weaker stress position and four in stronger stress position (and fifty-one in unstressed positions). These are two couplets:

> Teach me to feel another's Woe,
>   To hide the Fault I see;
> That Mercy I to others show,
>   That Mercy show to me.

Alexander Pope, 'The Universal Prayer', 1715 (Davis 1966:627)

In our terms this would mean that only the rhythmic explicature (19) can be developed from the text.

(19) This couplet has a rhythm x/x/x/x/x/x/x/.

Stewart argues that there is a sliding scale between fully dipodic (as in Kipling) and fully non-dipodic (as in Pope). This fits with the approach suggested here, that dipodism is a matter of implied form rather than generated metrical form. The generated metrical forms of both Kipling and Pope texts are similar; where they differ is in the rhythmic explicatures which can be developed from them.

Dipodism can also be seen in trochaic verse. Thus Tarlinskaja (1976:106) argues that in a normal performance of Longfellow's *Hiawatha* the first position in the line is stressed in 59.5 percent of cases while the third position is stressed in 88 percent of cases. (Tarlinskaja suggests a functional explanation for this, based on the notion that the line normally corresponds to a phrase, and a phrase normally begins with a weak syllable.) The tendency towards a dipodic pattern can for example be seen in the following lines, where grammatical monosyllables project to gridline 1 but not to gridline 2.

```
From his wanderings far to eastward,
(*    * (*    Δ*    (*  *(*    *(    0
(*    *         (*    *    (    1
(     *               *    (    2
                      *
From the regions of the morning,
(*    *(*  *   (*   *   (*  *(    0
(*    *    (*      *   (    1
(     *               *  (    2
                      *
```

Henry Wadsworth Longfellow, *Hiawatha*, 1855 (S:66)

If performed with sufficiently differentiated stress these lines could have the following rhythmic explicature:

(20) This line has a rhythm \x/x\x/x.

It is worth noting that exactly the same performance could also be said to have the rhythmic explicature in (21); this would be a more general explicature.

(21) This line has a rhythm /x/x/x/x.

In general, wherever there is a more specific explicature, more general explicatures are also present. This means that like any kind of tendential or variable form, lines which communicate dipodism also allow for non-dipodic readings. This is another kind of ambiguity built into metrical form, and dependent on metrical form being communicated (rather than being a determinate fact of the text).

This shows that different rhythmic explicatures can be drawn from the same line by expanding the vocabulary in which explicatures are formulated, from two to three differentiations of stress. Now I show that another way of developing explicatures from the line can add the grouping of syllables to an explicature. Consider for example this line from Browning's poem in chapter 1:

Say thou dost love me, love me, love me – toll

This is generated by the rules for iambic pentameter, and by the usual inferential processes communicates that it is in iambic pentameter. However, the repetition and punctuation of the latter part of the line enables us to extract out a sub-pattern 'love me, love me, love me, – toll' which gives rise to a rather different explicature:

(22) This line-part has a rhythm /x , /x , /x , /.

Here, the explicature involves a grouping of stressed and unstressed syllables into 'falling feet', or 'trochees'. Thus there is evidence for two different metres at the same time. Localised or acute ambiguities of this kind are characteristic of communication, and justify a communicative approach to metre.

The possibility of developing mutually incompatible explicatures from the same text can be understood as an instance of Empson's (1953:30) 'first type of ambiguity'. He discusses a line by Housman (similar in some respects to Pope's line B on p. 88), showing that there are different ways of developing an explicit 'rhythmic' grouping for the line.

Horror and scorn and hate and fear and indignation;

He claims that the preferred rhythm gives 'hate' strongest stress and 'fear' second strongest stress, and this encourages a grouping of the line into two units, divided after 'hate'. But he claims that there is also another grouping, a different 'rocking' rhythm for the line, which pairs 'horror and scorn' and 'hate and fear' and then adds 'indignation'. Rhythm, in this sense, is partly a matter of stress differentiation between words, and partly a matter of how the words are grouped into phonological phrases. The conjoined structure of this sentence means that there are alternative ways of grouping. These different groupings can nevertheless be understood as different explicatures which can be extracted from a text.

Summary: complexity and explicatures

In principle, there is no relation whatsoever between the generated metre and the communicated metre. A line which has no generated metre can neverthe-less communicate that it is in a metre, a line which has a generated metre can fail to communicate its metricality, and a line which is in a specific generated metre can communicate an apparently completely different metre. I will con-sider these dissociations in section 4.3, but here I consider the fairly common situation where there does appear in practice to be some relation between the generated and communicated metres. The fact that I have used the terms 'iambic pentameter' for both is irrelevant; the generated metre does not need to have a name in order to work, and the communicated metre has whatever name it is assigned as part of the interpretive procedures.

The communicated metre (iambic pentameter) has one of its templatic forms expressed as part of the thought (23):

(23) This line has a rhythm x/x/x/x/x/.

The generated metre (also called iambic pentameter) has as part of its grid:

$$* * * * * * * * * * \quad 0$$
$$* \quad * \quad * \quad * \quad * \quad 1$$

The two patterns share the number of basic elements (ten) and a differentiation between odd and even positions. We might expect some relation between the generated and the communicated metre only because the generated metre and the communicated metre relate to the same set of lines; the generated metre says what characteristics they must have and the communicated metre offers a template which they are likely to resemble.

The account of metrical form proposed in this section aims to fill the explana-tory gaps left by the generative approach of chapter 1. The generative account said nothing about the distribution of monosyllables. Now we can say that monosyllables are distributed in such a manner that the explicature describing the line's rhythm provides fairly strong evidence, usually via interpretive use, for the conclusion that the text is in iambic pentameter. Could this approach explain *all* aspects of metricality? This would mean dispensing with the gener-ative rules, so that metricality is entirely a kind of communicated form, holding as part of the set of thoughts implied by a text, and without any given structure. There are two basic arguments against this, which I think are sufficiently strong to maintain the split account of metricality. One argument against this unified approach to metricality comes from the fact that there is a division in metricality between invariance and tendencies. Thus the distribution of polysyllables is subject to invariant rules, while the distribution of monosyllables is not. The second argument relates to counting. The problem of how the line is counted out is not solved by the communication approach; even if we dispensed with the generative metrical rules we would still have to say how the line is counted up to ten syllables. This brings us back to the arguments of chapters 1 and 2, which suggested that there is good evidence that counting involves grid construction, hence generative rules. Thus the characteristics of metrical verse (particularly when considered cross-linguistically) suggest strongly that there is a specific kind of rule system at work.

Thus I conclude that a line of metrical verse may be characterised by two different kinds of form. The counting out of projected syllables and the invariant aspects of the rhythm are determined by generative metrical rules. In contrast, general rhythmic tendencies and other variable aspects of the lines are driven by the goal of communicating a certain metrical form.

4.2   Local irregularities

Generative metrical rules do not permit irregularities because they are invariant. Later in this section I will suggest some ways of dealing with lines in which the rules are broken. First, I look at lines which from a generative metrical perspective are fully metrical but which are irregular from the communicated metrical perspective.

Irregularities involving monosyllables

Monosyllables are a rich resource for local irregularities, because they are uncontrolled by generative rules; thus the line can be fully metrical while having a performed rhythm which is irregular. Poets exploit this in various ways. Thus the following lines are fully regular as far as the generative rules for iambic pentameter are concerned, but there is still a problem with them: either they have irregular rhythms which reflect a natural pronunciation of the words, or they have regular rhythms which sound very unnatural (in some cases almost incomprehensible).

```
But (Got wot) wot not what they mean by it;
)*     *)  *   *)  *    *)   *   *)  *  *)
        *        *        *        *     *
```

Sir Philip Sidney, 'I Never Drank . . . ' 1591 (J:312)

So that in her orb there is left for kings
)*   *)*   *)*   *) * *) *   *)
     *   *   *   *   *

Fulke Greville, 'Of Peace', 1670 (F:9)

Conveys about it could mix. But when death
)*   *) * *) * *)   *   *)   *   *)
     *   *   *   *   *

George Chapman, *Homer's Odyssey*, 1614 (F:25)

All whom the flood did, and fire shall o'erthrow,
)*   *)   * *)   * *)   *   *) *   *)
     *   *   *   *   *

John Donne, 'Sonnet VII', 1633 (F:117)

Since she whom I loved hath paid her last debt
)*   *)   *   *)*   *)   *   *) *   *)
     *   *   *   *   *

John Donne, 'Sonnet XVII', early seventeenth century (F:119)

Rocks, Caves, Lakes, Fens, Bogs, Dens, and shades of death,
)*   *)   *   *)   *   *)   *   *)   *   *)
     *   *   *   *   *   *

John Milton, *Paradise Lost*, 2.621, 1667 (Darbishire 1952:I,43)

Of a poor marmoset, nought but bone, bone.
)* *) *   *) * *) *   *) *   *)
     *   *   *   *   *

Richard Lovelace, 'La Bella Bona Roba', 1649 (F: 569)

Another option is to repeat a word sometimes in head and sometimes in non-head position, as in the following examples.

Yet use I not my foes as I use Thee.
)* *) * *) * *) * *)*   *)
     *   *   *   *   *

George Herbert, 'Unkindness', 1633 (F:320)

When thou hast done, thou hast not done,
)*   *)   *   *)   *   *)   *   *)
     *   *   *   *

John Donne, 'A Hymn to God the Father', 1633 (F:124)

Say all, and I with them, 'What doth not Time!'
But they, who knew Time, Time will find again;
I that fair times lost, on Time call in vain.

Robert Sidney, 'Forsaken Woods', early seventeenth century (J:699)

Another interesting practice of some poets is to italicise or capitalise mono-syllables, presumably to indicate stressing in performances. Italicisation of

monosyllables generally appears to ignore the periodicity of the rhythm, and
often seems explicitly to violate it, as in the following example.

> To-night, *his* mother's parting syllables?
>)*   *)   *   *) *   *) *   *)* *)
>   *   *   *   *   *
>
> William Allingham, 'In Snow', late nineteenth century (Fuller 2000:185)

> *Then* order your ascension robe!
>) * *) *   *) * *) *   *)
>   *   *   *   *
>
> Oliver Wendell Holmes, 'Latter-Day Warnings', 1857 (S:121)

> Where will *they* find their parent element?
>)   *   *) * *)   *   *)* *)* *)
>   *   *   *   *   *

> What will receive *them,* who will call *them* home?
>)   *   *) * *)   *   *) * *)   *   *)
>   *   *   *   *   *
>
> Matthew Arnold, 'Empedocles on Etna', 1852 (Allott 1986:105)

In the following quatrain, Fitzgerald capitalises otherwise weak monosyllables
to imply a trochaic ending to the normally iambic line.

> The Ball no Question makes of Ayes and Noes,
> But Right or Left, as strikes the Player goes;
>   And He that toss'd Thee down into the Field,
> *He* knows about it all – HE knows – HE knows!
>)*   *)   * *) * *)   *   *)   *   *)
>   *   *   *   *   *
>
> Edward Fitzgerald, *Rubáiyát of Omar Khayyám*, stanza 50, 1859 (K:125)

'Sultán' in the Rubáiyát of Omar Khayyam

In this section I look at Fitzgerald's deployment of the word 'sultan' in his
Rubáiyát of Omar Khayyám (first printed 1859). The word 'sultan' has been used
in English since the sixteenth century, always with stress on the first syllable.
Fitzgerald writes it 'sultán'. In a letter to G.B. Cowell, Fitzgerald explains that
he uses the accent in Persian words to indicate a long vowel (1856, Terhune
1980:II,205). In the word 'sultán' this will have the effect of shifting the stress
on to the second syllable, contrary to its normal pronunciation.

In the *Rubáiyát* Fitzgerald has many words with accented syllables: Pehleví,
Kaikobád, Khayyám, Kaikhosrú, Hátim, Parwín, Ramazán, Ferrásh, Zál,
Naishápúr, etc. These words in general are aligned with the grid so that it

is the accented syllable which is in head position:

> With old Khayyám the Ruby Vintage drink:
>)* *) * *) * *)* *) * *)
>   *   *   *   *   *

Edward Fitzgerald, Rubáiyát of Omar Khayyám, stanza 48, 1859 (K:124)

This fits with the notion that the accent has the effect of making this a stress maximum. But there is a striking mismatch which involves the word 'sultan'. This word is always written with the final syllable accented but in all its seven instances the accented syllable is placed in non-head position:

> Where name of Slave and Sultán scarce is known,
>) * *) * *) * *)* *) * *)
>   *   *   *   *   *
>
> And pity Sultán Mahmud on his Throne.
>)*   *)* *)* *) * *) * *)
>   * *   *   *   *

Stanza 10 (K: 117)

If we take 'Sultan' to have final stress, then this would appear to violate the metrical rules because it would be a stress maximum which does not project to gridline 1. However, 'sultan' is a word which has been used in English at least since Shakespeare, and always with stress on the first syllable, so if we go by the expected stress the line is fully metrical. The printed accent on the second syllable is invisible to generative rules if these rules take only lexical stress into account; however, the printed accent guides performance and thus gives the second of the above lines a rhythmic explicature something like this:

(24) This line has a rhythm x/xx//x/x/.

The accenting of the syllable thus creates rhythmic irregularity at the level of the communicated metre while the line is fully regular at the level of the generated metre. It might be claimed that Fitzgerald was caught between needing to indicate authentic Persian pronunciation and using the word in lines where inevitably it then falls in non-head position, but this claim fails for various reasons (not least that Fitzgerald does not in fact accent all foreign words: he does not mark stress on 'muezzin' or 'mushtara'). The arhythmic use of the word 'sultan' is not only consistent, it is also highly noticeable; it is used in the first stanza, which makes it both the first foreign word and the first accented word in the poem. In all its other uses it is used twice in the same stanza, again drawing attention to its use (in the first edition, stanza 10 twice, stanza 16 twice, stanza 70 twice).

To summarise, for Fitzgerald's use of the word 'sultan', if it is given its normal English stress it always falls in head position, but Fitzgerald marks a stress for it which pushes it systematically into non-head position. From the perspective of the generated metre, the line is fully regular, but from the perspective of the communicated metre it is irregular. We might take two routes in understanding what Fitzgerald is doing here. First, this might be a novel instance of the general strategy of making metrical verse complex; in this case the complexity comes from the contrary pulls of English and foreign stressing of the word and head and non-head position. Second, it might be a source of other inferences; perhaps by focusing uncertainty on a familiar instance of the exotic – the word 'sultan' – Fitzgerald aims to destabilise the comfortable exoticism with which his Victorian readers view the Orient.

Polysyllables which violate the metrical rules

In a polysyllable, one syllable has the strongest stress, and for the iambic pentameter rules this is defined as a stress maximum only if it is preceded by a syllable in the same line. A stress maximum must project to gridline 1.

The following lines illustrate trochaic inversion, where a syllable which might otherwise be defined as a stress maximum is in first position and hence is not subject to the metrical rules. I have chosen lines or pairs of lines which repeat the polysyllable. This shows two things: unless the words have variable stress, only one of the two instances can be in head position; and poets are ostensibly exploiting the possibility of trochaic inversion.

Holiday (boys), cry holiday!
```
* *)*    *)    *  *)**)          0
   *    *      *  *              1
```
John Lyly, *Sapho and Phao, c.*1582 (J:350)

Poorly provided, poorly followed,
```
)*  *)  * *)*   *)  * *)*  *)     0
    *    *    *    *    *          1
```
Samuel Daniel, *The Civil Wars,* 1595 (J:512)

Empty of pleasures? Empty of all graces,
```
)*  *)*   *) *    *)   **)*   *)Δ   0
    *    *      *    *      *       1
```
George Chapman, *Euthymiae Raptus,* 1608 (F:11)

Vary, re-vary; tune and tune again
```
)* *) * *)* *)  *   *) * *)       0
    *   *  *      *    *          1
```
Joshua Sylvester, 'Variable', 1621 (F:62)

Whether in princes' palaces he be
)* *) *   *) *   *)* *) * *)   0
    *   *   *   *   *   1
Or whether to his cottage he retire;
)*   *) * *) * *) *   *)* *)   0
     *   *   *   *   *   1

Sir Henry Wotton, 'To J D . . .', mid seventeenth century (F:74)

Thou with Eternal wisdom didst converse,
)*   *) * *) * *) *   *) * *)   0
    *   *   *   *   *   1
Wisdom thy Sister, and with her didst play
)*   *)   * *)* *)   *   *) * *)   0
    *   *   *   *   *   1

John Milton, *Paradise Lost*, 7.9, 1667 (Darbishire 1952:I,148)

Thousand rich slanders, thousand useful lies.
) * *)   *   *) *   *) * *) * *)   0
     *   *   *   *   *   1

Abraham Cowley, *The Civil War*, mid seventeenth century (F:562)

The lines above do not violate the metrical rule. But sometimes a polysyllable
does violate the metrical rule by having a syllable defined as a stress maximum
which does not project to gridline 1.

Into this prince gently, oh gently slide
)* *) *   *)   * *)*   *) * *)   0
    *   *   *   *   *   1

John Fletcher, 'Care Charming Sleep', 1647 (F:172)

He fishers made fishers of men;
)* *) *   *) * *) *   *)   0
    *   *   *   *   1

William Basse, 'The Angler's Song', 1653 (F: 201)

Those other two equalled with me in Fate,
) * *) *   *)* *)   * *) * *)   0
    *   *   *   *   *   1

So were I equalled with them in renown,
)*   *) **) *   *)   * *) * *)   0
    * *   *   *   *   1

John Milton, *Paradise Lost,* 3:33–4, 1667 (Darbishire 1952:I,54)

And when he comes among his friends at feasts,
```
)*      *)  *  *)    *  *)    *  *)    *  *)        0
        *     *     *     *       *            1
```
'Tis as an orphan among prosperous boys.
```
) * *)* *)  * *) *    *)   *    *)        0
    *    *    *     *     *            1
```

Matthew Arnold, 'Empedocles on Etna', 1852 (Allott 1986:78)

Still hungrier for delight as delights grow more rare.
```
) *  *)  *  *)  * *)  *  *)*    *)   *   *)   0
    *     *   *    *     *     *    1
```

Matthew Arnold, 'Empedocles on Etna', 1852 (Allott 1986:92)

The only thing we can say about these lines from a generative metrical perspective is that they are not generated by the rules for iambic pentameter. A reason for claiming that generative metrical rules exist is the consistency with which they apply; this suggests that they involve the highly efficient kind of linguistic processing which is otherwise seen in phonology and syntax. However, generative rules do not prescribe behaviour; it is possible to produce words which violate phonological rules, sentences which violate syntactic rules, and – as here – lines which violate metrical rules.

When we look at one of these lines in its context, it is not immediately obvious that it is suddenly and categorially unmetrical.

> Pass by his troubled senses; sing his pain
> Like hollow murmering winds or silver rain.
> Into this prince gently, oh gently slide,
> And kiss him into slumbers like a bride.

John Fletcher, 'Care Charming Sleep', 1647 (F:172)

The fact that the third line still feels metrical (even though from the perspective of generative metrical rules it is not) can only be explained by reference to the communication of metrical form. The line continues to communicate that it is in iambic pentameter, just slightly more weakly than the surrounding lines. The following rhythmic explicature can be developed from it:

(25) This line has a rhythm /xx//xx/x/.

This resembles and thus weakly implies the /xx/x/x/ rhythm which in turn implies iambic pentameter. Incidentally, it might be legitimate to construct another conditional which feeds directly from the rhythmic explicature and leads in a rewarding direction:

(26) If a line has a rhythm /xx//xx/x/ then it imitates the rocking of a cradle.

All of these implicatures will be developed quite independently of the fact that the line is, from a generative metrical perspective, unmetrical.

4.3   Metrical ambiguity

Why rising/falling ambiguities are possible

Blest with Sense, with Temper blest

Lines with this rhythmic sequence /x/x/x/ are sufficiently common in English verse to be given a name (sometimes these are called 'sevens'). In chapter 1, I showed that this kind of seven-syllable line can be generated either by the iambic rules or by the trochaic rules and so is structurally ambiguous. The iambic rules build feet from right to left, and can thus leave the initial foot short; the trochaic rules build feet from left to right and can thus leave the last built (rightmost) foot short. I will show the ambiguity by putting one grid above the line and the other below the line (the relation between grid and line is the same in both cases).

```
     *       *         *         *    1
  *)  *   *)     *   *  )*   *)   0   iambic
  Blest with Sense, with Temper blest
  (*   *  (*      *  (*   *   (*   0   trochaic
   *       *         *         *   1
```

The same general phenomenon can be found in longer and shorter lines with binary metres, and can also be found in ternary metres:

```
      *           *           *           *    1
   *) *   *    *)   *   *   *)   *  *    *)   0   anapaestic
   Midnight and moon light and bright shineing stars
  (  *  *   *  (*     *   *  (*   *  *  (*   0   dactylic
      *           *           *         *   1
```

Emily Bronte, 'High waveing heather . . .', 1836 (Roper 1995:31)

The line 'Blest with Sense, with Temper blest' is cited by John Rice (1765: 128) as part of his argument against foot structure. Rice cites an analysis by John Mason in which the line is scanned as trochees (which is also Puttenham's analysis, 1589:137), and Rice points out that the line could equally be scanned as iambs (if there is a short initial foot): 'would not both the Sound and Sense be equally consistent?'. Similarly, Attridge (1982:11) argues that the question of whether lines of this type are iambic or trochaic is 'without substance, of course, unless feet are regarded as having a real existence for the reader'.

For us, the possibility of scanning either as iambic or trochaic is a type of structural ambiguity: there are two distinct scansions for a single surface form.

An interesting, but for the moment unanswerable, question is whether the hearer maintains two simultaneous scansions, or chooses one and rejects the other. The basic structural ambiguity comes from the fact that the foot can fall short at either end of the line. But there is a further complication, built into the generative rules, which involves the non-projection of syllables at the edge of the line, and thus means that syllables at the edge might not be counted by the metre. Consider, for example, the ending of Nicholas Breton's 'In the merry month of May', which is in sevens until it gets to line 23. These are the last six lines:

Such as silly shepherds use,	21
When they will not love abuse,	22
Love, which hath been long deluded,	23
Was with kisses sweet concluded:	24
And Phyllida with garlands gay	25
Was made the Lady of the May.	26

Nicholas Breton, 'In the Merry Month of May', 1591 (J:232)

Lines 23 and 24 look like trochaic tetrameter lines but they might also be iambic tetrameter lines with a short initial foot and the rightmost syllable not projected (because it comes between a stressed syllable and the end of the line):

```
      *           *        *        *          1
      *)      *   *)   *    *)    * *)Δ         0    iambic
      Love, which hath been long deluded,
      (*       *   (*   *    (*   *(* *(         0    trochaic
      *           *        *        *          1
```

The simpler scansion (because it involves projection of all syllables and has no short feet) is trochaic, but the iambic scansion is a possibility. The same might be said for the last two lines, where an iambic scansion is the simplest but where a trochaic scansion would require a projection rule saying that an initial syllable would be non-projected if it immediately preceded a stressed syllable (i.e. a kind of initial extrametricality, called anacrusis in traditional metrics):

```
          *   *        *        *    1
      )*      *)* *)  *   *)  *     *)   0    iambic
      And Phyllida with garlands gay
      Δ     (* *(*  *  (* *     (*       0    trochaic
          *   *        *        *    1
```

Thus leftmost or rightmost extrametricality can reintroduce the possibility of structural ambiguity into lines which seem to be straightforwardly iambic or trochaic.

This relates to the question of whether there is a genuine distinction between iambic and trochaic verse in English. Atkins (1942) argues that 'in English and German there is no natural trochaic verse, but only trochaic lines in which the falling rhythm is maintained deliberately by the use of a very definite and consciously employed linguistic material'. Atkins suggests, for example, that in *Hiawatha* the trochaic rhythm is asserted particularly by employing trochaic words (i.e. words with penultimate stress, often disyllables; or compounds with penultimate stress) at the end of the line; 80 of the first 100 lines in *Hiawatha* have this ending. Furthermore, Longfellow makes particular use of tetrasyllables with penultimate and initial stress, particularly at the end of lines; the name 'Hiawatha' is an example of this, and 474 lines end with names with this phonological structure. Translated into the terms of the present book, trochaic metre is strongly communicated by the use of trochaic words, but the underlying grid might be iambic (exploiting the options of short initial feet and extrametricality). Thus the grid for the lines quoted earlier might instead be:

```
     From his wanderings far to eastward,
       *)    *    *) Δ*     *) **)    Δ     0
       )*        *)        *    *)           1
       )         *                *)         2
                                  *          3

     From the regions of the morning,
       *)    * *) *    *)    *    *) Δ       0
       )*       *)     *        *)           1
       )        *                *)          2
                                  *          3
```

Atkins's point is an interesting one, and would mean that the communication of trochaicity requires more cognitive work (because more inferencing) than the communication of iambicity. However, I suggest that we should continue to assume that there are generative rules generating grids specific to trochaic verse; this is much more economical for the generative rules than always having to arrange the basically iambic lines so that they consistently present evidence for trochees. But in cases where there are occasional trochaic lines in otherwise iambic texts, the iambic grid could be allowed to match a 'trochaic' line as an exception.

It is not just in the generative metrical structure that the line is ambiguous; it is also ambiguous in the metre it communicates. John Mason takes the metre of the 'sevens' line to be trochaic tetrameter (1749: 61), Rice himself allows it to be iambic tetrameter, while Watts (1721:80) identifies it as its own distinctive (unnamed) metre. This ambiguity in metre could arise if there were different conditionals. We might take the explicature of rhythm for a line in sevens such as 'Blest with Sense, with Temper blest' (from Fitzosborne's *Letters*) to be as in (27), which would then combine with one of various possible conditionals to derive a particular conclusion.

(27) This line has a rhythm /x/x/x/.
(28) If a line has a rhythm /x/x/x/ then it is in trochaic tetrameter.

(29) If a line has a rhythm /x/x/x/ then it is in iambic tetrameter.
(30) If a line has a rhythm /x/x/x/ then it is in sevens.

By Rice's description, Mason allows only (28) as a conditional; another analyst
might in principle allow only (29). Rice entertains but then apparently rejects
both (28) and (29), thus refusing to formulate a conclusion about the metre in
these terms. Alternatively we might in principle allow both (28) and (29) but
allow for the possibility that other aspects of the text will strengthen one against
the other – if this is the only line in an otherwise fully trochaic text, then there
is strong evidence for the conclusion that this line is in trochaic tetrameter and
hence in this context this strengthens the premise (28). Attridge (1982:108ff.)
suggests that 'rising' and 'falling' (and hence the difference between iambic
and trochaic) are perceived on the basis of a variety of characteristics of the
line rather than being inherent to the line. This seems to me correct, restating
'perceived' as 'inferred'. (However, Attridge's conclusion that there is therefore
no foot structure is based on the view that foot structure functions primarily
to structure rhythm, while in the present theory, foot structure is used to count
the syllables in the line; thus the fact that there are seven syllables in the line
is the consequence of building binary feet which project heads into a full grid
structure.)
      Ambiguities might thus arise because of a choice between generative rule sets
or because of the choice between conditionals. A third place where ambiguity
might arise is in the rhythmic explicature.

> In the hour of my distress,
> When temptations me oppress,
> And when I my sins confess,
>   Sweet Spirit comfort me!
>
> Robert Herrick, 'His Litany, to the Holy Spirit', 1648 (F:281)

The first three of these lines have a weak initial syllable (not uncommon in
sevens), which gives rise along with (31) to other possible rhythmic explicatures,
including (32).

(31) This line has a rhythm /x/x/x/.
(32) This line has a rhythm xx/x/x/.

We might treat (32) as having an interpretive relation to the thought (33), and
thus as weakly implying it (and thus eventually weakly implying the conclusion
(35) that the line is in iambic trimeter).

(32) This line has a rhythm xx/x/x/.
            by resemblance
(33) This line has a rhythm x/x/x/. [weak]

(34) If a line has a rhythm x/x/x/ then it is in iambic trimeter.
            by *modus ponens*
(35) This line is in iambic trimeter.

While the 'sevens' line is in general ambiguous both in its generated form and in its communicated form, it might be possible in particular cases to disambiguate either the generated or communicated form of the line. One kind of disambiguation comes from the tendency to mix sevens with eight-syllable lines. A use of sevens is as occasional short lines in otherwise predominantly iambic or trochaic texts. Thus Henry Baker's 'Love' is a poem in two verse paragraphs, all in trochaic tetrameter except for the first and last pair of lines in the first paragraph (the whole poem is quoted, p. 178). These are the first four lines:

> Love's an headstrong wild desire
> To possess what we admire:
> Hurrying on without reflecting,
> All that's just or wise neglecting.

Henry Baker, 'Love', 1725 (L:163)

Because the text is generally in trochaic tetrameter, we could most economically say that the two lines in sevens are also generated by the rules for trochaic tetrameter. It is not so clear that at the level of communication of form these lines would be treated as trochaic rather than iambic; this depends on the conditionals invoked. Thus lines in boundary positions (as here) show a slight tendency towards metrical irregularity, which could be formulated as a conditional allowing these lines to be other than trochaic. This might outcompete some other conditional requiring metrical uniformity across the text. The complementary situation is seen where the whole text is in sevens except at its boundaries; here in principle the boundary metres can determine the metre of the whole. Thus Shakespeare's *The Phoenix and Turtle* is mainly in sevens with a few trochaic tetrameter lines, but the last line is iambic tetrameter. These are the last two lines:

> Co-supremes and stars of love,
> As chorus to their tragic scene.

William Shakespeare, 'The Phoenix and Turtle', 1601 (J:602)

Similarly, Wotton's 'Upon the sudden restraint . . .' is all in sevens except that the last line is full iambic tetrameter. These are the last two lines:

> Virtue is the roughest way,
> But proves at night a bed of down.

Henry Wotton, 'Upon the Sudden Restraint . . .', 1651 (F:72)

The following stanza includes the one eight-syllable line in a poem otherwise entirely in sevens. The exclamation which fills in the missing initial syllable in the second line draws the hearer's attention and thus perhaps offers it as a key to disambiguating the metre.

> Amarantha sweet and fair,
> Ah, braid no more that shining hair!
>   As my curious hand or eye,
> Hovering round thee let it fly.
>
> Richard Lovelace, 'Song. To Amarantha . . . ', 1649 (F:564)

Where sevens are mixed with eight-syllable lines, the eight-syllable line can in principle help disambiguate the text as a whole. However, one of the problems for disambiguation is that the unstressed leftmost or rightmost syllable in eight-syllable lines might be treated as extrametrical, and thus the line falls back to being metrically just a seven-syllable line. Thomas Parnell's 'A Hymn to Contentment' is a seventy-eight-line text generally in what appears to be iambic tetrameter but with some lines in sevens. Here we might suspect that the apparently iambic lines actually have extrametrical initial syllables and thus that the lines might be trochaic, except for a key fact that the iambic lines show initial inversion:

> Whither, O whither art thou fled,
>
> Thomas Parnell, 'A Hymn to Contentment', 1714 (L:113)

Here, the first syllable of the eight-syllable line cannot be treated as extrametrical because it carries stress; furthermore this is 'trochaic inversion', a characteristic specifically of iambic verse, thus proving that the line is iambic. Something similar can be seen in 'To His Love When He Had Obtained Her', a thirty-line text of which lines 1–9 are all in sevens and the rest of the lines are eight-syllable lines in full iambic tetrameter. Line 14 begins with a trochaic inversion, thus confirming the iambic status of the eight syllable lines.

> Nature her bounties did bestow
>
> attr. Walter Ralegh, 'To His Love When He Had Obtained Her', pub.1931 (J:391)

My last example is from a sixteen-line text with the first fourteen lines in sevens and the final lines in iambic tetrameter with an extrametrical syllable at the end of each line and a trochaic inversion in the last line:

> Let these be well together blended –
>) *   *)   *   *) * *) *   *) Δ
>   *   *   *   *
> Dodsley's your man – the poem's ended.
>) *   *)   *   *)   * *)*   *) Δ
>   *   *   *   *
>
> Anonymous, 'To a Gentleman . . . ', 1763 (L:512)

There is some critical debate about inherent differences between iambic and trochaic verse, with suggestions, for example, that the stressed syllable is longer in iambic verse than in trochaic verse, or that the rhythm in trochaic verse is more consistently periodic over stretches of the text (see Newton 1975, based on work by Hascall and Beaver). If these claims are true then they might help disambiguate the rhythm of texts in sevens. Consider for example the following complete text:

Aestas

When summer's heat hath done his part,	iambic
The husband hath a gladsome heart;	iambic
Sith golden treasures of the plains	iambic
Make large amends for all his pains.	iambic
But th'idle lubber, labour-loathing	iambic + ext.
Walking, talking, wishing store,	sevens
Sowing naught but wind before,	sevens
Shall, but wind behind, reach nothing.	trochaic

Joshua Sylvester, 1621 (F:62)

The first four lines have eight syllables, and appear to be clear instances of iambic tetrameter; the fifth line adds an extrametrical syllable (giving nine syllables). The sixth and seventh lines cut the first syllable from the tetrameter (giving seven syllables). The eighth line continues the pattern of cutting the first syllable but adds the final extra syllable, to give eight syllables now in a trochaic tetrameter pattern. In terms of the generated metre, we could see the whole poem as in iambic tetrameter throughout, with various adjustments in the second part; however, in terms of the communicated metre we might see a gradually mediated shift in the course of the second part from iambic to trochaic. Incidentally, if it is true that iambic and trochaic metres have inherent differences, this text might show them. We might for example expect some change in the balance between head and non-head syllables from beginning (where we should find the iambic balance of a 1:2 length ratio of unstressed to stressed syllables) to end (where we should find the trochaic balance of a 1:1 length ratio of unstressed to stressed). If this were the case, then we might ask at what point the balance shifts: is line 5 with its x/x/x/x pattern iambic or trochaic and are lines 6 and 7 with their /x/x/x/ iambic or trochaic? I do not find a perceptual difference between the lines of this kind; it would be interesting to test this experimentally. It is however notable that in the first half of the text the lines are less periodic than in the second, which might perhaps reflect an iambic to trochaic shift. It is not clear whether these claimed characteristics of iambic versus trochaic relate to the metrical grid or to the communicated metre (and if to the communicated metre, if they relate to the rhythmic explicature or some aspect of the inferences).

Joshua Sylvester's poem demonstrates a characteristic use of sevens to effect a shift between iambic and trochaic sections of a poem, whether at the level of communicated or generated form. This can be seen again in Dryden's

'Alexander's Feast', a poem (on the Pindaric Ode model) in mixed-length lines, predominantly iambic. Syllable counts and explicit foot type are indicated.

He chose a Mournful Muse	6 (iambic)
Soft Pity to infuse:	6 (iambic)
He sung *Darius* Great and Good,	7
By too severe a Fate,	6 (iambic)
Fallen, fallen, fallen, fallen,	8 (trochaic)
Fallen from his high Estate	7
And weltring in his Blood:	6 (iambic)
Deserted at his utmost Need,	8 (iambic)
By those his former Bounty fed:	8 (iambic)

John Dryden, 'Alexander's Feast', 1697 (Kinsley 1958:III,1428)

The text is generally iambic, but the line 'Fallen, fallen, fallen, fallen', while it might be attached to an iambic grid, nevertheless strongly communicates trochaic tetrameter. The next line begins as though it is also in trochaic tetrameter, but ends short, raising the possibility that it is actually iambic. The line which follows loses another syllable to give a clearly iambic trimeter line, and now we are back to the iambic norm of the verse. Thus the seven-syllable line 'Fallen from his high estate' mediates between trochaic and iambic at the level of communicated metre.

Tennyson's 'The Lady of Shalott' is an example of a much more pervasively metrically ambiguous text (which became more ambiguous in the 1842 revised version of the 1833 original publication). These are the first two stanzas of the 1842 version.

1	On either side the river lie	8 iambic
2	Long fields of barley and of rye,	8 iambic
3	That clothe the wold and meet the sky;	8 iambic
4	And through the field the road runs by	8 iambic
5	To many–tower'd Camelot;	8 iambic
6	And up and down the people go,	8 iambic
7	Gazing where the lilies blow	7
8	Round an island there below,	7
9	The island of Shalott.	6 iambic
10	Willows whiten, aspens quiver,	8 trochaic
11	Little breezes dusk and shiver,	8 trochaic
12	Through the wave that runs for ever	8 trochaic
13	By the island in the river	8 trochaic
14	Flowing down to Camelot.	7
15	Four gray walls, and four gray towers,	7 (?)
16	Overlook a space of flowers,	7 (?)
17	And the silent isle imbowers	7 (?)
18	The Lady of Shalott.	6 iambic

Tennyson, 'The Lady of Shalott', 1842 (Ricks 1969:355)

Lines in the poem as a whole vary in length from five to nine syllables, with seven- or eight-syllable lines the most common. The lines with odd numbers of syllables are the most metrically ambiguous; five- and seven-syllable lines tend to begin and end with stresses (suggesting a short foot at one end) while nine-syllable lines tend to begin and end on non-stressed syllables (suggesting an extrametrical syllable at one end):

```
    *    *      *
   *) * *)   * *)              iambic
   Lady of Shalott                        line 36
   (*  *(*     *(*             trochaic
    *    *      *


   *        *      *    *
   *)*      *)    *  *)*  *)    iambic
   Gazing where the lilies blow           line 7
   (* *     (*     *(*  *  (*   trochaic
    *        *      *    *


       *     *      *     *
   )*  *)  * *)    * *) *  *)Δ   iambic
   The helmet and the helmet feather       line 93
     Δ(*   * (*    *(*  * (*  *  trochaic
       *     *      *     *
```

The lines with six or eight syllables strongly communicate either trochaic or iambic structure (but might at some cost be underlyingly either, for reasons outlined earlier).

```
       *   *     *
   )*  *)**)   * *)             iambic
   The lady of Shalott                    line 18
     Δ(* * (*    *(*            trochaic
       *   *     *


       *    *       *    *
   )*  *)*  *)  *    *) * *)     iambic
   To many-towered Camelot               line 5
    Δ  (* *(*    *    (* *(*    trochaic
       *    *       *    *


    *     *      *      *
   *) *  *)  *    *) *    *)Δ    iambic
   Only reapers, reaping early            line 28
   (*  * (*  *   (* *  (* *(    trochaic
    *      *      *      *
```

Note also that some lines are additionally ambiguous in metre depending on whether syllables are projected. Thus lines 15–17 of the text cited above are trochaic tetrameter if the rightmost syllable is projected; but if the rightmost syllable is not projected because of the phonology of the words 'towers', 'flowers', 'imbowers', then the line will have seven syllables and be in sevens.

As the cited example shows, the text tends to move in blocks of lines which can be grouped together as iambic or trochaic. Lines in the 1833 version which break the sequence tend to be removed or changed in the 1842 version. Thus in the 1833 version, line 11 is 'The sunbeam showers break and quiver' which is iambic with extrametricality in an otherwise trochaic sequence and is therefore revised to trochaic in the 1842 version. There is no reason to think, here, that the metrically ambiguous lines act to bridge between the trochaic and iambic lines; perhaps they are best thought of as potentiating the presence of both types of line in a stanza. In this regard, it is worth noting that trochaic lines appear only in stanzas which also have ambiguous lines (in both versions of the text).

A major metrical change between the 1833 and 1842 versions is an increase in the number of seven-syllable lines, from twenty to thirty-four (and in a text which is otherwise shortened). This can be seen primarily as an increase in overall ambiguity since seven-syllable lines are always ambiguous between iambic and trochaic. Many of the new seven-syllable lines are in the last two stanzas, suggesting some building up of ambiguity towards the end (for unclear reasons). A comparison between the 1833 and the slightly shorter 1842 version shows that any aperiodicities which disrupt a regular binary rhythm are removed. Thus Tennyson removes lines 6 and 7 of the original 'The yellow-leaved waterlily/The green-sheaved daffodilly' which do not fit well into the binary metre. He also removes all clear cases of trochaic inversion. Thus line 24, 'Piling the sheaves in furrows airy', is removed, and line 43, 'Therefore she weaveth steadily', is changed to 'And so she weaveth steadily'; similar changes are made to lines 44, 47 and 147, all of which begin with trochaic inversions which do not survive into the revised text. Lines beginning with lexical-grammatical monosyllabic sequences (i.e. aperiodicities similar to trochaic inversion) are also edited out; thus 'Mute with a glassy countenance' (1833:139) becomes 'with a glassy countenance' (1842:130). The only line in the 1842 edition which might be said to have trochaic inversion involves the word 'sometimes' (in lines 55, 57, cf. also 60) but as this might be analysed as a compound it is not a fully clear example of trochaic inversion. I suggest that these changes have two functions. First, they emphasise binarity of metre; this is the one thing which is certain in the text, more than headedness. Second, they remove evidence for iambicity: iambic texts are more associated with aperiodicity than are trochaic texts, and in particular 'trochaic inversion' is a characteristic marker of iambic metre. Thus trochaic and iambic lines are made more alike in the later version in order to increase the metrical ambiguity.

Why binary/ternary ambiguities are possible

Feet can be binary or ternary in both generated and communicated metres. In this section I look at metres where the line is ambiguously binary or ternary. Ambiguities of this kind can arise for various reasons, relating to characteristics of strict and loose iambic metres.

Strict iambic metres can have trochaic inversion, which means that the first five syllables in an iambic line can have this rhythmic pattern:

> / x x / x

Up to this point, the metre is in principle ambiguous between iambic or dactylic metres. Where the lines are five syllables, the ambiguity cannot be resolved. Even where the lines are six syllables, the difference between a binary metre and a ternary metre is minimal:

> / x x / x /   binary (iambic)
> / x x / x x   ternary (dactylic)

Thus for short lines, particularly with a lot of trochaic inversion, metrical ambiguity is always a possibility. This is illustrated for the following poem; here six- and five-syllable lines alternate, and these might be interpreted as iambic trimeter or dactylic dimeter, alternating with iambic dimeter with extrametricality or dactylic dimeter with a short rightmost foot.

> *His Prayer to Ben Jonson*
> When I a verse shall make
> Know I have prayed thee,
> For old religion's sake,
> Saint Ben to aid me.
>
> Make the way smooth for me,
> When I, thy Herrick,
> Honouring thee, on my knee
> Offer my lyric.
>
> Candles I'll give to thee,
> And a new altar;
> And thou 'Saint Ben' shalt be
> Writ in my psalter.

> Robert Herrick, 1648 (F:274)

The lines are structurally ambiguous in the sense that they could be generated by either set of generative rules; I suggest they are also ambiguous in the metre they communicate. A further complication, characteristic of texts in short lines, is that the couplets might be run together as metrical units, in effect treating the 'metrical line' as a pair of printed lines (see chapter 5). This has the effect of strengthening the evidence for the dactylic metre, because the iambic scansion has a stress maximum on 'offer' which does not project to gridline 1.

```
        *        *       *     *      *     1
   *   *)   *   *)   *   *)  *  *)   *  *)Δ   0
Honouring thee, on my knee Offer my lyric.
(*    *    *  (*    *    * (*  *    *(*  *    0
   *              *            *        *     1
```

Where the line is longer, ambiguity is possible only if there is some redis-
tribution of stresses in positions 6, 7 and 8, which is legitimate only if these
positions are filled with monosyllables, as in the following line:

```
Strangers to slander, and sworn foes to spite,
  )*  *)  *  *)  *  *)     *   *)  *   *)
      *     *    *         *     *
```

John Pomfret, 'The Choice', 1700 (L:3)

This line is fully metrical from the generative perspective. As it is in a text
which is otherwise entirely in iambic pentameter, we could say that it has
iambic pentameter as its generated metre. This line also permits a rhythmic
explicature (36) which implies that the line is iambic pentameter.

(36) This line has the rhythm /xx/x/x/x/.

But the arrangement of monosyllables also permits a different rhythmic explicature:

(37) This line has the rhythm /xx/xx/xx/.

This rhythmic explicature resembles the stereotyped rhythm for iambic pentameter, but only weakly, and thus only weakly implies iambic pentameter (the
implicature of iambic pentameter is however strengthened by the fact that the
surrounding lines are also iambic pentameter). However, it also directly combines with conditional (38), deriving the conclusion that the line is anapaestic
tetrameter (with a short initial foot), a ternary metre.

(38) If a line has a rhythm /xx/xx/xx/ then it is in anapaestic tetrameter.

Thus there is competition between the ternary metre, strongly implied by the
line in isolation, and the binary metre, more strongly implied by the line in its
context. A binary–ternary ambiguity of this kind is made possible, occasionally,
by exploiting the possibility of placing stressed syllables in non-head positions
in iambic pentameter verse. Tarlinskaja (1976:130) shows the same type of
ambiguity in a different context; she cites the following text which in our terms
has anapaestic tetrameter as its generated metre.

> For only last night, as they whispered, I brought
> My own eyes to bear on her so, that I thought
> Could I keep them one half minute fixed, she would fall,
> Shrivelled; she fell not; yet this does it all!
>
> Robert Browning, 'The Laboratory', 1849 (Pettigrew 1981:I,420)

But several of the lines, including the final line, could also be scanned as iambic pentameter. Thus the final line might have the rhythmic explicature:

(39) This line has the rhythm /xx/x/x/x/.

And this would imply iambic pentameter. Again, trochaic inversion turns out to have a key role in allowing a metrical complexity.

As a final example of this kind of binary/ternary ambiguity, which exploits coincidences in the patterns of strict iambic and anapaestic metres, consider the following lines.

> That none beguiled be by time's quick flowing,
> Lovers have in their hearts a clock still going,
>   For though time be nimble, his motions
>   Are quicker
>   And thicker
>   Where love hath his notions:
>
> Sir John Suckling, 'That None Beguiled . . . ', 1646 (F:471)

The first two lines can be scanned as iambic pentameter (with an extrametrical syllable and trochaic inversion in the second line). But the third breaks down as iambic on the word 'nimble', which has its stressed syllable in a line-internal odd-numbered position, and thus means that the line is best scanned as in a ternary metre, perhaps anapaests. This encourages us to reanalyse lines 4 and 5. These at first look like iambic monometer with extrametricality, but lines 4, 5 and 6 can be scanned as continuations of line 3 in a long anapaestic sequence. This in turn raises the possibility of looking back and rescanning the first two lines as anapaests.

Another source of binary/ternary ambiguities is the presence of extra syllables between iambic feet. There are two different sources for these. One possibility is that the metre is loose iambic, which permits an unfooted syllable between feet.

> I closed my lids, and kept them close,
> And the balls like pulses beat;
> For the sky and the sea, and the sea and the sky
> lay like a load on my weary eye,
> and the dead were at my feet.
>
> Samuel Taylor Coleridge, *The Rime of the Ancient Mariner*, 1798 (W:163)

The first line can be scanned as strict iambic tetrameter or as loose iambic tetrameter. The third and fourth lines can be scanned as strict anapaestic tetrameter or as loose iambic tetrameter. The second and fifth lines can be scanned as strict iambic trimeter with an extra initial syllable or as loose iambic trimeter. I illustrate with the fourth line, which incidentally is also open to a dactylic scansion; I project 'weary' as three syllables.

```
lay  like a load on my weary  eye,
*]  *  (* *]  *  (*   *]*(**]     loose iambic
*       *          *   *

*)  *  * *)  *  *   *)* * *)      anapaestic
*       *          *   *

(*  *  *(*  *  *   (* * *(*        dactylic
*       *          *   *
```

In 'The Ancient Mariner' the lines are ambiguous throughout the poem in a constantly shifting manner, between loose and strict iambic and between iambic and anapaestic (and sometimes dactylic). At the level of the line, this is a structural ambiguity for the generated metre: often more than one generated metre will fit any given line. However, for the text as a whole we could be consistent and say that the text is in loose iambic tetrameter and trimeter throughout. The effects of strict iambicity, anapaests and dactyls (and perhaps trochees) can then be understood in terms of the communicated metre; the line quoted above will give rise to rhythmic explicatures which can derive several different metres as conclusions. Loose iambic metre is a rich source of metrical ambiguity, allowing a wide range of rhythms to appear in lines which from a generated perspective are all in the same metre. Thus for example Christina Rossetti's 'Goblin Market' is in a loose iambic metre which gives the effect sometimes of iambs, sometimes of dactyls, and often just of rhythmic uncertainty.

The other source of binary/ternary ambiguities is when syllables are not projected. This, incidentally, can be a source of some ambiguity between a strict metre with non-projected syllables and a loose metre with unfooted syllables.

> I stand on the mark beside the shore
>   Of the first white pilgrim's bended knee,
> Where exile turned to ancestor,
>   And God was thanked for liberty.
> I have run through the night, my skin is as dark,
> I bend my knee down on this mark:
>   I look on the sky and the sea.
>
> Elizabeth Barrett Browning, 'The Runaway Slave at Pilgrim's Point', 1850
> (Browning 1889:II,192)

In these lines the 'extra' syllables are monosyllabic grammatical words. The generated metre might deal with these lines in one of two ways. One option is to exploit the possibility of projecting only one syllable from a sequence such as 'of the' or 'on the', and similarly projecting 'I have' and 'skin is' as one syllable (by contracting the auxiliaries). These kinds of non-projection are all seen in strict iambic verse. They would permit the lines to be scanned as strict iambic tetrameter:

> I have run through the night, my skin is as dark,
>)* Δ *)   Δ   * *)   * *)Δ * *)
>   *   *   *   *

However, given that there are so many instances of extra syllables, a better alternative may be to treat the line as in loose iambic tetrameter (p. 26). Thus 'run' and 'skin' are both identified as stress maxima because they are both followed by two grammatical monosyllables. When brackets are iteratively inserted, unfooted syllables legitimately appear in the middle of the line.

> I have run through the night, my skin is as dark,
> *(*   *]   *   (* *   (*   *]*(* *

The last of the quoted lines is interesting; if we treat the metre as a strict metre we can choose to project all syllables and so get a perfectly metrical iambic tetrameter line. This thereby justifies the previous analysis as strict iambic tetrameter but at the cost of some inconsistency as regards projection, and producing an irregular rhythm.

> I look on the sky and the sea.
>)* *) *   *) * *)   * *)

Or we could treat this line also as loose, but in this case the line falls short, which also introduces some inconsistency.

> I look on the sky and the sea.
>)* *] * (*   *]*   (* *]

Neither option thus maintains the uniformity of the stanza. Again, we have disruption, exploiting a metrical ambiguity (between strict and loose metre) which cannot be fully resolved. The consequence of either not projecting syllables or using a loose iambic metre is to give the effect of anapaests emerging in an otherwise iambic line (hence the traditional notion that anapaests are substituted for iambs, or that the metre is iambic-anapaestic).

4.4   Metrical imitation

The generated metre and the communicated metre are in principle distinct. This means that any of the following combinations are possible:

(a) The text has a generated metre but does not have a communicated metre.
This would be true of texts whose generated metre is concealed. An example might be the Hebrew psalms, which we know as prose texts but in some cases the texts appear to be generated by a syllable-counting metre. The metricality is not salient in the texts as they survive; but if written out as metrical, some of the texts additionally reveal that they are pattern poems (Halle 1987). Another example of 'metrical concealment' can be seen the prose printings of 'Ossian' published by Macpherson, where at least some of the text is clearly in loose iambic trimeter but is written out as prose perhaps to distance it from ballad verse (p. 140).

(b) The text has a communicated metre but does not have a generated metre.
This would be true of free-verse texts which mimic (usually in short stretches) metrical texts. I consider this in more detail shortly.

(c) The text has a generated metre and a communicated metre, and the two types of metre are similar.
This is the case for most iambic pentameter texts, where there is a clear relationship between the grids and constraints involved in the generated metre and the rhythmic patterns implied as part of the communicated metre. I discussed this on p. 100.

(d) The text has a generated metre and a communicated metre, but the two types of metre are different.
I consider two cases of this: verse in a generated syllable-counting metre which communicates iambic pentameter, and verse in iambic pentameter which communicates sapphic metre.

Later in this section, I explore cases (b) and (d), where imitation is involved. In the former case, a text which by the generative rules is unmetrical nevertheless imitates a metrical text; in the latter case a text in one generative metre imitates a text in a different metre.

The imitation of musical rhythm

First, I consider other ways in which the gap between generated metre and rhythmic explicature allows imitation of something other than the underlying metre. I begin with metrical texts which imitate a musical rhythm, a practice associated particularly with Robert Browning but here illustrated using a complete poem by Sebastian Evans. The poem communicates a loose iambic tetrameter for the first eleven lines, after which it communicates the rhythm of the music played by the trumpet. Though the poem shifts in what it communicates, throughout it can be generated by the rules for loose iambic metres, though the line lengths vary. Until line 12 there are four feet in each line; after this there are between one and six feet to the line.

What the Trumpeter Said
1855

At a pot-house bar as I chanced to pass
I saw three men by the flare of the gas:
Soldiers two, with their red-coats gay,
And the third from Chelsea, a pensioner grey,
With three smart hussies as bold as they.   5
Drunk and swearing and swaggering all,
With their foul songs scaring the quiet Mall,
While the clash of glasses and clink of spurs
Kept time to the roystering quiristers,
And the old man sat and stamped with his stump: 10
When I heard a trumpeter trumpet a trump: –
'To the wars! – To the wars!
'March, march!
'Quit your pretty tittle-tattle,
'Quit the bottle for the battle,   15
'And march!
'To the wars, To the wars!
'March, march with a tramp!
'To the wars!
'Up, you toper at your tipple, bottle after bottle at the tap!   20
'Quit your pretty dirty Betty! Clap your garter in your cap,
'And march!
'To the trench and the sap!
'To the little victual of the camp!
'To the little liquor of the camp!   25
'To the breach and the storm!
'To the rolling and the glory of the wars!
'To the rattle and the battle and the scars!'
Trumpeter, trumpet it out!   29

Sebastian Evans, 1865 (K:472)

Two interesting questions arise, one about the metre of the whole text and the other about the rhythm of the lines from 12 onwards. The first eleven lines are in loose iambic tetrameter: there are four syllables which can be stressed in each line, with one or two unstressed syllables between each stressed syllable (giving the impression of shifting between anapaests and iambs); as legitimate variants in this metre, lines 3 and 6 begin (and end) on the stressed syllable (giving the impression of ambiguous falling/rising metres). If we now consider lines 12–29 we see that these also can be analysed as loose iambic metres: one or two syllables fall between stressed syllables, and there are some lines which begin and end on a stressed syllable. Where these lines differ significantly from lines

1–11 is that there are variable numbers of stressed syllables to the line. Thus by preceding the mimicry part of the text with a loose (rather than strict) metrical section, there is some metrical continuity underlying the rhythmical shifts.

This has consequences for the second point of interest, which relates to the rhythm itself. We are given reason to think that lines 12 onwards mimic a trumpet rhythm, but in fact it is possible to construct plausible patterns in different ways. Thus while line 12 most plausibly has two major stresses on 'wars' and 'wars', does line 13 have two stresses on 'march' and 'march' (justified by parallelism with the preceding line), or just one stress on the second 'march'?

```
   x   x   /      x   x   /
'To the wars! – To the wars!   12
   /        /
'March, march!                 13

   x   x   /      x   x   /
'To the wars! – To the wars!   12
   x        /
'March, march!                 13
```

If we take there to be a loose iambic metre underlying the lines, then both are possible variants; the former retains two feet at the cost of having two stresses adjacent while the latter has one foot. The metrical ambiguity here is perhaps accentuated by the repunctuation and development of the lines as 17 and 18.

The text up to line 12 has shifted between having one syllable between stressed syllables and two syllables between stressed syllables; from line 14 onward we have a tension between two possible readings, one a trochaic reading and the other retaining an iambic rhythm but with three rather than two syllables between stressed syllables. While loose iambic metres do not allow three projected syllables between stressed syllables, note that one of these syllables consists just of a syllabified consonant (l), raising the possibility that it is not projected. Thus we have two possible scansions for line 14, one of which shifts the underlying metre to trochaic, and the other retains a loose iambic metre (the latter reading is potentially motivated also by the term 'tittle tattle', which implies rapidity of speech, thus with large numbers of syllables between stressed syllables):

```
     /        /   /   /
Quit your pretty tittle-tattle,
   (*   *   (*   * (* *  (* *(   0
     *       *    *     *       1

     /        /
Quit your pretty tittle-tattle,
   * (*      *] * (* Δ  *] Δ    0
             *        *         1
```

This iambic/trochaic ambiguity, which is both a structural ambiguity (i.e. different underlying metres) and a problem for performance, continues throughout the text, and is crystallised by lines which begin and end on stressed syllables, a classic locus for rising/falling ambiguity in the English tradition as seen in sevens. It is worth noting, incidentally, that the final line has a fully determinate rhythmic explicature: stress on the first, fourth and seventh syllables, but that this rhythm is about as structurally ambiguous a rhythm as could be found in English. This is the only seven-syllable line in the poem and this is one reason for its being in principle analysed as loose iambs, as anapaests or as dactyls. In all cases, the grid will have this partial structure:

```
Trumpeter, trumpet it out!
  *   * *   *   * *   *     0
  *         *         *     1
```

But it can be built in three different ways, by different bracketing rules:

```
Trumpeter, trumpet it out!
  *]  *(*  *]  *(*  *  (   0    loose iambs
  *        *        *   1
```

```
Trumpeter, trumpet it out!
  (*  * *   (*  * * (*     0    dactyls
   *         *       *     1
```

```
Trumpeter, trumpet it out!                 anapaests
  *)  * *   *)  * * *)     0
   *         *       *     1
```

This text shows that mimicry of a non-metrical rhythm is possible, that such texts can be underlyingly metrical, and that mimicry can introduce formal complexity into a text, creating structural ambiguity in rhythm and uncertainty in performance.

The imitation of sapphics

The sapphic is a Greek metre governing several lines in a stanza, which was adapted by Horace, and it is in its Horatian form that it is most influential. As a Latin metre, as used by Horace, the sapphic stanza has four lines, three of eleven and one of five syllables, with the following quantitative patterns (– is a heavy syllable, u a light syllable).

```
– ˘ – – –˸˘ – ˘ – – –
– ˘ – – –˸˘ – ˘ – – –
– ˘ – – –˸˘ – ˘ – – –
– ˘ ˘ – –
```

The long lines have an obligatory word boundary (marked here with a colon) after the fifth syllable. Quantitative sapphics of this kind have occasionally been imitated in English verse, as in the following example by Webbe.

$$- \smile - \quad - \quad - \smile \quad \smile - \smile - -$$

O ye Nymphes most fine, who resort to this brooke,

$$- \smile - \quad - \quad - \smile \smile \quad - \quad \smile - -$$

For to bathe there your pretty breasts at all times,

$$- \quad \smile \quad - - \quad - \quad \smile \smile \quad - \quad \smile - -$$

Leaue the watrish bowres, hyther and to me come

$$- \quad \smile \smile - \quad -$$

at my request nowe.

William Webbe (1585:287)

Quantitative verse is difficult to scan (and hence write and read) in English, probably because of the complexities of deciding which syllables count as heavy, and hence the problem of developing a rhythmic explicature for the line. Webbe apparently marks syllables as heavy if they contain a clearly long vowel, or a vowel followed by two consonants (unless the two consonants can constitute a complex onset, as in 'pretty breasts', where '-y' is counted as light). Grammatical words tend to be counted as light even where they have long vowels (such as 'my'), but note that 'O' is counted as heavy. Some writers help out with the rhythmic explicature; thus Campion's sapphic text 'Come let us sound' (1601) is set to music with one note for each syllable, in a pattern which exactly reproduces the classical sapphic sequence, made from quarter notes (crotchets) for short syllables and half notes (minims) for long syllables (Ing 1951:117).

Most English sapphics in fact imitate not the quantitative pattern of Horace's sapphics, but a characteristic stress-based pattern for the sapphic. Horace's stanzas tend to have a fairly regular stress pattern, a result of the fact that stress in Latin is influenced by syllable weight and word boundaries; the stress pattern tends to relate to the long and short lines like this:

/ x x / x   / x x x / x
$$- \smile - - : \smile \smile - \smile - -$$

/ x x / x
$$- \smile \smile - -$$

The sapphic metre and stanza structure was widely used in mediaeval Latin verse, but with the metre usually reanalysed as a stress-based metre based on the pattern seen in Horace. Thus Attridge (1974:212) quotes a ninth-century stanza with this pattern:

```
/ x x / x : / x \ x / x
/ x x / x : \ x / x / x
/ x x / x : / x / x / x
/ x x / x
```

This accentual pattern was then adapted as the basis of Protestant hymns, such that we can formulate some conditionals (reducing the differentiation of stress to two levels):

> (40) If this line has a rhythm /xx/x/x/x/x then it is a long line in a sapphic stanza.
>
> (41) If this line has a rhythm /xx/x then it is a short line in a sapphic stanza.

Note that, as an accentual metre, the long lines have much in common with iambic pentameter with initial trochaic inversion and an extrametrical rightmost syllable; the rhythm /xx/x/x/x/x is also a rhythm found in some iambic pentameter lines. Bridges actually suggests that trochaic inversion entered English iambic verse as a strategy by adapting the /xx/ beginning of sapphic hymns (Bridges 1921:42). The similarity between the rhythmic templates means that an iambic pentameter line can be used to imitate a sapphic line.

> Story! God bless you! I have none to tell, sir,
> Only last night a-drinking at the Chequers,
> This poor old hat and breeches, as you see, were
> > Torn in a scuffle.
> Constables came up for to take me into
> Custody; they took me before the justice;
> Justice Oldmixon put me in the parish –
> > – Stocks for a vagrant.
>
> George Canning with John Hookham Frere, 'Sapphics. The Friend of Humanity
> and the Knife-grinder', 1797 (L:824)

This text implies that it is in sapphic metre just by having three long lines and a short line, and by being explicitly called 'sapphics'. It also has eleven syllables in the long lines, and five in the short, and almost every line begins on a trochaic inversion. This gives the lines rhythmic explicatures which resemble the explicatures for sapphics and thus imply sapphics, though the distribution of monosyllables means that the rhythms are either regular and unnatural-sounding or irregular and natural-sounding (which is part of the comic effect of the poem).

This poem thus implies that it is in sapphic metre. However, this mimicry is achieved by lines which from a generative metrical perspective are iambic pentameter (and dimeter in the short line). The final syllable in each case is extrametrical and so not projected, so that there are ten projected syllables in all lines. All line-internal polysyllables are aligned so that their stressed syllables project to gridline 1. And almost every line has trochaic inversion.

Constables came up for to take me into
)*   *)*   *)   *   *) * *)   *   *) Δ
    *   *   *   *   *

Custody; they took me before the justice;
)*   *)*   *)   *   *) * *)   * *) Δ
    *   *   *   *   *

Justice Oldmixon put me in the parish –
)*   *)   *   *)*   *)   * *)   *   *)Δ
    *   *   *   *   *

            – Stocks for a vagrant.
)   *   *) * *) Δ
                  *   *

The generative metrical rules stipulate certain aspects of the lines but leave many other aspects uncontrolled. This poem exploits every loophole in the generative metrical rules: almost every line has trochaic inversion, and every line has extrametricality. This demonstrates the aesthetic and communicative advantages of having the generated metrical form of a metrical line significantly underdetermined by the rules.

English poems can imitate sapphics less directly than the examples given here (Jay and Lewis 1996). In some other cases, the generated metre and the communicated metre clearly do not coincide, with the rhythm entirely consistent with a generated metre and the communication of 'sapphic' left to the arrangement of three long lines and one short line, often with a salient enjambment between the third and fourth lines. John Hall wrote a sapphic with three iambic tetrameter lines followed by an iambic dimeter line; Pope's 'Ode on Solitude' has the same structure. Robert Herrick's 'The White Island' has three lines in sevens followed by a three-syllable line with stress on the second syllable:

> In this world, the world of dreams,
> While we sit by sorrow's streams,
> Tears and terrors are our themes
>   Reciting;

> Robert Herrick, 'The White Island', 1648 (F:284)

Robert Brownings 'A Grammarian's Funeral', cited p. 95, has one iambic pentameter line followed by a five-syllable line with /xx/x stress, and thus might weakly imply sapphic structure. John Hollander's 'After An Old Text' has lines in syllable-counting metre (eleven- and five-syllable lines) but without a periodic rhythm. Unmetrical lines can also imply sapphic metre by their shape. Thus William Carlos Williams has a free-verse sapphic in *Paterson* (1958, Book V. II) with the long lines varying in length from nine to four syllables and the short lines varying in length from two to three syllables.

Wherever we find verse in apparently 'classical' metres in English it is always worth asking whether the lines are generated by a specialised set of quantitative rules (which is sometimes the case), or whether instead the lines are in one of the familiar accentual metres and are structured to imply that they are in the quantitative metre. For example, Samuel Wesley has a poem which he titles 'Anacreontic, On Parting with a Little Child'. The classical anacreontic metre is an eight-syllable line with the pattern ˘˘–˘–˘––. But Wesley's poem is in sevens; that is, generated as iambic tetrameter with a short initial foot.

> Dear, farewell, a little while,
> Easy parting with a smile;
> Ev'ry object in thy way
> Makes thee innocently gay;
>
> Samuel Wesley, 'Anacreontic, On Parting with a Little Child', 1736 (L:179)

It would be possible to perform most of the lines fairly naturally in a way which de-stresses the initial syllable, which gives a rhythmic explicature which quite closely resembles the rhythmic explicature for the anacreontic, and thus weakly implies it.

> (42) This line has a rhythm xx/x/x/.
>   by resemblance
> (43) This line has a rhythm ˘˘ – ˘ – ˘ – –.

Thus this text is generated as iambic tetrameter and yet implies that it is in the completely different metre of anacreontics.

Resemblance (in interpretive use) is in principle unconstrained, like any relation between thoughts. Thus it is worth noting that a line with a rhythm xx/x/x/ here is interpreted as resembling the anacreontic quantitative rhythm, but previously has been interpreted as resembling the sevens metre and also an iambic trimeter (p. 111).

The imitation of rhythm in a syllable-counting text

Some texts which might be thought of as iambic pentameter in fact violate the stress maximum condition; that is, while there are ten metrified syllables and a loosely periodic rhythm, polysyllables are not strictly controlled. I suggest that texts of this kind are not generated by the iambic pentameter rules. Instead they are generated by rules for a ten-syllable syllable-counting metre (basically the iambic pentameter rules without the stress maximum condition). The tendency towards a periodic rhythm nevertheless suggests that at the level of implicature, the lines imply that they are in iambic pentameter. In texts of this kind, periodicity can be much reduced, while still present. Hollander (1975:264) comments: 'In syllabic verse, a momentary accentual cadence can function like a momentary rhyme in a strictly controlled blank-verse situation.' Tarlinskaja (1976) suggests that there is a gradient variation between fully iambic pentameter verse and fully decasyllabic syllable-counting verse, depending on the regularity of the rhythm. In my terms, this gradience might hold at the level of implicature of metre, but not at the level of generated metre, where distinctions are categorial: the generated metre is either iambic pentameter or syllable counting (or neither).

Hollander (1975:272) offers another example of this, a non-rhythmic syllable-counting poem by Auden, 'In Memory of Sigmund Freud', which is nevertheless 'a poem-shaped poem' and in fact is shaped like a rhythmic poem by Hölderlin in a German metre – itself imitating a Greek metre. The visual mimicry in turn fits with the occasional emergence of periodic rhythm in Auden's text, which mimics Hölderlin's metrical line – but without actually being itself metrical. Reinterpreting Auden, we can say that Auden's syllable-counting poem offers weak evidence that it is in Hölderlin-style iambic hexameter.

The imitation of metre in a non-metrical text

We also find verse which is not metrical at all from a generative perspective but which nevertheless approximates to a metrical pattern. Thus T. S. Eliot's 'The Love Song of J. Alfred Prufrock' is not sufficiently consistent from line to line to be generated by metrical rules. Nonetheless, as Smith (1968:148) argues, there is an approximation to iambic pentameter, which she calls 'the most probable line', a type of line which emerges and submerges in the text; thus for example the final line in the poem is a perfect iambic pentameter line. One way of understanding this text would be to say that it is not constrained by generative metrical rules (from this perspective it is unmetrical) but that it nevertheless provides evidence which is stronger or weaker from line to line that it is in iambic pentameter. Something similar is achieved by Swift in his 'Humble Petition of Frances Harris'. This is a text in long lines which vary in length and in rhythm, and thus from a generative perspective is non-metrical. But as each line nears its end it appears to be metrical; Swift wrote four poems of this type, and one of the others begins 'Dear Tom, this verse, which however the beginning may appear, yet in the *end's good metre*' (1721, Williams 1958:1022). Here are the first nine lines:

> That I went to warm my self in Lady *Betty's* Chamber, because I was cold,
> And I had in a Purse, seven Pound, four Shillings and six Pence, besides
> Farthings, in Money, and Gold;
> So because I had been buying things for my *Lady* last Night,
> I was resolved to tell my Money, to see if it was right:

> Now you must know, because my Trunk has a very bad Lock,
> Therefore all the Money, I have, which, *God* knows, is a very small Stock,
> I keep in a Pocket ty'd about my Middle, next my Smock.
> So when I went to put up my Purse, as *God* would have it, my Smock was
>   unript,
> And, instead of putting it into my Pocket, down it slipt:
>
> Jonathan Swift, 'The Humble Petition of Frances Harris', 1701
> (Williams 1958:69)

The text gives the impression of being in anapaests because most lines end
on an anapaestic foot (some end on iambs), and the lines can quite often be
scanned from right to left to produce a short sequence of anapaestic feet.
In the case of the line beginning 'Therefore' the whole line can be scanned
as anapaestic hexameter (and the final two lines of the whole poem are very
close to anapaestic hexameter). This is not consistent enough to allow for the
lines to be generated. But it is entirely consistent with the implicature of anapaests. The first two lines might be performed to give them these rhythmic
explicatures:

> (44) Line 1 has the rhythm xx/x/x/x/x/xx/xx/.
> (45) Line 2 has the rhythm xx/xx/xx/x/xx/xx//xx/xx/.

We could formulate a conditional:

> (46) If a line ends on the rhythm xx/xx/ then it is in anapaests.

This conditional would probably be held somewhat weakly, and it would then
give us the weak conclusion that the line is in anapaests.

4.5   'Tension'

Taylor (1988:32) shows that Victorian and early twentieth-century prosodists
were interested in the idea of a difference between the phonetic rhythm of the
text and the metrical pattern, and saw this as a source of aesthetic experience
of verse. In much twentieth-century theory this has been called '(metrical)
tension'. In our terms metrical tension is the difference between the rhythmic
explicature developed from a performance of the text and a metrical template,
formulated as part of a thought:

> (47) Line A has a rhythm /xx/xxx/x/. [explicit form]
>   by resemblance
> (48) Line A has a rhythm x/x/x/x/x/. [implied form]

R. L. Stevenson speaks of the 'rare and special pleasure' which comes from the use of 'the double pattern of the texture and the verse'; 'we see the laws of prosody have one common purpose: to keep alive the opposition of two schemes simultaneously followed' (1885, cited Taylor 1988:44). Henry Newbolt says 'most of the beauty of the lines and all their variety is gained by the skill with which the woof of speech-rhythm is continually thrown athwart the warp of the metrical type' (1912, cited Taylor 1988:33). This difference between spoken rhythm and metrical template is a characteristic of literary texts which has been associated with the notion of 'tension' in both literary critical and generative metrical accounts. Thus Thompson (1961:7) says 'The difference between the patterns of the line as speech and as metre is often recognised today as *tension* and is usually highly prized.' Wimsatt and Beardsley (1959:596) see tension as built into metrical form: 'There is no line so regular (so *evenly* alternating weak and strong) that it does not show some tension. It is practically impossible to write an English line that will not in some way buck against the meter.' Halle and Keyser (1971:142) formulate rules for measuring the complexity of a line of metrical verse and suggest that more complex lines are more perceptually difficult, and that this perceptual difficulty correlates with tension. Attridge (1982:18) speaks of metre as formalising and controlling a natural tension in speech between the freedom to arrange phonetic characteristics freely and the 'pull towards simple patterns and recognitions', and says that 'the more complex the realisation [of the metrical pattern], the greater the feeling of metrical tension' (1982:155).

In broad terms, 'metrical tension' is exemplified by all the cases described in this chapter where a reader or hearer entertains simultaneous different representations of the metrical or rhythmic form of a text. This can arise through weak resemblance between rhythmic explicature and metrical template, through the ambiguities which are basic to metres such as sevens, and the ambiguities of texts which are in one metre and mimic another. These are all kinds of contradiction, with the strength of the contradictions depending on the relative strength of the competing metrical representations. Empson suggests: 'if there is contradiction, it must imply tension; the more prominent the contradiction, the greater the tension' (1953:235). The experience of metrical tension is thus an experience of the relation between inferences. In chapter 3 I cited Sperber and Wilson's view that entertaining a certain set of inferences (weak implicatures) counts as having a kind of aesthetic experience. Metrical tension would seem to be another situation in which having a set of thoughts counts as a kind of aesthetic experience.

This inference-based approach solves one of the problems with earlier accounts of 'tension', which is the question of whether metrical tension is a characteristic of the text or a characteristic of the reader's experience of the text. The former would be implied by taking tension to be the relation between two characteristics which are external to the reader: the phonetic rhythm and the metrical template. But the word 'tension' itself implies that the reader is somehow made tense by this textual tension. Thus Smith (1968:3) says: 'all we can say, and even this may be too much, is that varying degrees or states of tension seem to be involved in all our experiences, and that the most gratifying ones are those in which whatever tensions are created are also released'. If we take the phonetic rhythm to be the content of a thought (the explicit form) and the metrical form also to be the content of a thought (the implied form), then the relation between these is a relation between thoughts, and hence the metrical tension is a relation between thoughts, both a fact about the reader's cognitive state and, because these are thoughts about the text, a fact about the text.

4.6   Summary

Most metrical texts will have three kinds of form. The performance of the text will have explicit form, including its rhythmic explicatures. The rhythmic explicatures may resemble metrical templates and thus imply them; thus a text may imply that it is in iambic pentameter, which is its implied form. This is the source of rhythmic periodicity in the performance of the line. Alongside these fairly overt kinds of form, there is also another kind of form which is hidden from introspection; this is the metrical form which holds of the linguistic representation of the text, and fixes certain invariant characteristics including the number of projected syllables and the placement of stress maxima. Thus formal tendencies and rigid form are accounted for by different kinds of explanation.

The explanation of iambic pentameter offered in chapter 1 was reductionist. Like any generativist account, it takes a modular and not a holistic view of language, explaining some aspects of iambic pentameter and saying nothing about other aspects of iambic pentameter. This account of iambic pentameter has 'explanatory gaps', areas of the metre which are so far untouched, most centrally the fact that there is a tendency towards periodicity of rhythm in the iambic pentameter line. In this chapter I filled these gaps by using the pragmatic approach outlined in chapter 3.

The word 'reductionist' might be used negatively as a criticism of the fact that generative linguistics limits the aspects of language which it seeks to explain. This negative view assumes that uniform or holistic explanation of language is both possible and desirable. This is basically the view of Cureton (1992:1):

Rhythmic experience is essentially multidimensional. While the basic elements of a rhythmic pattern are often simple, each simple pattern can be combined in a variety of ways into comparable (or larger) patterns, with these further patterns arrayed variously within the rhythmic experience as a whole.

While Cureton carefully emphasises the multiple sources of rhythmic experience, he has nonetheless a unifying goal, and he suggests that 'The major task of
a prosodic theory should be to model and motivate this coherent diversity'(6).

In this chapter I have suggested that there is no unified prosodic theory and
indeed that the diversity is not 'coherent'; instead the best account of metre is
modular and non-holistic. This is because there is a categorial distinction between obligatory and optional characteristics of metre, requiring different kinds
of explanation. Thus a reductionist modular account which seeks different explanations for different kinds of fact better explains metre than a holistic account
which seeks a unified explanation. Reductionism and modularity also have an
advantage in traditional literary critical terms: by dividing the explanation of
metre between generative and pragmatic rules we can thereby demonstrate a
much greater complexity and ambiguity for metrical practice than is allowed
by more traditional or holistic approaches. Metre turns out to be both more
interesting and more complex than it might otherwise seem.

5   Lines

5.1   Lineation is implied

In this chapter I will show that lineation, the division of a text into lines, is a kind of implied form, not an inherent fact of the text. Because there are many kinds of evidence for the division into lines, there are usually many competing options for how the text is divided up. In most texts, one lineation is dominant but I will suggest that other alternative lineations remain weakly present. This can be assimilated to Sperber and Wilson's suggestion that poetic effects involve a mass of weak implicatures; here I propose that the weak implicatures of alternative lineations are experienced as aesthetic. In some texts, no single lineation is dominant, and the text is ambiguous in lineation, which is a kind of high-level complexity, which in turn may be experienced as aesthetic. Thus verse is inherently contradictory and complex and thereby inherently aesthetic.

The apparent determinacy of lineation comes from the fact that there are strong implicatures relating to lineation both in writing and in speech. For writing we might have explicatures such as (1) and conditionals such as (2):

> (1) This word has no words on the page to its right.
> (2) If a word has no words on the page to its right then it is at the end of a line. [weak]
> by modus ponens
> (3) This word is at the end of a line. [weak]

Note that on its own conditional (2) is weak, because paragraphs in prose also end on words which have no words to their right. For spoken performances, we might have explicatures like (4) and conditionals like (5):

> (4) This word is followed by a pause.
> (5) If a word is followed by a pause then it is at the end of a line. [weak]
> by modus ponens
> (6) This word is at the end of a line. [weak]

Again, conditional (5) holds fairly weakly because there are also pauses internal to lines. Like any conditional about form, its strength can vary from tradition to tradition and from author to author; thus it holds fairly strongly for Whitman, who tends to end lines on a pause (Hollander 1975:277), and weakly for Milton, who often avoids ending lines on a pause.

All the conditionals relating to lineation are weak, with the exception of the following:

> (7) If a section of text is a line then it will be preceded or followed by another
>   line. [strong]

While this is a strong condition it does not guarantee the truth of a conclusion; no condition can do this, no matter how strong. In principle, there can be one-line texts, but they are rare: hence the strength of the conditional. The weakness of most of the individual conditionals means that inferences about lineation need more than one source of evidence. Thus we find both metre *and* rhyme, or both metre *and* line-final punctuation. It is rare to find texts in which there is just one source of evidence for lineation; where such texts exist – some free-verse texts offer just layout in print or pausing in speech – lineation is correspondingly weakly evidenced. In contrast, some kinds of text have very strongly evidenced lineation; heroic couplets in English verse tend to offer multiple sources of evidence for the line.

The strength of visual evidence

Because we are so used to seeing very strong evidence for lineation – by the way that lineated texts are printed on the page – it is difficult to conceive of lineation as holding only by implicature. If there was ever an apparent fact-of-the-matter about a text it would seem to be its division into lines; nevertheless, I will suggest that this is just a strong implicature.

A text is a set of performances which resemble each other, where 'performance' means any instantiation of a text, in any medium. The set of performances which constitute the text might consist of just one performance (e.g. for a text which is spoken only once and never performed again, never written down), or many (e.g. a play printed in different forms and performed in speech many times). For most readers and most English verse texts, the text is a performance in print and a performance in speech (perhaps 'spoken under the breath').

Performances can be ranked, though there is no universal or natural ranking; ranking of performance depends on cultural assumptions about medium, author, etc. This ranking correlates with the 'authority' of the performance. An author's reading aloud, a director's cut of a film, a performance of a play overseen by the author; all can in principle be taken to have greater authority than other performances of the text. There is also a relation between the strength of a thought about a text and the medium of the performance from which the thought is derived. The spoken version of a text might be thought to be more 'authoritative' than the written version; this is often held to be true for 'folk' performances and their transcriptions, and more generally characterises an ethnopoetic approach to verbal art. In Elizabethan England, poems were owned as manuscripts, but when printed versions appeared the manuscripts were thrown away on the assumption that the printed version is a more authoritative performance of the text (Marotti 1995:230). For most of the poetry discussed in this book, the printed version of a text has generally been held to be more authoritative than the spoken version.

The more 'authoritative' a performance is held to be, the stronger the thoughts derived from it. The strength of a thought is the degree to which the thought is held to be true; the more authoritative the source of the thought, the more it is held to be true. This applies in particular to explicatures, such that explicatures from an authoritative performance may be stronger than exactly the same explicatures from a less authoritative performance. Thus in an author's reading a line may be given a particular rhythm, which allows the development of a rhythmic explicature. This explicature is likely to be held more strongly than exactly the same rhythmic explicature developed from a performance by someone who is not the author.

Lineation, perhaps more than any other formal characteristic of a text, feels like a fact about a text, not an inference or interpretation of the text. I suggest that this is because the printed version of the text allows the development of explicatures (of the type 'there are fourteen words with no words to their right') from which thoughts about lineation can be very directly derived. The thought about lineation is strengthened by being derived from the printed form of the text, if this is taken to be authoritative. Perhaps there is also some priority given to vision: if the formal explicature is developed from what we see rather than what we hear, perhaps we make it stronger. It is worth comparing the apparently determinate fact of lineation, visible in the printed text, with the less clearly determinate rhythm of a text. Any spoken performance of a text has an actual rhythm, but while this rhythm is just as much 'there' in the spoken performance as is the lineation of a written performance, there is likely to be more acknowledgement that rhythms are variable and multiple. In contrast, lineation is often held to be fixed and singular. This derives from prejudice about medium.

It is mainly in the past century that ways have been found of overcoming the strength of visual evidence for lineation (Rothenberg and Joris 1995). The key text in this regard is perhaps Stéphane Mallarmé's 'Un coup de dés jamais n'abolira le hasard' (1897), of which this is part of a page:

SOIT
      que
          l'Abîme

   blanchi
       étale
        furieux
             sous une inclinaision
               plaine désespérement

(Hartley 1965:216)

Here, words which are in different vertical positions nevertheless sometimes seem to continue a horizontal sequence, but there are also horizontal overlaps and horizontal gaps which might or might not be taken as boundaries between lines. Mallarmé's text thus significantly weakens the visual evidence for lineation; in his preface Mallarmé suggested that in his poem the page replaces the line as the basic unit of the poem.

Texts which are 'both verse and prose'

In this section I look at texts which are scannable as verse (by the generative metrical rules) but which are laid out on the page as prose. This is a way of weakening the evidence for lineation.

Rice (1765:179–80) cites a translation from the contemporary Swiss poet Salomon Gessner which he says is 'poetry imposed on us for prose':

Led by the Murmers of refreshing Streams, and silent Shades of sacred Groves, she strays: Now by the Brook, whose Banks are lin'd with Reeds; now in the Walks, thick shaded o'er with Trees; trampling the Flowers: Or now, reclining on the mossy Bank, she sits at Ease and meditates the Song.

Rice shows that this is actually iambic pentameter (with one short line), but with visual evidence for lineation removed; thus he rewrites part of it (showing sensitivity to the trochaic inversion on 'trampling').

> Now in the Walks, thick shaded o'er with Trees;
> Trampling the Flowers:——
> Or now, reclining on the mossy Bank,

The prose layout of the text implies 'this text is not in lines' but the fact that it can be assigned metrical form implies 'this text is in lines'. Translation is always an interesting practice when it comes to implicatures involving form, because what were once formal explicatures (e.g. involving the lineation by layout of the original text) are now removed from the text, but can still be implied. The common practice of translating verse into prose can be taken as giving rise to complex implicatures about the special status of the original formulation of a text, and its special relation to the language (and by implication the 'folk' from which it emerges). The practice of translating verse into prose which is also verse, or more accurately into a text which implies both that it is in verse and in prose at the same time, can be seen as a way of complicating the implicatures, giving the text even more of a 'dual nationality'.

One of the most interesting eighteenth-century practitioners of this kind of prose translation is James Macpherson, who translated Homer's *Iliad* into prose in 1773, and most famously 'translated' Gaelic poetry into English prose as *The Poems of Ossian*. Though presented in prose, at least some of his prose text is scannable as loose iambic trimeter. In Laing's (1805) printing of Macpherson's work, he places the prose version (as printed in *The Poems of Ossian*) next to a verse version which appears to be Macpherson's original and which was passed to some of his literary contacts before any of his work was published:

> From the tree at the grave of the dead,
> The *lonely screech*-owl *groans*.
> I see a dim form on the plain,
> 'Tis a ghost! it fades, it flies;
> Some *dead* shall pass this way.

From the tree at the grave of the dead the *long howling* owl *is heard*. I see a dim form on the plain! It is a ghost! it fades, it flies. Some *funeral* shall pass this way: *the meteor marks the path*. (James Macpherson, 'The Six Bards'/'Croma' (Laing 1805:II, 416–17))

Both versions of the text, whether written as verse or written as prose, can be scanned as loose iambic trimeter. The first thing this shows is that layout is not crucial for determining a text's status as divided into lines: there is evidence from the metre that both texts are divided into lines even though this is supported from layout in one case and not the other. Several interesting questions now arise. Why did Macpherson use loose iambic trimeter? One possibility is that this is close to the loose iambic tetrameter characteristic of ballads without actually being in ballad metre; thus it weakly implies 'folk' (in the nationalistic eighteenth-century notion of the folk) and so connects back to the idea that these are texts somehow emerging from the spirit of the nation. However, the lines are not divided into stanzas, which both weakens the implicature that they are generically ballads and strengthens the implicature that they are generically epic. (In a sense Macpherson predates the lyrical ballads of Coleridge and Wordsworth with the contradictory implicatures of genre in what we might call his 'epic ballads'.) Most interestingly of all, why did Macpherson not lineate his text throughout, particularly since much of it is demonstrably metrical?

Macpherson explains why he chooses prose rather than iambic pentameter in rhyming couplets. (He does not acknowledge the possibility that the texts are in a loose metre, something which seems first to have been explicitly theorised by Coleridge.)

The following Poems, it must be confessed, are more calculated to please persons of exquisite feelings of heart, than those who receive all their impressions by the ear. The novelty of cadency, in what is called a prose version, tho' not destitute of harmony, will not to common readers supply the absence of the frequent returns of rhime. This was the opinion of the Writer himself, tho' he yielded to the judgement of others, in a mode which presented freedom and dignity of expression instead of fetters, which cramp the thought whilst the harmony of language is preserved. His intention was to publish in verse ... It is, however, doubtful, whether the harmony which these poems might derive from rhime, even in much better hands than those of the translator, could atone for the simplicity and energy, which they would lose. (James Macpherson, 'Preface to *The Poems of Ossian*', 1773 (Gaskill 1996:410)

We might interpret Macpherson's use of prose which is at the same time verse ('not mere prose' as he described his translation of the *Iliad*) as the construction of a text which leads to various contradictory implicatures of form. This contradiction can be experienced as aesthetic, and also as symbolising the (implied) unbridgeable gap between the original and the translation.

Lineation and generated metrical form

In metrical verse, line boundaries must be established in order for the text to be scanned. We know that the generative metrical rules are sensitive to the line boundary because the scansion starts by projecting an initial syllable and moves right or left along the syllables until it reaches a terminal syllable. Sensitivity to the line boundary can also be seen in the fact that the line is a domain for the definition of stress maximum. A stressed syllable in a polysyllabic word is defined as a stress maximum if the syllable which precedes it is in the same line, but not if the syllable which precedes it is in a different line. But if a line boundary exists by implicature and is not a determinate fact of the text, how do the generative rules 'know' where the boundary is? This is a problem addressed by Levin (1971:182), who concludes that metre is not a linguistic phenomenon because it depends on the division of a text into lines, and lines are not linguistic entities: 'When the line is defined for the hearer it is defined by conventional features of poetry and is thus itself a convention; it has no linguistic relevance.' We might restate Levin's 'linguistic' as 'generated': lines are not generated and so the metre is not generated. The account of communicated metre outlined in chapter 4 fits with Levin's view that lines are communicated and metre is also communicated; the implicature of metre and the implicature of lineation and line boundaries belong in the same explanatory domain and are interrelated. But in chapters 1 and 2 I have argued that in a different sense of metre, metre is *also* generated, which means that we must explain how generated form (the metrical grid) can be related to communicated form (the location of the line boundaries). In this approach, generated metrical form is assumed to be built in a specialised cognitive system which in Fodor's terms is 'encapsulated' in the sense that it is linked only in limited ways with other kinds of cognition. I now explore two possible explanations.

One possibility is to order the generative rules after the inferential processes, allowing the generative rules to have access to the conclusions of the inferential processes. First the reader or hearer infers the presence of line boundaries, and these are then used to cut the text's linguistic representation into sections (lines), which are then scanned by the generative rules. One reason for being cautious about accepting this order is that specialised cognitive processes are considered to have limited access to general cognition, and it is not obvious that there is access into these specialised cognitive processes from general cognition; Fodor calls the specialised cognitive processes 'encapsulated'. The second reason for being cautious is that inferential processes do not always produce determinate outcomes; as we will see in this chapter, lineation can be ambiguous or uncertain in a metrical text, but the generative rules cannot deal with uncertain or ambiguous inputs. This suggests some separation in principle between generative and inferential processes. A third reason for rejecting this approach is that the alternative approach, which I now consider, offers a new explanation for one of the deep facts about metre.

The alternative is to separate the generative rules from the inferential processes. This means that the input to the generative rules will be a continuous (i.e. unlineated) phonological sequence, part of the phonological representation of the text. A generative rule system is chosen (from the range of possible ones, including, e.g., iambic pentameter, iambic tetrameter, trochaic tetrameter, anapaestic trimeter, etc.) and an initial and terminal syllable are specified, and the grid is built by projecting the sequence from initial to terminal syllable. But how is the generative rule system chosen and how are the initial and terminal syllables specified? One possibility is that all options are simultaneously pursued, with scansions rejected when they fail, until the text can be coherently scanned (but allowing also for the possibility of structural ambiguity).

This might explain a cross-linguistically attested fact about metre, which is that a metre always fixes at least two characteristics of the line. The metre always fixes the length of the line (with controlled variation), and I have argued that this is its primary function. But it seems that every metre always fixes something else as well. In English, stress maxima are fixed in place. In Welsh, rhyme is fixed in place. In Irish, word boundaries are fixed in place (relative to the end of the line, by specifying how many syllables the rightmost word must be). It is not immediately obvious why the metre should fix something in addition to the counting out of the syllables, unless the metre must also have a means of anchoring itself to the phonological sequence. This would be necessary if the metrical rules applied in an encapsulated or modularised manner to the phonological sequence as suggested in the previous paragraph, without being 'told' which metre the text was in or where the line boundaries were. Fixing two characteristics of the line rather than just one is thus a kind of 'triangulation' strategy whereby the right metre can be enabled to scan the right section of text. The possibility that these extra constraints relate to the anchoring of the metre to the phonological sequence also explains why the extra constraints often relate to the edge of the line. Thus the English rule for stress maxima makes special reference to the beginning of the line, and in Irish, word boundaries are placed relative to the end of the line.

In combination, lines can vary in length, which in effect means that different lines are in different (though usually related) metres. English odes are in iambic metres with variable length lines; Welsh and Irish poems based on syllable-counting often mix line lengths in the same stanza. In all these cases, variation in length is possible because for each individual line, at least two aspects of the line are controlled by the metre. If we found a text which had varying numbers of syllables in every line and no other constraints, this would not be a 'variable length syllable-counting text' (i.e. by analogy to 'variable length iambic texts' exemplified by English odes); instead, it would be unmetrical.

5.2   Evidence for the line

The following is a list of some of the characteristic kinds of evidence for the line, some of which are found in English verse and some in other traditions. Some of these kinds of evidence are boundary characteristics, telling us where the line begins or ends, and others are extent characteristics, holding across the text between the line boundaries (but not crossing over them).

- Parallelism between lines. This is an extent characteristic. In some traditions it is fully systematic; Jakobson (1987) calls this 'canonic parallelism' (Fox 1988, Fabb 1997:137–64).
- Parallelism within the line. Welsh verse may offer the best example of this, with its rules for *cynghanedd*, where a sequence of sounds in the first half of the line is repeated in the second half of the line (Williams 1953, Rowlands 1979, Fabb 1997:119).
- Alliteration at the beginning of the line. This is rarely systematic but it is fairly common, for example in Mongolian poetry (Poppe 1958, Fabb 1997:118,160).
- Alliteration within the line. In *Beowulf* the line always includes either two or three alliterating stressed syllables. While this is an extent char-acteristic, in some ways it also functions as a boundary characteristic,

because the rightmost stressed syllable is never part of the alliteration pattern; thus it indicates that the line is ending (Russom 1987).

- The initial letter in the line can be part of a pattern. Thus, for example, in the *altus prosatur*, a Hiberno-Latin text from Iona, the first line in each stanza begins with a 'letter' which together add up to the complete alphabet (Clancy and Márkus 1995).
- Rhyme.
- Metre. This is mainly an extent characteristic, but also a boundary characteristic because there are metrical irregularities at line edges.
- Layout on the printed page.
- Boundaries at line ends (e.g. syntactic or phonological phrase boundaries, pauses, punctuation).
- Size. While there can be short lines and long lines, there are normative expectations relative to the tradition that lines will be a certain length, which means that evidence for a line boundary will be strengthened if it falls close to the normative length of the line. Similarly it has been argued that in *Beowulf* the parts of the long line are characteristically balanced so that shorter half-lines combine with longer half-lines.

While it is possible to list general kinds of evidence for the line, it is not possible to give a complete list, because evidence can be emergent, specific to a text and perhaps never seen again. Thus, for example, Hollander comments that the first line of *Paradise Lost* has a balance between three monosyllables, a polysyllable and three monosyllables (1975:94):

Of Man's first Disobedience, and the Fruit

This pattern is evidence that the syllables in question form a complete unit, a line. In terms of inferencing, we might develop an explicature:

(8) This is a sequence of three syllables followed by a polysyllable and three syllables.

Or more abstractly:

(9) This sequence of syllables is in a symmetrical pattern.

We might then formulate a weak conditional:

(10) If a sequence of syllables is in a symmetrical pattern then it is a line.

This leads to the conclusion that this sequence is a complete line. This weak conclusion is added to the strong conclusion based on layout that it is a line, but is counteracted by the fact that there is no line-final pause which weakly implies that it is not a line. Here the explicatures (8) or (9) and the conditional (10) are not part of some general inventory of 'kinds of evidence for the line' which Milton draws upon; they just emerge as a plausible explicature and conditional for this text.

Linguistic constituent boundaries and the line boundary

The linguistic representation of a text divides the text into constituents which have beginnings and ends. These include syntactic constituents such as the word, the phrase and the sentence, and phonological constituents such as the phonological word, the phonological phrase and the utterance. Syntactic constituents often coincide with phonological constituents: a syntactic phrase can also be a phonological phrase, and a syntactic word and a phonological word are often the same (Nespor and Vogel 1986). But there can also be differences. The English 'I've' or 'didn't' or 'wanna' are each a single phonological word but two syntactic words. In Greek drama, bridge rules require that a particular pair of syllables must be in the same word; Devine and Stephens (1984) show that in Greek tragedies this is the syntactic word, while in Greek comedies this is the phonological word. In principle, any kind of syntactic or phonological constituency can be involved in literary form (but for a contrary view see Hayes (1989), who argues specifically for the primacy of phonological constituency).

There is a tendency for linguistic constituent boundaries to coincide with line boundaries. In some traditions, the end of the sentence and the end of the line coincide. Rubin (1995:106,194) claims that this is generally true in orally composed epic (for functional reasons because lines are remembered as syntactically complete chunks). In other traditions, they do not (i.e. they allow enjambment, where a syntactic constituent boundary does not coincide with a line boundary). The relation between linguistic constituent boundaries and line boundaries can be expressed by conditionals. A conditional which links the end of a sentence with the end of a line might be phrased as (11); in English verse this is generally weak.

(11) If this is the end of a sentence then it is the end of a line.

A conditional which links the end of a word with the end of a sentence will have to be phrased differently (because there are many words within the line), but it is generally very strong.

(12) If this is the end of a line then it is the end of a word.

When a strong explicature like (12) can be developed from the text which also gives rise to a explicatures which contradict it, the contradiction is very strong, as in the following text:

> To separate these twi–
> Lights, the Dioscuri;
>
> Ben Jonson, 'To the Immortal Memory . . . Sir H. Morison', 1640 (F:147)

Relevance Theory tells us that in communication, if we are invited to expend inferential effort then we should expect cognitive rewards. Is contradiction a cognitive reward? I suggest that in our experience of literary texts, contradiction is experienced as aesthetic, and thus is a cognitive reward. But there are other rewards to be gained from this contradiction. Further inferential effort will deliver some rewards, such as recognising the pun relating 'twi' to the twin Dioscuri (Castor and Pollux), or recognising an allusive echo of a split word in an ode by Horace (Hollander 1975:143). Jonson exploits both phonological form (twi– rhymes with –ri) and written form in generating this contradiction.

Sometimes just written form is enough, as seen in this stanza:

That rabble rout that in this castle won	1
Is Ireful – ignorance, Unseemly – zeal,	2
Strong – self – conceit, Rotten – religion,	3
Contentious – reproach – gainst – Michael –	4
If – he – of – Moses' – body – aught – reveal –	5
Which – their – dull – sconces – cannot – easily – reach,	6
Love – of – the – carcass, An – inept – appeal –	7
To – uncertain – papers, A – false – formal – fetch –	8
Of – feigned – signs, Contempt – of – poor – and – sinful – wretch.	9

> Henry More, *Psychozoia*, 1642 (F:526)

More here writes whole noun phrases as though they are words. Lines 4–6 are all a single name split across three lines. Note that this splitting of a word is purely at the level of the layout and implicature; this is not really a single word of English. The (written) performance of the text introduces a contradiction which does not hold at the level of linguistic form.

The performance of the text in speech or writing might also strengthen the evidence for lineation. Ing (1951:83-4) shows this for sixteenth-century punctuation of printed poems, where there is a tendency to put a comma or heavier stop at the end of the line (even where not syntactically needed). In the first stanza of 'Shep. Tonie's answer to *Harpalus Complaynt on Phillidaes Loue Bestowed on Corin*' (Anonymous 1573) every line ends on a punctuation mark, but punctuation is not used to mark line-endings in later stanzas where the same kind of syntactic break is involved; thus punctuation is used in the first stanza to establish divisions clearly, then eases off.

The relation between linguistic structure and performance in writing or speech was a matter of great interest to eighteenth-century rhetoricians, focusing particularly on how to perform Milton's blank verse. Some writers prescribe a pause in performance at the end of every line. Thus Watts (1721:77) suggests putting a pause at the end of a line without punctuation 'about half so long as a Comma, just to give notice that the Line is ended'. Thomas Sheridan (1781: 127–30) says that verse and prose are distinguished by the pause at the end of the verse line. Interestingly, he describes various ways in which readers of Milton choose to perform the end of the line. Most readers make no pause at all unless there is a pause in sense, as though it is prose. Some give the end of the line the intonational fall characteristic of the end of the sentence, while others innovate intonationally by raising the pitch on the final syllable. Sheridan's own advice is to lengthen the final syllable in the line while keeping the pitch level, which he calls a 'pause of suspension' (1781:111). All these approaches treat lineation as a problem for performance, where various kinds of evidence can be used to indicate the end of the line; they also attempt to disambiguate lineation, and so both Watt and Sheridan try to develop special performance techniques which give the end of the line a unique quality, thus permitting the development of a strong conditional.

Perhaps the most interesting and substantial of these discussions is by John Walker (1781:207–20; see also 1785:333–43). Walker (1781) criticises Sheridan's insertion of a pause at the end of the line, for three interesting reasons. First, he says that performance should be true to authorial intention:

for in the first place, if the author has so united the preceding and following lines in verse as to make them real prose, why is a reader to do that which his author has neglected to do, and indeed seems to have forbidden by the very nature of the composition? (John Walker (1781:207))

Second, he says that the pause by itself will always be short in comparison to the pauses at the ends of major syntactic/phonological units, and hence that it will become almost or completely imperceptible: an important claim that evidence must be noticed in order to count as evidence, which fits with the idea that form is implied. Third, he takes rhythmic periodicity to be the primary evidence for verse: thus he has a notion of 'the most central evidence' for form. He then ties periodicity to metricality and takes this as supplementary evidence for lineation, assuming equal-length lines. In an important supplementary claim, he allows that form is a matter of degree:

This prosaic air in these lines may have a very good effect in point of expression and variety, but if too frequently repeated, will, undoubtedly render the verse almost imperceptible. (John Walker (1781:209))

(Walker does some rather modern things in his exposition. He cites examples and asks the reader to make a judgement as to whether his claims are right : 'an appeal may be made to every ear for the truth of what has been just observed'. He also alters examples and asks for judgements on them, analogous to the practice of modern linguists. And he relineates texts so that the major phonological pauses do come at the ends of lines, and asks the reader to practise performing the texts in these forms in order to avoid the habit of pausing at line-end.)

For these reasons Walker proposes not to insert pauses at the ends of lines, unless licensed by the phonology of the text. His primary aim is to keep the performance relatively unmarked in linguistic terms, while a secondary aim is to achieve 'expression and variety' – in other words, an aesthetic effect. It is worth noting that Walker does not emphasise the contradictory aspects of performance: it is his rewritten text, with punctuation added at the end of a line without phonological boundary, in which 'the eye puts a cheat upon the ear, by making us imagine a pause to exist where there is only vacancy to the eye', and thus 'cheats' of this kind are to be avoided.

Walker makes two further comments about the end of the line: he describes 'affectations' whereby there is particular effort to remove evidence for the end of the line.

Writers of blank verse affect to end the line without any pause, or with as small a pause as possible, and readers are too apt, where they see no pause at the end of the line, to run the lines together, without attending to such pauses as they would make in prose, for fear we should suppose they do not know how to read blank verse: this makes them frequently pronounce the words at the end of one line and the beginning of the next much more swiftly than any other part of the verse, to the utter ruin of the harmony. (John Walker (1785:343))

And the printer

will often omit placing a pause at the end of a line of verse, where he would have inserted one in prose; and this affectation is still carried farther by the reader, who will generally run the sense of one line into another, where there is the least opportunity of doing it, in order to show that he is too sagacious to suppose there is any conclusion in the sense because the line concludes. (John Walker (1781:217))

In these practices, the speaker and the printer of the text (both types of performer) work to remove evidence for line-endings, seeking a formal contradiction which they value as a poetic characteristic.

One of the ways in which form works is to be contradictory, which I suggest is experienced as aesthetic. Enjambment is so widespread in English verse that it must be seen as having some general function, and I suggest that its general function is to give rise to a kind of low-level contradiction which is experienced as aesthetic. But enjambment can also be the basis of further inferences. An implicature of form can imply other thoughts about form: enjambment between the third and fourth line of a four-line stanza implies 'this stanza is in sapphic metre' (p. 129). And an implicature of form can imply thoughts about content. In my account, both form and meaning are the content of thoughts about the text, and so we would expect a free interplay between thoughts about form and thoughts about meaning. Consider for example Sidney's sonnet 'I Never Drank ... ', every line of which has a punctuation mark at the end except for these:

> How falls it then, that with so smooth an ease
> My thoughts I speak, and what I speak doth flow
> In verse, and that my verse best wits doth please?
>
> Sir Philip Sidney, 'I Never Drank ...' 1591 (J:312)

Here the enjambment can be interpreted as an imitation of the flowing of water. The word 'flow' encourages us to invent a conditional like (13), and so engage in a deduction:

(13) The text has enjambment.
(14) If a text has enjambment then it flows like water.
    by *modus ponens*
(15) The text flows like water.

Spiller (1992:183) suggests that enjambment is 'the Romantic sense of the pressure of energy against form' and cites Blake, who says 'The cistern contains; the fountain overflows.' I suggest that we see it as a somewhat conventional example of the relation between inferences about form and inferences about meaning.

Mid-line boundaries which resemble end-of-line boundaries

Where a certain feature is associated with the end of a line, it may also be deployed in the middle of the line. In principle this means that there is some competition for where the end of the line is located; the middle of the line is in effect staking a claim to be treated as the end of the line. This is exemplified by the manuscript punctuation of *Paradise Lost* book 1, as described by Treip (1970:56): 'Especially often marks fall at the caesura, this emphasising primarily the movement of the verse from mid-line to mid-line, and setting this long forward movement against the other basic movement of the recurring pentameter line.' Treip shows that the line is lightly punctuated, omitting most punctuation even if grammatically required, and usually leaving just one punctuation mark in each line either at the end or in the middle. This means that the middle of the line is characterised by a feature which is also evidence for the end of the line. One way of understanding this is to take a fairly conventional conditional such as (16), and apply it to this text, with the result that there will be extensive contradictory evidence for the line boundary.

(16) If a word is followed by a punctuation mark it is at the end of a line.

An alternative is to formulate a new conditional (17), which will create an equal amount of structural uncertainty.

> (17) If a word is followed by a punctuation mark it is at the end or the middle of a line.

Milton's practice, as throughout his writing, seems designed to create formal complexity. But we can see similar complexities to a lesser degree in other writing.

Thus Chapman, in his translation of the *Iliad*, favours lines which lack punctuation at the end of the line, but usually have punctuation after the fifth, sixth or eighth projected syllable in the fourteen-syllable line:

> The general yet bore no such mind, but viciously disgraced
> With violent terms the priest, and said: 'Dotard, avoid our fleet,
> Where lingering be not found by me, nor thy returning feet
> Let ever visit us again, lest nor thy godhead's crown
> Nor sceptre save thee. Her thou seekst I still will hold mine own
> Till age deflower her. In our court at Argos, far transferred
> From her loved country, she shall ply her web, and see prepared
> (with all fit ornaments) my bed. Incense me then no more,
> But, if thou wilt be safe, begone.
>
> George Chapman, *Homer's Iliads*, 1598 (F:16)

The line boundary can be inferred for Chapman's text by the presence of rhyme and a conditional like (18):

> (18) If a word has no words to its right it is at the end of a line. [strong]

But a conditional like (19) is also available; an experienced reader will hold it to some extent (because it will have been reinforced by other readings).

> (19) If a word is followed by a punctuation mark it is at the end of a line. [weak]

Given this conditional, Chapman's lines consistently throw up weak evidence for an alternative lineation, in contradiction to the printed lineation. Chapman's metre might be seen here as in part an aesthetic practice, producing a consistent and chronic complexity of lineation throughout his text. It is also probably intended to imitate the practice in Homer's verse of requiring a word boundary to fall near the mid-line.

Mid-line punctuation is fairly common in English texts, particularly for longer lines (such as those used by Chapman). Ing suggests that there was a general tendency in late sixteenth-century printing to add a punctuation mark after the eighth syllable in the heptameter and the sixth syllable in the hexameter (even where there is no syntactic reason to do so). As a weak tendency this can also to some extent be seen in iambic pentameter. Consider for example the Elizabeth Barratt Browning poem used in chapter 1. Punctuation marks are found after syllables in the following positions.

Position of syllable in line	1	2	3	4	5	6	7	8	9	10
Number of pauses after this syllable	1	0	2	6	3	1	2	0	2	8

Thus the most common positions for punctuation marks are after the fourth and tenth syllables. This makes some sense in terms of our metrical grid because the syllables in positions 4 and 10 are the two syllables which project to gridline 2. But because this is a tendency rather than a rigid requirement, we cannot make it part of the generative rules. We can control the presence of these punctuation marks, just as we dealt with the periodic rhythm, by a conditional:

> (20) If the line is in iambic pentameter then there will be a punctuation mark after the fourth syllable.

(There are, as always, other ways of constructing the conditional: we could say that there is a pause here, or we could identify the position as 'after the second stressed syllable' or as 'just before the middle of the line'. Any of these conditionals are likely to get similar effects.) As before, the use of a mid-line punctuation mark can be interpreted as a way of confusing the evidence for lineation, implying alternative possible lineations to those seen in print.

Other metrical traditions find other ways of putting boundaries characteristic of line-ends in the middle of the line. Lines usually end at the end of a word, but some traditions also have caesura rules which require a word boundary to fall at a specific position at or near the middle of the line. In dramatic dialogue, speakers usually change at the ends of lines, but speakers can also be made to change in the middle of a metrical line without interrupting the metre:

> K. RICH. Then, by my self –
> Q. ELIZ.   Thy self is self-misus'd.
> K. RICH. Now, by the world –
> Q. ELIZ.   'Tis full of thy foul wrongs.
>
> William Shakespeare, *Richard III*, 4.4, 1591

Mid-line speaker change is another way of complicating the evidence for the line.

Rhyme

Rhyme is strong evidence for the end of a line, which might be formulated in a conditional such as (21):

> (21) If this word rhymes with another word, then this word is at the end of a line.

As always, there are complications, with rhyme sometimes used line-internally. In Welsh and Irish verse, complex rhymings of end-of-line with middle-of-line are a built-in complexity. In English verse, mid-line rhymes can raise the question 'one line or two', which I look at in chapter 5, section 3. Where end-of-line rhyme is used systematically it is strong evidence; where end-of-line rhyme is used in irregular patterns, the evidence is less easy to use. English odes quite often complicate the evidence for their lineation, already complex because of line-length changes, by having irregularly distributed rhymes.

As an example of how rhyme is used as evidence for lineation, consider Spenser's *Epithalamion* (1595). The first stanza has a pattern:

$$5\ 5\ 5\ 5\ 5\ 3\ 5\ 5\ 5\ 3\ 5\ 5\ 5\ 5\ 4\ 5\ 6 \quad \text{number of feet}$$
$$\text{A B A B C } \underline{\text{C}} \text{ D C D E E } \underline{\text{E}} \text{ F G G F } \underline{\text{F}} \text{ H } \underline{\text{H}} \quad \text{rhyme}$$

I have underlined lines in which the length changes away from the iambic pentameter norm. Note that these lines are always the second line in rhyming couplets. In the later *Prothalamion* (1596) the pattern for stanza 1 is:

$$5\ 5\ 5\ 5\ 3\ 5\ 5\ 5\ 5\ 3\ 5\ 5\ 5\ 5\ 3\ 3\ 5\ 5 \quad \text{number of feet}$$
$$\text{A B B A } \underline{\text{A}} \text{ B C B B } \underline{\text{C}} \text{ D D E D } \underline{\text{E}} \text{ E F F} \quad \text{rhyme}$$

We could see this as a complication of the strategy used in the earlier poem, which slightly weakens the cueing of the short line; here the variant line still rhymes with an earlier pentameter line but not always with the preceding line.

Metre and rhythm

In metrical verse, the metrical grid extends from the beginning to the end of the line (except for any unprojected syllables at either end). In an isometric text, where every line is of the same length, the metre can thus provide strong evidence for the line. This would involve a conditional such as the following:

> (22) If a section of text can be divided into equal-length units then each of the units is a line.

Strong evidence can also come from the fact that metrical disruptions are particularly associated with line edges. Thus trochaic inversion is a line-initial phenomenon, and in iambic verse, extrametricality is a line-final phenomenon. Trochaic inversion is most reliably a marker of the line beginning if it involves a polysyllable. We might formulate a conditional like this:

> (23) If a polysyllabic word has its main stressed syllable immediately follow-
> ing another stressed syllable, then it is at the beginning of a line.

Earlier, I showed the usefulness of this conditional in determining lineation in *Paradise Lost*.

Another type of line-edge irregularity is extrametricality, an unstressed sylla-ble at the end of the line which is not projected into the metrical grid. In iambic verse the evidence for extrametricality and hence the end of a line overlaps with the evidence for trochaic inversion and hence the beginning of a line. Thus trochaic inversion characteristically has a line-initial sequence of /xx/ and ex-trametricality characteristically has a sequence of /x + x/ split across two lines. The fact that there is competing evidence is not necessarily a problem; we could just allow for competition in the drawing of conclusions about lineation, and indeed this kind of competition might be another example of a built-in complexity. Thus we might use a weak conditional (25).

> (25) If this syllable is preceded by a stressed syllable and followed by an
> unstressed-stressed syllable sequence then it is at the end of a line. [weak]

While extrametricality can be used as a way of marking line boundaries, it is also possible to use extrametricality to conceal line boundaries, in 'enjambed rhythms'. Enjambed rhythms are rhythms which appear to be continuous (thus removing evidence for lineation), and can arise one of two ways. One involves lines without headlessness or extrametricality, in which the line ends at the end of a full foot and the next line begins with the beginning of a full foot; this is a situation which is fairly common in Milton and indeed is one reason for claims that Milton is 'harmonious prose'. The second involves a matching of headlessness to extrametricality, so that an extra syllable at the end of one line fills a gap at the beginning of the next. This can be seen as an emergent property of the following stanza:

> When thou dost return
> On the wave's circulation,
> Beholding the shimmer,
> The wild dissipation,
> And, out of endeavour
> To change and to flow,
> The gas becomes solid,
>
> Ralph Waldo Emerson, 'Motto to "Illusions" ', 1860 (S:50)

The first line has a pattern of x/xx/; the second line begins with two unstressed syllables xx/xx/x so that if the two are added together we get x/xx/xx/xx/x. Then the next few lines begin and end on a single unstressed syllable, which join up: x/xx/x + x/xx/x = x/xx/xx/xx/x. Only at the word 'flow' (perhaps an irony) does the sequence become disrupted because the line does not end on an extrametrical syllable. Note that the punctuation at the ends of the lines contradicts the flow. Shakespeare does something similar in 'Who is Silvia..' All the lines are in seven syllable lines but they alternate headless tetrameter /x/x/x/ with trimeter with extrametricality x/x/x/x to give a rhythm which can continue through the whole stanza.

> Who is Silvia? what is she,
>> That all our swains commend her?
> Holy, fair, and wise is she;
>> The heaven such grace did lend her,
> That she might admired be.

William Shakespeare, from The Two Gentlemen of Verona, 1623 (J:569)

Sometimes run-on rhythms can be a source of more disruptive ambiguities. Consider the ending of Shakespeare's 'Ariel's song'.

> Full fathom five thy father lies;
>> Of his bones are coral made;
> Those are pearls that were his eyes:
>> Nothing of him that doth fade,   4
> But doth suffer a sea-change
> Into something rich and strange.
> Sea-nymphs hourly ring his knell:
>> Ding-dong   8
> Hark! now I hear them.
>> Ding-dong, bell.

William Shakespeare, from The Tempest, pub.1623 (F:64)

The poem begins with an iambic tetrameter line; lines 2–7 are headless iambic tetrameter (i.e. sevens). In the last three lines things get complicated. If we carry the rhythm of 'Ding-dong' (line 8) forward into the next line then 'Hark' will be stressed, and the combination line will be in sevens like the preceding lines:

> /   x   /   x   / x   /
> Ding-dong Hark! now I hear them.

Or we could instead choose to stress not 'hark' but 'now', giving a line which would continue rhythmically into the final line, giving a line which now matches the first line of the poem.

> x   / x /   x   /   x   /
> Hark! now I hear them. Ding-dong, bell.

Here both ways of reading the line are justified in terms of a match with other lines in the poem; the ambiguity arises because the words in the final three lines are all monosyllables. The generated metre need not change; all that shifts is the communicated metre.

Metre in texts with varying length lines

Where the length of the line is regulated, metre can constitute evidence for the line; this is because we know in advance how long each line should be and thus where its end is relative to its beginning. A way of complicating this is to write texts in which lines vary in length, which Milton's Satan calls 'various-measured verse' (*Paradise Regained* 4:256) and of which Cowley says 'The *Numbers* are various and irregular' (Spingarn 1957:II,86). English texts which are metrical but with irregularly varying lines are usually based largely on the classical ode, and particularly on those of the Greek poet Pindar (Jump 1974, Heath-Stubbs 1969). Texts of this type almost always rhyme, though usually with irregular rhyme schemes (which further weakens the evidence for lineation). Here is an example from Emerson:

```
Great is the art,                        27
Great be the manners, of the bard.
He shall not his brain encumber
With the coil of rhythm and number;      30
But, leaving rule and pale forethought,
He shall aye climb
For his rhyme.
"Pass in, pass in," the angels say,
"In to the upper doors,                  35
Nor count compartments of the floors,
But mount to paradise
By the stairway of surprise."            38
```

Ralph Waldo Emerson, 'Merlin I', 1847 (S:47)

Each line is metrical, but the metre varies between dimeter, trimeter and tetrameter, and some of the lines have short initial feet. From a generative perspective the lines can all be scanned as in iambic metre; stress maxima are all in place; however, lines 29 and 30 imply that they are trochaic. Thus the shifts in metre from line to line are unpredictable. The rhyme pattern also varies, with some couplets, some longer-distance rhymes and some lines (31 and 34) not rhyming at all. Because the metre of each line cannot be predicted in advance, it constitutes only weak evidence for lineation. The weakened evidence for lineation is in some ways similar to the practice of writing verse as prose, by removing one of the key kinds of evidence, and this is reflected in Sprat's comment on the genre of the ode that 'that for which I think this inequality of number is chiefly to be preferr'd is its near affinity with Prose' (Sprat 1668:132).

Accounts of mixed-length metrical lines have often argued that there is a special experiential effect associated with them. Thus here Emerson claims surprise. Sprat says of Cowley's 'irregular numbers' that 'the frequent alteration of the Rhythm and Feet affects the mind with a more various delight, while it is soon apt to be tyr'd by the settled pace of any one constant measure' (1668: 132). The ode can also 'perplex':

> The Character of these late Pindariques, is, a Bundle of rambling incoherent Thoughts, express'd in a like Parcel of irregular Stanza's, which also consist of such another Complication of disproportion'd, uncertain and perplex'd Verses and Rhimes. (William Congreve, *A Discourse on the Pindaric Ode*, 1706 (Hodges 1964:214))

These accounts all suggest that there is an emotional reaction to a complex kind of lineation. This supports my general proposal in this chapter that we experience complexity in lineation as aesthetic.

Line-initial and line-final words

One of the less frequently noted kinds of evidence for lineation is the use of specific words. This is often emergent evidence; specific texts use specific words at line boundaries, as I show shortly. But there are also certain characteristic ways of using specific kinds of word at line boundaries. These include the use of a one-word command or exclamation, as in the following lines:

> I can interpret where the mouth is dumb.
> Speak, and I see the side-lie of a truth.
>> George Meredith, *Modern Love* XXVII, 1862 (K:443)

> Dead! one of them shot by the sea in the east,
>> Elizabeth Barrett Browning, 'Mother and Poet', 1862 (Browning 1889:V, 49))

This practice seems to be particularly common in iambic pentameter, perhaps because it characteristically has an effect similar to trochaic inversion. Collins's 'Ode on the Poetical Character' has its first stanza in iambic tetrameter and its second stanza in iambic pentameter. The shift to iambic pentameter is accompanied by a line-initial monosyllabic exclamation:

> Lo! to each other nymph in turn applied
>> William Collins, 'Ode on the Poetical Character', 1746 (L:379)

Thus the one word exclamation is evidence not just for a new line but for a new metre. We might formulate a conditional:

> (26) If a word is preceded and followed by a punctuation mark then this word
>   is at the beginning of a line.

Another characteristic technique for using words to mark line edges is anadiplosis, the practice of repeating a line-final word at the beginning of the next line.

> How wonderful is Death,
> Death and his brother Sleep!
>
> Shelley, The Daemon of the World, 1815 (W:234)

> Blest pair! whose union future bards shall tell
> In future tongues: each other's boast! farewell.
> Farewell! whom joined in fame, in friendship tried,
> No chance could sever, nor the grave divide.
>
> Thomas Tickell, 'To the Earl of Warwick.
On the Death of Mr Addison', 1721 (L:157)

Note that Tickell uses both the one-word-exclamation and anadiplosis to mark the beginning of what is the final couplet in the poem. Like all evidence for the line, anadiplosis on its own is weak evidence.

Inferencing does not operate according to pre-set rules or stipulated conditionals. In principle, new conditionals can be developed as the text is being read; in this sense form is emergent. As an example of this, consider *Paradise Lost*, a text which to some extent demands new assumptions about form. Evidence for lineation is apparently sparse; unlike some of the other texts of the period, there is not good evidence from pausing or punctuation or from rhyme (but there is evidence from metre, as I discuss shortly). However, there are certain tendencies for specific words to be line-initial or line-final in the poem. Consider the beginning of the poem:

> Of Man's first disobedience, and the fruit
> Of that forbidden tree whose mortal taste
> Brought death into the World, and all our woe,
> With loss of Eden, till one greater Man
>
> John Milton, Paradise Lost, 1:1–4, 1667 (Darbishire 1952:I:5)

The beginning of a text is a good place to establish some thoughts about form; it is a part of the text, where the reader can assume that extra thought will be rewarded. Here we have a poem which begins with the word 'of', and then the next line also begins with 'of'. Based just on the first two lines we might formulate a conditional:

(27) If a word is 'of' then it is at the beginning of the line.

We would have to formulate this as a weak conditional because it is not satisfied by the lines which follow, but I suggest that it is worth holding active as a weak conditional. It turns out that 28 percent of this poem's lines which contain 'of' have 'of' at the beginning. Thus while the conditional is weak, it might be taken as evidence for lineation; in a third to a quarter of cases, if the word is 'of' then indeed it is at the beginning of the line. The conditional does have some validity beyond Milton's text, in texts perhaps influenced by Milton. Thus consider Barbauld's 'To Mr C–ge', which is a poem of forty-three lines, in blank verse. Barbauld uses the word 'of' fourteen times, and of these seven are line-initial. Thus for example lines 13–18:

> Scruples here,
> With filmy net, most like the autumnal webs
> Of floating gossamer, arrest the foot
> Of generous enterprise; and palsy hope
> And fair ambition with the chilling touch
> Of sickly hesitation and blank fear.
>
> Anna Laetitia Barbauld, 'To Mr C–ge', 1799 (L:817)

Similarly, in Wordsworth's 'Tintern Abbey' there are sixty uses of 'of', of which twenty-three are line-initial, thus showing a similar tendency to place 'of' at the beginning of a line, which we can also interpret as the use of 'of' as weak evidence for a line-beginning. An even more dramatic example is found in Akenside's 'Pleasures of the Imagination':

> Oh! blest of heav'n, whom not the languid songs
> Of Luxury, the siren! not the bribes
> Of sordid wealth, nor all the gaudy spoils
> Of pageant honour can seduce to leave
> Those ever-blooming sweets, which from the store
> Of nature fair imagination culls
> To charm th'enliven'd soul! What though not all
> Of mortal offspring can attain the heights
> Of envied life;
>
> Mark Akenside, 'Pleasures of the Imagination', 1744 (L:394)

All these texts suggest that there is a conditional relating 'of' to line-beginnings. But this conditional is fairly weak and derived inductively (as far as I know it is not codified anywhere). In English verse, Milton appears to be encouraging us to formulate it by the way he begins the poem, and it is possible that other writers assume our knowledge of *Paradise Lost* and hence that we are able to use the conditional. It is worth noting that having 'of' at the beginning of a line is not 'natural' for the language in any sense; this can be seen by considering texts which have very different proportions. Thus James Thomson's blank verse *Winter* has 'of' as a line-initial word in only 10 percent of its uses.

It is possible that in addition to encouraging us to formulate a conditional relating 'of' to lineation, Milton encourages us to formulate some other very weak conditionals relating specific words to line endings. Of the other boundary words in the first few lines, 'taste' appears (as a noun) as the final word in twelve lines out of twenty-three (i.e. 52 percent), while 'woe' is final in twenty-five lines out of thirty-seven (67 percent), so there is some reason to think that we are also being cued at the beginning to take these words too as weak evidence for a line-end. Other final words, 'fruit' and 'man', are line-final in about a quarter of their uses, and the same is true for 'with' at the beginning of the line. It is worth considering 'fruit' in rather more detail. The word appears (as a noun, singular or plural) in eighty-three lines, distributed relative to line-internal position as follows:

position	1	2	3	4	5	6	7	8	9	10
instances of 'fruit'	4	6	1	14	1	14	0	19	1	20

In eighth position, five of the instances are in the phrase 'fruit(s) and flower(s)', a phrase which only ever appears at the end of the line, and thus might again be taken as evidence of a line-ending. Five further instances in eighth position have 'fruit' followed by a bisyllabic modifier, again a sequence which only ever appears at the end of a line, such as 'fruit divine'. Thus the word 'fruit' on its own or in combination, is placed with some degree of systematicity in the line, to the extent that we can take its use as weak evidence of a line boundary.

Conditionals which relate specific words to line boundaries will usually be specific to a poem and will emerge in the course of reading the text. While 'of' as a line boundary word may have some currency beyond Milton, it is unlikely that his other boundary words do. But in other poems conditionals emerge which relate other words to line edges. Consider, for example, the way in which Matthew Arnold begins 'Sohrab and Rustum', an 892-line poem in blank verse. These are the first four lines:

> And the first grey of morning fill'd the east,
> And the fog rose out of the Oxus stream.
> But all the Tartar camp along the stream
> Was hush'd, and still the men were plunged in sleep;
>
> Matthew Arnold, *Sohrab and Rustum*, 1853 (Allott 1986:186)

Like Milton, Arnold uses certain words characteristically at line-ends. The word 'stream' is at the end of both line 2 and 3; this pattern continues, less densely, through the poem, with seven of its ten uses line-final. Similarly 'tent' ends lines 7, 9, 11, 22 and 25, and again with less density in nine of its twenty-three instances in the poem overall, 'tent' is line-final. 'Sleep' at the end of line 4 is found also at the end of line 29, 'strand' ends lines 13 and 16 (these are the only uses of these nouns in the poem, so no pattern is set). Note also that to a lesser extent lines begin in similar ways, something again signalled at the beginning, with the first two lines beginning with 'And' (also beginning lines 9, 10, 17, 26, 28, 30, etc.); 'but' begins lines 3 and 7. Again, these set a pattern: 426 lines have 'and' of which 180 are line-initial, while 88 lines have 'but' of which 49 are line-initial. Thus, as in Milton's poem, specific words are associated, by emergent conditionals, with the edge of the line. Just as in Milton's poem, too, these words are used with particular density at the beginning.

Any textual practice performs many functions at the same time, and it is possible to find other reasons for specific words being line initial or line final. For example, words might be line-initial or line-final because of their importance, exploiting the greater salience of line-edges. Perhaps the frequency with which 'woe' is used in *Paradise Lost* relates to its significance as a key term in the text; the same might even be claimed for 'taste'. Note that this does not lessen the force of the word as evidence for the line boundary (if anything, because the words are semantically salient, they provide even stronger evidence for the line boundary).

Putting the evidence together

The following text is Matthew Arnold's 'Philomela', originally laid out in verse, here laid out as prose.

Hark! ah, the nightingale – the tawn-throated! hark, from that moonlit cedar what a burst! what triumph! hark! – what pain! o wanderer from a Grecian shore, still, after many years, in distant lands, still nourishing in thy bewilder'd brain that wild, unquench'd, deep-sunken, old-world pain – say, will it never heal? And can this fragrant lawn with its cool trees, and night, and the sweet, tranquil Thames, and moonshine, and the dew, to thy rack'd heart and brain afford no balm? Dost thou to-night behold, here, through the moonlight on this English grass, the unfriendly palace in the Thracian wild? Dost thou again peruse with hot cheeks and sear'd eyes the too clear web, and thy dumb sister's shame? Dost thou once more assay thy flight, and feel come over thee, poor fugitive, the feathery change once more, and once more seem to make resound with love and hate, triumph and agony, lone Daulis, and the high Cephissian Vale? listen, Eugenia – how thick the bursts come crowding through the leaves! again – thou hearest? eternal passion! eternal pain!

Matthew Arnold, 'Philomela', 1853 (Allott 1986:215), rewritten as prose

I will now show how the various conditionals introduced in this chapter imply a lineation for this text. (I'll leave this to the next page in case you feel like trying to work this out for yourself!)

This is the actual lineation as printed by Arnold. The numbers in the right hand column refer to the conditionals which follow.

Hark! ah, the nightingale –	1, 3, 7
the tawn-throated!	3, 4, 7
hark, from that moonlit cedar what a burst!	1, 3, 7
what triumph! (3, 1) hark! – what pain!	2, 3, 6, 7
O wanderer from a Grecian shore,	7
still, after many years, in distant lands,	1, 5, 7
still nourishing in thy bewilder'd brain	5, 6, 7
that wild, unquench'd, deep-sunken, old-world pain	2, 3, 6, 7
Say, will it never heal?	1, 3, 7
And can this fragrant lawn	5, 7
with its cool trees, and night,	5, 7
and the sweet, tranquil Thames,	5, 7
and moonshine, and the dew,	5, 7
to thy rack'd heart and brain	5, 6, 7
afford no balm?	3, 7
Dost thou to-night behold,	7
here, through the moonlight on this English grass,	1, 5, 7
the unfriendly palace in the Thracian wild?	3, 5, 7
Dost thou to-night behold,	5, 7
with hot cheeks and sear'd eyes	5, 7
the too clear web, and thy dumb sister's shame?	3, 7
Dost thou once more assay	7
thy flight, and feel come over thee,	7
poor fugitive, the feathery change	7
once more, and once more seem to make resound	7
with love and hate, triumph and agony,	7
lone Daulis, and the high Cephissian Vale?	3, 7
listen, Eugenia –	1, 3, 7, 8
how thick the bursts come crowding through the leaves!	3, 7
again – thou hearest?	1, 3, 4, 7
eternal passion!	3, 4, 7
eternal pain!	2, 3, 6, 7

Conditionals

1 = initial isolated word (conditional 26)
2 = the word 'pain' only ever appears at the end of a line (an emergent
     conditional is needed)
3 = line-end is at dash or exclamation mark or question mark (similar
     to conditional 16)
4 = extrametricality (conditional 25)
5 = a section (for which there is independent evidence) can be split
     into two metrically identical lines (conditional 22), either iambic
     pentameter or iambic tetrameter.
6 = rhyme (conditional 21)
7 = layout (conditional 18)
8 = trochaic inversion (conditional 23)

There is one major disruption in line 4, where there are two kinds of evidence that 'hark' should be in the middle of a line. Otherwise, the evidence for lineation is at its weakest in the pre-final section (from 'Dost' to 'Vale'), where layout alone tells us where the line boundaries are; the weakness of lineation here might be taken as mimicking 'flight', and thus another connection between implicatures of form and implicatures of meaning.

To conclude I propose to choose another, shorter, text and look at how lineation is evidenced. This is the beginning of Wordsworth's 'Ode: On immortality', with printed evidence for lineation removed. Does the text retain sufficient evidence for lineation, and for the location of line boundaries?

There was a time when meadow, grove, and stream, the earth, and every common sight, to me did seem apparelled in celestial light, the glory and the freshness of a dream. It is not now as it hath been of yore; – turn wheresoe'er I may, by night or day, the things which I have seen I now can see no more.

I suggest trying to reconstruct the lineation yourself, before reading any further.

Evidence for a line boundary after 'stream' comes from two sources: first, this would be a stereotypical line type in English – an iambic pentameter line. Second, 'stream' rhymes with a word twelve syllables away, 'seem', which suggests line boundaries at these points, even though the second line is long and does not end on a pause.

> There was a time when meadow, grove, and stream,
> the earth, and every common sight, to me did seem

These would be a reasonable pairing of an iambic pentameter and iambic hexameter line, but now we have evidence that there is a boundary at 'sight' because eight syllables later we have 'light':

> There was a time when meadow, grove, and stream,
> the earth, and every common sight,
> to me did seem
> apparelled in celestial light,

There is some cost, or some conflict here, in that we have a very short line and furthermore a line which does not end on a pause, but with the benefit of maintaining an ABAB rhyme pattern. The next line-ending can also be found by rhyme and in fact gives us another iambic pentameter line, ending on a full stop, hence strong evidence for lineation.

> the glory and the freshness of a dream.

The next line boundary is not at first licensed by rhyme (though there will be one, several lines later) but perhaps by the fact that it can also be an iambic pentameter line and ends on a major pause:

> It is not now as it hath been of yore; –

The next line finds its boundary by rhyming with a word four syllables later, 'day':

> turn wheresoe'er I may
> by night or day,

But another possibility emerges, which is that 'night' rhymes with 'sight' and 'light' and thus is itself a line ending:

> turn wheresoe'er I may,
> by night
> or day,

In order to keep the rhyme, we must allow two very short lines. In the final part of the text, we might divide the lines as:

> the things which I have seen
> I now can see no more.

This takes 'seen' to rhyme with 'stream', 'seem' and 'dream'; there is not phonological identity, but whether a rhyme holds or not is a matter of inference. So if there is sufficient evidence to maintain this line division, we might divide the line like this into a couplet of iambic trimeters; note that both 'seen' and 'more' are at the end of a clause. Alternatively, we might take it as a single long line (with the division into two halves characteristic of the hexameter), but note that this is now the only hexameter line in the text; unusual, but at the same time at the end of a stanza, so this in turn might be taken as evidence for lineation.

> the things which I have seen I now can see no more.

The original printed layout of this section of the poem is:

> There was a time when meadow, grove, and stream,
> the earth, and every common sight,
> to me did seem apparelled in celestial light,
> the glory and the freshness of a dream.
> It is not now as it hath been of yore; –
> turn wheresoe'er I may,
> by night or day,
> the things which I have seen I now can see no more.

Summary

In this section I have argued that though the division into lines might appear at first to be a determinate fact of the text, in fact it is an implicature (or set of implicatures), a conclusion about the text based on a combination of different kinds of usually weak evidence. The search for lineation always generates a range of weak implicatures, a situation which Sperber and Wilson suggest might be experienced as aesthetic. Some texts make lineation more difficult to determine than others; these texts appear to be exploiting a particular way of giving rise to the aesthetic experience of form.

5.3   One line or two?

In this section I discuss a characteristic line boundary problem, found in many metrical traditions. This is where there are two sizes of constituent which compete for categorisation as the line, with the result that we have either a pair of short lines or a single long line.

Consider, for example, the following first stanza of a three-stanza poem by Suckling.

> Dost see how unregarded now
>   That piece of beauty passes?
> There was a time when I did vow
>   To that alone;
>   But mark the fate of faces:
> That red and white works now no more on me
> Than if it could not charm, or I not see.

Sir John Suckling, Sonnet I, 1646 (F:468)

The pattern of seven lines as laid out on the page can be represented like this:

```
4 3 4 2 3 5 5    number of iambic feet in the line
A B A – B C C    rhyme scheme
```

Given the conditional (28), we can eventually reach the conclusion that the above lineation is the lineation of the text.

(28) If a word has no words to its right then it is at the end of the line.

This is a strong conditional, so it leads to a strong conclusion that the lineation is as above. But the following conditional is also quite strong:

(29) If a word is at the end of a line then it rhymes.

This conditional leads to the conclusion that the word 'alone', which does not rhyme, is therefore not at the end of a line. Then there is another conditional, which captures the tendency towards isometricality (a sequence of lines all being in the same metre).

(30) If a sequence of syllables is of the same length as an adjacent line then
it is a line.

Given this conditional, since the sequence of syllables 'To that alone; But mark
the fate of faces' is of the same length as the next line, the conclusion is that it
too is a line. This now gives us a result which is compatible also with conditional
(29), and thus a reinterpretation of where the line boundaries fall:

> Dost see how unregarded now
>   That piece of beauty passes?
> There was a time when I did vow
>   To that alone; But mark the fate of faces:
> That red and white works now no more on me
> Than if it could not charm, or I not see.
>
> relineated version

The pattern of seven lines as laid out on the page can be represented like this:

4 3 4 5 5 5   number of iambic feet in the line
A B A B C C   rhyme scheme

Thus there is competition between the conclusion that there are two short lines
and the conclusion that there is one long line.

Suckling's *Sonnet II* carries out a complementary strategy. This is the first
stanza of three.

> Of thee, kind boy, I ask no red and white
>   To make up my delight,
>   No odd becoming graces,
> Black eyes, or little know-not-whats, in faces:
> Make me but mad enough, give me good store
> Of love for her I court,
>   I ask no more,
> 'Tis love in love that makes the sport.
>
> Sir John Suckling, *Sonnet II*, 1646 (F:469)

This poem's lineation can be represented either as:

Lineation A
5 3 3 5 5 5 4   number of iambic feet in the line
A A B B C C –   rhyme scheme

or as:

Lineation B
5 3 3 5 5 3 2 4   number of iambic feet in the line
A A B B C D C D   rhyme scheme

Layout here is somewhat ambiguous. By the criterion of 'no words to the right' we get lineation B, but the vertical arrangement of lines 6 and 7 suggests that they are to be read together as a single line (lineation A). Lineation B gives us a better result for the rhyme scheme in one sense, in that all the lines are then rhymed, but lineation A also offers an advantage in that it gives us a more regular rhyme scheme (except for the final line). The criterion of metrical uniformity favours lineation A. Thus there is evidence for both lineations, one with two short lines and one with a single long line.

I use the term 'size ambiguity' for this ambiguity of lineation between two short lines or one long line. As I claim throughout this book, formal ambiguity is an end in itself because it is experienced as aesthetic. But it can have other functions. Jump (1974:18) describes a size ambiguity at the end of Dryden's 'Threnodia Augustalis'; the poem ends with a sequence of 4 feet + 5 feet + 6 feet + 4 feet + 3 feet.

> While starting from his Oozy Bed,
> Th'asserted Ocean rears his reverend Head;
> To View and Recognize his ancient Lord again:
> And with a willing hand, restores
> The *Fasces* of the Main.
>
> John Dryden, 'Threnodia Augustalis. A Funeral-Pindarique Poem', 1685
> (Kinsley 1958:I, 442)

Jump suggests that the final 4 + 3 pair can be reanalysed as a single seven-foot line, 'So we have a hint of an ample, resounding conclusion simultaneously with an actual presentation that is compact and epigrammatic.'

Size ambiguities are built into some types of poetry. In *Beowulf* the 'verse' and the 'long line' each have some claim to be treated as the line; the two six-syllable lines of the Icelandic *dróttkvaett* metre might be treated as two lines or as together forming a single long line. The lines (*pada*) of classical Sanskrit verse might equally be treated each as compounds of several separate lines separated by caesurae, each with their own metrical grids, and when borrowed into Thai the sub-sections are clearly treated as separate lines, each ending in rhymes (Hudak 1990). The Japanese haiku sequence of 5+7+5 morae might be treated as a single line rather than as three. The Greek sapphic stanza ends on a long line which is split into two lines in its reanalysis by Horace (but sometimes allowing words to break across the split, thus keeping the ambiguity between one line or two). The reason that size ambiguities seem to arise relates to the centrality of the line as a basic unit in verse. Where there is some question about which unit is basic, as in these cases, we can reinterpret this as a problem of which unit is to be taken as the line.

Layout as one line or two

For us, layout is likely to be strong evidence for lineation, but it would probably have been taken as weaker evidence by sixteenth-century readers. Thus Webbe (1585:269) discusses the different ways of laying out lines either as a single long line or as two short lines, with various kinds of rhyme, implying that it is not a matter of great importance how the lines are laid out. And Puttenham (1589:76), speaking of the hexameter, requires 'that ye suffer him to runne at full length, and do not as the common rimers do, or their Printer for sparing of paper, cut them of in the middest, wherein they make two verses but halfe rime'. Barnabe Googe's *Eclogs, Epytaphes, and Sonettes* (1563) throws up some interesting problems in this regard. There is a tendency in this book to print the poems in very short lines, but other features suggest a different lineation in longer lines. Here are a few representative lines as originally printed:

> Good aged *Bale*:
> that with thy hoary heares
> Doste yet persyste,
> to turne the paynefulle Booke,

Barnabe Googe, 'To Doctor Bale', 1563 (Fieler 1968:91)

The twenty lines of the poem are laid out like this, with rhyme at the end of every second line.

```
2 3 2 3 2 3 2 3 2 3 2 3 2 3 2 3 2 3 2 3   no. of feet
– A – B – A – B – C – D – C – D – E – E   rhyme scheme
```

Rhyme here would support reanalysis as long lines in iambic pentameter:

```
5 5 5 5 5 5 5 5 5 5   no. of feet
A B A B C D C D E E   rhyme scheme
```

Odd lines begin with capital letters and even lines begin with small letters, and this also suggests a grouping into long lines. However, there is no indentation of even lines, and so in this way layout does not support the long-line analysis. Furthermore, the placement of line-initial words supports a short-line analysis. The word 'and' is found only at the beginning of three odd lines; the words 'that' and 'to' are found only at the beginning of (three and four of) the even lines. This pattern reinforces the lineation as printed. Marotti (1995:28) thinks that the splitting of lines in this book is a printer's decision forced by 'the exigencies of page and type size'. Kennedy (1989:28) acknowledges that the issue of the split lines (particularly pentameter and tetrameter) is not easily explained, but suggests that Googe was indifferent to long- or short-line printing by showing that there are variant printings of the same text in different forms. However, Thompson (1961:67) thinks that the splitting of pentameter lines in Googe is deliberate. I suggest that we see it as a practice which functions partly to make lineation complex, and hence as deliberate.

Rhyme in the middle of the long line

Rhyme is one of the more reliable sources of evidence for the end of the line. Thus the placement of rhymes at the mid-point of long lines can be a source of size ambiguity. (which is perhaps why Puttenham (1589:81) disapproves of it). We can see it in Poe's 'The Raven'.

> Once upon a midnight dreary, while I pondered, weak and weary,
> Over many a quaint and curious volume of forgotten lore,
> While I nodded, nearly napping, suddenly there came a tapping,
> As of some one gently rapping, rapping at my chamber door.
> " 'T is some visitor," I muttered, "tapping at my chamber door,
>   Only this and nothing more."
>
> Edgar Allen Poe, 'The Raven', 1845 (S:107)

The printed lineation is:

```
8  8  8  8  8  4    number of feet in line
–  A  –  A  A  A    rhyme scheme
```

But if we take the mid-line rhymes actually to be cueing the end of the line, then we can relineate to get both a more homogeneous metre (and furthermore a more familiar metre, which also strengthens the conclusion that the poem is in this metre) and a more elaborate (but still not perfect) rhyme scheme.

```
4  4  4  4  4  4  4  4  4  4  4    number of feet in line
A  A  –  B  C  C  B  –  B  B       rhyme scheme
```

Metrical considerations

A sequence of syllables written as a single line must sometimes be treated as two separate metrical lines. Thus consider the following lines, which were printed as anapaestic tetrameter.

> Let me have a warm house, with a stone at the gate,
> And a cleanly young girl to rub my bald pate.
> May I govern my passion with an absolute sway,
> And grow wiser and better as my strength wears away,
>
> Walter Pope, 'The Old Man's Wish', 1685 (F:709)

The problem with these lines is that the sequence of anapaestic feet is disrupted in the middle. Sometimes there is a syllable missing and sometimes an extra syllable. This can be resolved by reconstructing the lines as two short lines each with its own metrical grid, and thus as anapaestic dimeter. The missing syllable can now be seen as a line-initial short foot, and the extra syllable as a line-final extrametrical syllable (not projected).

> And a cleanly young girl
>)∗   ∗ ∗) ∗ ∗   ∗)
>   ∗   ∗
> to rub my bald pate.
>   ∗ ∗) ∗ ∗   ∗)
>   ∗   ∗
> May I govern my passion
>)∗   ∗ ∗)∗   ∗ ∗) Δ
>   ∗   ∗
> with an absolute sway,
>)∗   ∗ ∗) ∗ ∗   ∗)
>   ∗   ∗

While the generative metrical rules sometimes require the line to be divided into two, sometimes the communicated metre suggests a division of the line into two, even though the generated metre does not require it. Thus consider these lines:

> Still to be neat, still to be dressed,   (line 1)
> Give me a look, give me a face,   (line 7)
> Ben Jonson, 'Still To Be Neat . . .', 1616 (J:153)

These lines are in a text which can be generated by the rules for iambic tetrameter throughout. But these lines can be given a rhythm in performance which suggests (along with the mid-line pause) a splitting of the line into two metrical units: /xx/ + /xx/. Here there is evidence from the implied metre for line-splitting.

Extrametricality is characteristic of the end of the line, but sometimes it is apparently found line-internally after a pause, as in the following line:

> Though no man hear't, though no man it rehearse,
>)∗   ∗) ∗   ∗) Δ ∗   ∗) ∗ ∗) ∗ ∗)
>   ∗   ∗   ∗   ∗   ∗
> Abraham Cowley, *Davideis*, 1656 (F:558)

In some poems, extrametricality at the mid-line is found repeatedly throughout the text, thus creating a persistent size ambiguity. Joseph Addison's 'Song' is an eight-stanza poem with most of its lines clearly in iambic tetrameter, with occasional short initial feet and occasional extrametrical final syllables. But the third line in some stanzas seems to have an extra syllable in the middle:

> When all is over, she gives her lover,
>
> Joseph Addison, 'Song', 1713 (L:46)

The combination of mid-line extrametricality with mid-line rhyme here suggests that what is printed as a single line might equally be reanalysed as two. Different conditionals lead to different conclusions; conditionals involving metrical uniformity and layout tell us that this is a single line, while conditionals involving rhyme and extrametricality tell us that this is two lines.

The search for metrical uniformity can encourage us to reanalyse two short lines as a long line. This can be seen, for example, in Joseph Beaumont's 'The Gnat' (mid seventeenth century, F:535), which is in ten-line stanzas laid out as:

```
5  5  2  2  1  5  5  2  2  1   number of feet in line
A  A  B  B  C  D  D  E  E  C   rhyme scheme
```

This could be reanalysed as:

```
5  5  5  5  5  5
A  A  C  D  D  C
```

Reanalysis thus gives a satisfactory rhyme scheme, and it is worth noting that the only trochaic inversion (a line-initial phenomenon) ends up at the beginning of a pentameter line. Thus there is good reason to reanalyse the lines; but layout and the rhyme between the two short lines are evidence for the alternative analysis.

Systematic word boundary placement in the middle of the long line

One of the sources of potential size ambiguity is rigid placement of a mid-line word boundary. Thus Michael Drayton's *Poly-Olbion* is printed in iambic hexameter couplets, but always with a word boundary after the third foot (I base my comments here on the extracts in Fowler 1991:52–7). Iambic hexameters in English often have a word boundary in this place, but the systematicity here makes it possible to reinterpret the line as iambic trimeter (a metre also quite widely used by Drayton).

> Where she, of all the plains of Britain that doth bear
> The name to be the first, renowned every where,
>
> as printed

> Where she, of all the plains
> of Britain that doth bear
> The name to be the first,
> renowned every where,
>
> new layout

However, while the systematic placement of the word boundary gives some sense of iambic trimeter here, there are reasons overall to prefer an iambic hexameter reading. Apart from layout, rhyme comes at the end of every twelfth syllable and not every sixth (as we would expect for trimeter). But also there are occasional extrametrical syllables, after the twelfth syllable and not after the sixth, again suggesting that the twelfth syllable is the end of the line. And interestingly in the extract under consideration where there are cases of non-projection, these occur at the end of the hypothesised short line but not at the end of the long line (fitting the pattern of full projection at the end of the line, p. 46), thus justifying the hexameter lineation.

> Comparing these his spirits with those that went before
>)*   *)*   *)   *   *Δ) *   *)   *   *)   **)
>
> In climbing up towards heaven, her high-pitched hymns to sing
>)*   *) * *) *   * Δ)   *   *)   *   *)   * *)

Thus various sources of evidence lead to the strong conclusion that the lines are hexameter, which competes with a weak conclusion that the lines are trimeter.

Emergent conditionals: alliteration as a line-splitting device

Alliteration is not used systematically in English, though in traditions where it is used extensively it often relates to the one-line-or-two problem. In Icelandic *dróttkvaett* the line is either (loosely) six or twelve syllables; alliteration spreads across the twelve syllables but internal rhyme holds separately within each six syllable sequence. In the Somali song metre *gabay* the line is either (loosely) six or twelve syllables; there is metrical evidence to take the twelve-syllable sequence as the line, but alliteration operates so that a particular sound is found in every six-syllable sequence (Banti and Giannattasio 1996). The use of alliteration to complicate lineation in English is seen in a poem by Queen Elizabeth I, of which these are four lines:

> The doubt of future foes exiles my present joy,
> And wit me warns to shun such snares as threaten mine annoy;
> For falsehood now doth flow, and subjects' faith doth ebb,
> Which should not be if reason ruled or wisdom weaved the web.
>
> Queen Elizabeth I, 'The Doubt of Future Foes . . . ', 1589 (J:183)

The poem is in poulter's measure (alternating six-foot and seven-foot lines), with rhyme at the end of each line. There is a word boundary after the third foot in the six-foot line and after the fourth foot in the seven-foot line, which might justify some reanalysis into short lines. Further strengthening this is the fact that there is fairly dense alliteration within the half-line; while there is some leakage between the halves (and between lines), the potential for alliteration to divide the line into two is very clear in the fourth quoted line. This seems to be an example of emergent form; the writer in this case seems to have developed a new technique for complicating the formal structure of the text.

Line-pairs as superlong lines

Finally, I consider the possibility of reanalysing a two-line unit as a superlong line.

According to Spiller (1992:12) the earliest sonnets were written out in manuscript with each pair of lines in the octave written as follows, with a stop added at the end of each ten/eleven-syllable line, and C indicating 'cominciamento' (beginning).

> C xxxxxxxxxx . xxxxxxxxxx .

And the two tercets which make up the sestet were written as follows:

> C xxxxxxxxxx . xxxxxxxxxx .
> C xxxxxxxxxx

This makes the sonnet 'an accumulation of points', and links it to the genres of proverb, maxim and catalogue. It also makes the line-pair a kind of superlong line, even at the level of layout on the page.

One of the general reasons for thinking that pairs of lines might form a single line-like unit is that odd and even lines can have different metrical characteristics. (This is cross-linguistically attested: it is true, for example, of some of the classical Sanskrit metres.) If the metre controls the line, then metrical differentiation between adjacent lines might suggest that the metre controls the line pair. Thus it is common for the even line in English trochaic verse to have a short rightmost foot, giving a sequence of 8+7 syllables in the line pair, which might suggest that the fifteen syllables form a single superline.

> Fare thee well! and if for ever –
> Still for ever, fare *thee well* –
> Even though unforgiving, never
> 'Gainst thee shall my heart rebel. –
>
> Lord Byron, 'Fare Thee Well', 1816 (McGann 1981:III, 380)

Herman Melville often chooses to have rhymes at the end of some lines but not others in a poem. A characteristic pattern is to have every second line involved in a rhyme:

> From his saw-pit of mouth, from his charnel of maw
> They have nothing of harm to dread,
> But liquidly glide on his ghastly flank
> Or before his Gorgonian head;
>
> Herman Melville, 'The Maldive Shark', 1888 (S:298)

This rhyme pattern might encourage us to take the pair of lines as a single superline thus turning these four lines into rhyming couplets.

5.4   Loose beginning and strict ending

In English metrical verse there are differences between the beginning and the ending of the verse line. The beginning is more likely to be 'loose' and the ending 'strict' in ways now to be explained. This is an asymmetry between the beginning and the ending of the line.

At the beginning of the English iambic line we have the potential for trochaic inversion. Thus in the following example, 'Europe' has stress on its initial syllable; within the line, this syllable projects to gridline 1 but at the beginning of the line it does not. On p. 18 I explained this by suggesting that a line-initial syllable is not a stress maximum and is thus not controlled by the metrical rules.

> Europe he saw, and Europe saw him too.
>)* *)   * *) *   *) *   *) *   *)   0
>   *   *   *   *   * 1
>
> Alexander Pope, *The Dunciad*, 1742 (L:257)

There is nothing equivalent to this at the end of the line. Thus, for example, a trochaic tetrameter line cannot end on an 'iambic inversion', which would be a polysyllabic word with final stress projecting to a non-head position. *Hiawatha* has lines such as the following, with the stressed syllable in a polysyllable in penultimate position (projecting to gridline 1):

> Sends them hither on his errand,
> (*   * (* *(*   *(* *   0
> *   * *   *   1
>
> Henry Wadsworth Longfellow, *Hiawatha*, 1855 (S:68)

But there are no lines like the following in *Hiawatha*, where the stressed syllable in a polysyllable is in final position. This would be the equivalent of 'trochaic inversion' in the mirror-image structure of the trochaic line.

> Sends them hither in his canoe
> (*   * (* *(*   *(* *   0
> *   * *   *   1
>
> invented line

Trochaic inversion at the beginning of the line fits a cross-linguistically attested pattern, where the beginning of the verse line is rhythmically loose and the end of the verse line is rhythmically strict. Another manifestation of this in English is that all syllables in a word are more likely to project nearer the end of the line, even if they fall into non-projecting classes. Thus 'friar' is a word which can project as one or two syllables; following a general pattern it projects as two syllables later in the line.

> The knight and the abbot, friar fat, friar thin.
> * *) *   **) * *Δ *) **   *) 0
>   *   *   *   * 1
>
> Thomas Lovell Beddoes, 'Songs by the Deaths', *c*.1825 (W:317)

The phenomenon of final strictness is sometimes manifested in 'strict cadences'. In metres which show this, the line as a whole is often fairly rhythmically loose, but the final pair of feet are usually tightly controlled (with the exception that the final syllable is usually completely free or indifferent, a point returned to below). Thus in the Greek dactylic hexameter, each of the first four feet can be either a dactyl (heavy–light–light) or a spondee (heavy–heavy), but the final pair of feet must be a dactyl followed by a spondee: a strict metrical ending to a line which is otherwise fairly loose. In Vedic Sanskrit (Arnold 1905), most syllables can be indifferently heavy or light but the most common ending for the line is a sequence of light–heavy–light (and then an indifferent syllable at the very end). There also seems to be a very loose tendency to find strict quantitative cadences in otherwise non-metrical texts. Thus Cicero's prose appears to be characterised by the preference for certain quantitative patterns at the end of a sentence, called 'clausulae' including endings such as heavy–(indifferent), heavy–light–heavy (the 'cretic foot'), and heavy–light–heavy–(indifferent) (Raven 1965:170). On p. 132 I looked at a rare example of a strict cadence in a dubiously metrical text by Swift, which might possibly be read as an imitation of Ciceronian style.

Other languages show 'final strictness' and 'initial looseness' by controlling the line-final word. In Irish syllabic metres (Knott 1957), different metres place different requirements on the length of the final word in the line: *Rionnaird* builds a six-syllable line which must end on a disyllable; *Ae freislighe* builds seven-syllable lines which end alternately on a trisyllable and then on a disyllable. In contrast there are no Irish metres where the word at the beginning of the line is controlled. Irish may offer the most elaborate control over the number of syllables in the final word, but other metres have simpler constraints, often forbidding the line to end on a monosyllable. This is the case in the Serbo-Croatian decasyllable metre (Jakobson 1966) and in the metre of the Finnish *Kalevala*, for example (Kiparsky 1968), while the metre of Dyirbal *Marrga* songs requires the line to end on a disyllable (Dixon and Koch 1996).

Another possible manifestation of the loose-beginning and strict-ending pattern is the difference between alliteration and rhyme. We find both line-initial alliteration, linking lines together, and line-final rhyme, linking lines together. Cross-linguistically, line-final rhyme is much more common and is often systematically patterned in a way apparently not found with alliteration. One of the few traditions which has fairly extensive line-initial alliteration is Mongolian verse, and here there are only sequences of like sounds of some-what unpredictable length, not as structured as rhyme. In Fabb (1999) I argue that alliteration and rhyme differ as kinds of sound patterning, with alliteration holding only between adjacent units of text (usually lines or half-lines) and not able to engage in the kinds of cross-rhyming ABAB or ABBA patterns which are common with rhyme. This might possibly relate just to differences between alliteration and rhyme and the relative salience of the beginning and end of the syllable, but it is also possible that the beginning of the line is a different kind of place from the end of the line. Thus line-initial alliteration is less accessible for complex operations than line-final rhyme.

The loose-beginning and strict-ending pattern is seen in metrical verse, but it may not be true of non-metrical verse. In some literary traditions there is systematic parallelism between verse lines (e.g. in Indonesia, see Fox 1988) and no metre. In these traditions there does not appear to be a requirement that one end of the line is strict (e.g. requiring closer parallelism) than the other. Thus, loose beginning and strict ending seem to be characteristics of specifically metrical verse structure rather than verse structure in general.

The looseness of the final syllable

While there is a general tendency for the end of the line to be metrically strict, there is also a general tendency for the very final syllable to show some metrical looseness. This is manifested in English iambic verse by the possibility of having an unprojected syllable at the end of the line. In many quantitative verse traditions, it is seen in the possibility of having a light syllable in what should be a heavy syllable's position. This is called 'brevis in longo' (short in long), and is a kind of metrical indifference. The final syllable in the Greek hexameter line is in a heavy position (because it follows a heavy syllable) but can be heavy or light. The same is true of classical Sanskrit metres; the final syllable in a sub-line section is almost always heavy but at the end of a line can be heavy or light (p. 54). This can be seen, for example, in the deployment of a sub-line section such as the seven-syllable sequence ⌣⌣⌣⌣⌣– (six light syllables and a heavy). This sequence is found line-internally and line-finally in various metres; when it is line-internal the seventh syllable must be heavy but when it is line-final the seventh syllable must be light.

There is a functional explanation of 'brevis in longo', which is that the line ends in a pause, and thus the timing difference between heavy/long and light/short syllables is neutralised at the end of the line. This kind of functional explanation might also be used to explain line-final extrametricality in English; the extra syllable falls into the pause. This functional explanation might be correct. Nevertheless, it is an oddity that while in general the metrical line ends on a strict sequence, the very final syllable can often be loose.

Asymmetries in sub-line units

As we have seen (p. 168), sub-units within the line can sometimes show the loose-beginning and strict-ending characteristic seen in the line more generally. Prince (1989) makes this point for Greek iambic trimeter, where the line is divided into three sub-units (metra), each of four syllables; the first syllable in each sub-unit is either heavy or light, which can be seen as a type of looseness. English shows a very slight tendency towards looseness at a mid-line division. On p. 39 we saw that trochaic inversion is sometimes found after a mid-line pause, which suggests that the domain for defining a stress maximum can sometimes be defined as part of a line. In discussions of where variation is permitted in the iambic pentameter line, it is usually agreed that of the five iambic feet, the second and fifth are the strictest. This might correlate with a mid-line division after the second foot.

Just as lines can end on an unprojected (extrametrical) syllable, so sub-units can also end on an unprojected syllable. This is seen in English lines where an extrametrical syllable seems to be permitted before a mid-line pause. However, it is worth noting that this does not seem to be true for quantitative metres; positions filled by heavy syllables at the end of mid-line units cannot alternatively be filled by light syllables. This is very clear for Sanskrit, where a mid-line unit always ends on a heavy syllable, with substitution of a light syllable possible only at the end of the line. This mismatch between extrametricality in English and brevis in longo in quantitative metres might suggest that they are actually to be explained by different principles (and also raises problems for functional explanations which try to connect them).

Explaining asymmetries

A key question about line-internal looseness and strictness and related asymmetries is whether they involve just the edge of the line or whether lines change continuously throughout. Does a line become increasingly strict towards the end, or suddenly strict? (I will suggest the latter.)

On the whole, these asymmetries seem to involve just the edge of the line. Initial looseness is focused on specific syllables; where more than one syllable is involved, they do not become 'less loose' as they get further from the beginning of the line. The same applies to final strictness; in Greek dactylic hexameter it is specifically the last five syllables which are strictly constrained (and all constrained to the same extent). Furthermore, the notion that the line moves from loose to strict does not fit with the fact that in most metres, there is either final strictness or initial looseness but not both. In English iambic pentameter the first syllable is 'rhythmically variable' (here, a stressed syllable in a polysyllabic word is not a stress maximum). But the rest of the line is fully strict; there is no specifically 'final strictness'. In Greek dactylic hexameter, the last two feet are stricter than the first four feet, but the first foot is not looser than the next three; thus there is no 'initial looseness'. This suggests that most kinds of looseness and strictness involve constraints on particular parts of the line, which means that they can be built into the generative rules. This was the approach I took to trochaic inversion, defining the key rhythmic notion of 'stress maximum' so that it is sensitive specifically to the beginning of the line. This is in contrast to approaches which suggest that trochaic inversion is a manifestation of a general initial looseness, as has been suggested (Hayes 1989: 223, 251, Hanson and Kiparsky 1996:293). Similarly, where specific parts of the metrical line are specifically strict this can be built into the rules by special constraints. By building the asymmetries into the metrical rules, we thereby explain why asymmetries are found only in metrical lines. This also explains why, as pointed out earlier, lines structured by parallelism rather than metre do not show these asymmetries.

As always, we can supplement the generative rules with a pragmatic account of asymmetries. The generative rules fix the actual asymmetries permitted in a metre, but they do not explain why they exist and are cross-linguistically found specifically at the beginning or end of the line. Perhaps the explanation is that these asymmetries are clues to the presence of the line boundary, as I argued earlier in this chapter. This kind of explanation can then explain why there are (loose) asymmetries which are not controlled by the generative rules, such as the fact that a word is most likely to project all its syllables at the end of the line.

5.5   Summary

In this chapter I have argued that lineation is always implied. Some texts (e.g. printed texts) provide very strong evidence for a particular lineation; others (spoken texts, and particularly non-metrical spoken texts) provide relatively weak evidence for a particular lineation. But lineation is still always implied. Alternative lineations can hold weakly, even when they contradict a dominant lineation; these alternative lineations exist as a mass of weak implicatures which are experienced as aesthetic. There are some kinds of text whose aesthetic appears to be based on a fundamental ambiguity as to the size of the line (the 'one line or two' situation). The composition of verse is thus a very flexible aesthetic practice; not only does it allow for the complexities of metricality, but is also a source of complexity through its status as the content of implicatures. In the next chapter I look at another way in which lineation is exploited for its inherent complexities, which involves the grouping of lines into stanzas.

6   Line-groups in metrical verse and in narrative

For most verse texts, lines are grouped into stanzas or verse paragraphs. In the previous chapter I argued that the division of a text into lines and the location of line boundaries holds only by implicature. In this chapter I argue the same for the organisation of lines into line-groups and the location of line-group boundaries. Organisation into stanzas or other groupings of lines is an implied form of the text, and not an observer-independent fact of the text.

6.1   Line-grouping is implied

In this section I undertake a detailed analysis of three texts to show that line-grouping is implied. I begin with a poem in which line-grouping is implied both by layout and by other means; then a poem in which layout tells us that there is no line-grouping but there is other evidence which tells us that there is; I conclude the section by looking at a poem in which there are simultaneous but contradictory line-groupings.

Line-grouping is unambiguously implied by layout and other means

Love

¶A   Love's an headstrong wild desire
        To possess what we admire:
        Hurrying on without reflecting,
        All that's just or wise neglecting.   4
        Pain or pleasure it is neither,
        But excess of both together;
        Now, addressing, cringing, whining,
        Vowing, fretting, weeping, pining,   8
        Murm'ring, languishing and sighing,
        Mad, despairing, raving, dying:
        Now, caressing, laughing, toying,
        Fondling, kissing and enjoying.   12
        Always in extremes abiding,
        Without measure, fond or chiding:

> Either furious with possessing,
> Or despairing of the blessing: 16
> Now transported; now tormented;
> Still uneasy; ne'er contented.
> None can tell its rise or progress,
> Or its ingress or its egress,   20
> Whether by a look produced,
> Or by sympathy infused.
> ¶B   Fancy does so well maintain it,
> Weaker reason can't restrain it,   24
> But is forced to fly before it,
> Or else worship and adore it.

Henry Baker, 'Love', 1725 (L:163)

This is a continuous twenty-six-line poem with an indentation at line 23. A conventional and fairly strong conditional is invoked to tell us that the poem is split into two line-groups, which I mark as ¶A and ¶B in the left-hand margin:

> (1) If this line is indented then it is at the beginning of a line-group. [strong]

The division is reinforced by another kind of evidence, which is that lines 1–2 end on a short foot (i.e. are headless) and so do lines 21–2 (and these are the only short lines in the text). It is not uncommon for headless lines to mark line-group boundaries for which there is other evidence, though it is also the case that short lines sometimes come in the middle of line-groups. This supports a weak but somewhat conventionalised conditional (2).

> (2) If this line ends on a short foot then it is at the beginning or end of a line-group.

Both conditionals hold for more than just this text, and are part of the knowledge which a reader may carry from text to text. But group ¶B also has another distinctive characteristic, which is that every line ends on 'it'. This might be interpreted in terms of the following emergent conditional:

> (3) If this sequence of lines ends on the same word, then this sequence of lines is a single line-group.

This conditional emerges only because there is another reason to think that the last four lines constitute a line-group. To summarise, we have conventional and strong conditionals which are evidence that the last four lines constitute a distinct group, and because of this, other uniform characteristics of the last four lines also emerge as kinds of form.

Henry Baker's poem has unambiguous line-grouping with strong evidence for two verse paragraphs from layout and from other sources. Like many stichic texts of this period, the lines are also grouped into couplets by rhyme. The smaller line-groups fit unproblematically into the larger groups. It is nevertheless worth noting that other line-groupings emerge weakly at various points in the poem, and in particular there is a slight tendency towards the emergence of quatrains.

Line-grouping is unambiguously implied without being evidenced by layout

Nicholas Breton's 'Who Can Live in Heart So Glad' is a continuous text seventy-four lines long, in iambic tetrameter and rhyming couplets. Though it is printed as though it is a single line-group, I suggest that there is evidence for a line-group boundary at the beginning of line 35:

> Fair Aglaia, in whose face
> > Nicholas Breton, 'Who Can Live in Heart So Glad', 1604 (J:235)

The conclusion that this is a line-group boundary relates primarily to the fact that there is a shift in content in this line; the lines before have been general praise of a shepherdess, and this line introduces Aglaia for the first time (who will be praised for the rest of the poem). Thus this conclusion relates to a conditional such as (4):

> (4) If this line introduces a new kind of content then it is at the beginning of a line-group.

This conditional in fact justifies a division of the text into line-groups such as this:

¶A	General praise of a shepherdess	1–34	thirty-four lines
¶B	Bridge section introducing Aglaia	35–8	four lines
¶C	Specific praise of Aglaia	39–72	thirty-four lines
¶D	Coda	73–4	two lines

This division of the text into line-groups ¶A and ¶C (which are both thirty-four lines long) is then further strengthened by appeal to the following conditional:

> (5) If this is a line-group then it will be of the same length as another line-group in the same poem.

Evidence that lines 39–72 are a single line-group is that they form a single sentence which praises Aglaia, thus exploiting conditional (4) and a conditional such as (6):

> (6) If this is a line-group boundary then it will coincide with a syntactic boundary.

The evidence for line group ¶D is in part that the penultimate line names 'Aglaia' for only the second time in the poem and thus exploits conditional (4) but also by appeal to conditional (7), which is somewhat conventionalised (e.g. by its use in the Shakespearean sonnet):

> (7) The last two lines of a text form a distinct line-group.

Furthermore, the final two lines, 73–4, have only four words in each line, which makes them among the shortest in the poem (no line has fewer than four words, and only lines 57–9 also have four words).

> In Aglaia's only eyes,   73
> In my worldly paradise.   74

Thus there is something distinctive about them, though this is a fairly unique kind of form such that we might formulate an (emergent) conditional for just this text:

> (8) If these lines have the fewest words in the text then they form a line-group.

Given that there is other evidence that the final pair of lines is a distinct unit, the shortness of the pair of lines further strengthens the evidence that it is a final couplet.

Thus this is a text which is not laid out to provide evidence for line-grouping but where various kinds of evidence, of which coherence of meaning is particularly significant, conspire to suggest line-grouping.

Line-grouping is implied, and is ambiguous

If line-groups are implied then it should be possible for a text to have simultaneous but incompatible divisions into line-groups. Verse which is divided by layout into at most verse paragraphs rather than stanzas sometimes offers evidence for smaller line-groups emerging in contrast to the larger structure. Consider Margaret Cavendish's 'A Landscape', a stichic text mainly in iambic pentameter rhyming in couplets. This is the complete text with the verse paragraphs marked in the right margin along with line numbers, and my suggested grouping in the left margin.

A Landscape

¶1   Standing upon a hill of fancies high,   ¶A
    Viewing about with curiosity's eye,
    Saw several landscapes under my thoughts to lie
        Some champians of delights where there did feed   ¶B

¶2   Pleasures, as wethers fat, and ewes to breed;   5
    And pastures of green hopes, wherein cows went,
    Of probability give milk of sweet content.
    Some fields, though ploughed with care, unsowed did lie,

¶3   Wanting the fruitful seed, industry.
    In other fields full crops of joys there growed,   10
    Where some ripe joy's fruition down had mowed.
    Some blasted with ill accidents looked black,

¶4   Others blown down with sorrow strong lay flat.
        Then did I view inclosures close to lie,   ¶C
    Hearts hedged about with thoughts of secrecy.   15
    Fresh meadow of green youth did pleasant seem:

¶5   Innocency, as cowslips, grew therein.
    Some ready with old age to cut for hay,
    Some hay cocked high for death to take away.
    Clear rivulets of health ran here and there,   20

¶6   No mind of sickness in them did appear.
    No stones or gravel stopped their passage free,
    No weeds of pain, or slimy gouts could see.

¶7   Woods did present my view on the left side,   ¶D
    Where trees of high ambition grew great pride.   25
    There shades of envy were made of dark spite,
    Which did eclipse the fame of honour's light.

¶8   Faults stood so close, not many beams of praise
    Could enter in: spite stopped up all the ways.
    But leaves of prattling tongues, which ne'er lie still,   30
    Sometimes speak truth, although most lies they tell.

¶9   Then did I a garden of beauty view,   ¶E
    Where complexions of roses and lilies grew;
    And violets of blue veins there growed,
    Upon the banks of breasts most perfect showed.   35

¶10   Lips of fresh gilliflowers grew up high,
    Which oft the sun did kiss as he passed by.
    Hands of Narcissus perfect white were set,
    The palms were curious tulips, finely streaked.

¶11   And by this garden a lovely orchard stood,   ¶F 40
    Wherein grew fruit of pleasure rare and good.
    All coloured eyes grew there, as bullace grey,
    And damsons black, which do taste best, some say.

¶12   Others there were of the pure bluest grape,   45
    And pear-plum faces of an oval shape.
    Cheeks of apricots made red with heat,
    And cherry lips, which most delight to eat.

¶13   When I had viewed this landscape round about,
       I fell from fancy's hill, and so wit's sight went out.   49

Margaret Cavendish, Duchess of Newcastle, 1653 (F:633)

Conditional (1), relating indentation to line-grouping, leads to the strong conclusion that the line-groups begin at lines 4, 14, 24, 32 and 40; I mark these line-groups as ¶A–F in the right-hand column.

(1) If this line is indented then it is at the beginning of a line-group. [strong]

Further evidence for these line-groupings comes from coincidence between line-group boundaries and syntactic boundaries, and also from conditional (5), which relates similarity in length to line-grouping, thus reinforcing the evidence that ¶B and ¶C are line-groups because they are both ten lines, and that ¶D and ¶E are line-groups because they are both eight lines.

(5) If this is a line-group then it will be of the same length as another line-group in the same poem.

Thus there is strong evidence for this line-grouping.
   But there is also evidence for a different line-grouping. This comes from conditional (9), in combination with conditional (5).

(9) If this line begins with a trochaic inversion then it is at the beginning of a line-group.

I have underlined trochaic inversions in the text. Based on this conditional we have evidence for line-groups beginning at lines 1, 2, 5, 9, 13 and 17 (and line 45) which all have trochaic inversions at the beginning of line-groups. If we also make use of conditional (5) then we have two kinds of evidence both giving the conclusion that four-line line-groups begin at lines 1, 5, 9, 13 and 17; I have marked these as line-groups ¶1–5 in the left-hand margin. We now invoke conditional (10) (which is related to conditional (3), involving lines which end on the same word):

(10) If this sequence of lines begins on the same word, then this sequence of lines is a single line-group.

This tells us that lines 21–3 are a single line-group. Confirming evidence comes from conditional (1), which tells us that line 24 initiates a new line-group. At this point the two kinds of line-grouping, quatrains and verse paragraphs, coincide. Until this point they have been out of alignment, and after this they will be in alignment, with the quatrains falling inside the verse paragraphs.

Now we return to quatrains, and keep grouping the lines into fours. Evidence for this comes from conditional (1), in combination with conditional (9), involving trochaic inversion on monosyllables (i.e. in the rhythmic explicature): ¶7 new paragraph and 'Woods did', ¶8 'Faults stood', ¶9 new paragraph and 'Then did', ¶10 'Lips of', ¶11 new paragraph and a possible inversion on 'And by'. Section ¶12 reinstates the pattern of trochaic inversion on a polysyllable with which the poem begins, and the final section ¶13 is a couplet with a coherent closing meaning, which perhaps also exploits a conditional like (7):

> (7) The last two lines of a text form a distinct line-group.

I have suggested that the poem in the first half has its quatrains out of alignment with its verse paragraphs, and in the second half has its quatrains fitting into the verse paragraphs; throughout, the text is ambiguous in line-grouping but with a different kind of ambiguity in the first and second halves, with a movement from contradiction to compatibility. There are further ambiguities in line-grouping at the very beginning and end which show the same pattern of initial contradiction and final compatibility. Consider the first four lines. I conclude that this is a line-group basically because the line-groups which follow have trochaic inversion every four lines, and thus the first four lines, by conditional (5) (equal length) are also taken to be a line-group. But there is also a trochaic inversion in line 2, which might suggest that lines 2–4 are a line-group, and lines 1–3 are the only rhyming triplet in the poem, which might suggest that lines 1–3 are a line-group (as does the fact that line 4 begins with an indentation). Thus there are three incompatible ways of dividing up the beginning of the text into small line-groups. The end of the text is also ambiguous but in a different way. There is evidence that the last six lines are a quatrain followed by a couplet; this is justified by conditional (5) and also by a conditional which might be formulated as (7). However, there is evidence for another division with a line-group starting in line 47:

> Cheeks of apricots made red with heat,

The evidence that this is the beginning of a line-group is that it is the only line in the poem which is headless (the poem shows some rhythmic irregularities, but nevertheless I believe this is true). Thus it might involve conditional (11), related to conditional (2), because metrical variation can be evidence for a line-group boundary.

> (11) If this line begins on a short foot then it is at the beginning or end of a line-group.

Furthermore, this line begins on a monosyllabic 'inversion' and also imitates the beginning of line 36 with 'Lips of', and thus might invoke a conditional like (12):

> (12) If this line parallels a line which is at the beginning of a line-group then this line is at the beginning of a line-group.

The final ten lines are thus a combination of different line-groupings as follows: 10 lines, or 4+4+2 lines, or 4+2+4 lines. This ambiguity shows a 'fit' between the possibilities not seen at the beginning, primarily because this ambiguity involves multiples of two (in a poem organised in couplets). Thus there is some reason to think that the micro-organisation of the end of the poem shows an ordered ambiguity in contrast to the disordered ambiguity of the beginning.

The analysis which I have just presented is basically a traditional literary critical account of the poem, formulated in a way which allows us to understand it as a cognitively realistic model of how the poem is interpreted by the reader. A literary critical account would now probably go on to ask whether the poem's formal complexities relate to its content (i.e. the emotional states it describes). This is a legitimate question to ask, but I suggest that the formal complexity has a function irrespective of whether it is mirrored in the content of the poem; I suggest that we experience these shifting formal contradictions and complexities as aesthetic. Hymes (1981) and others have shown that formal analysis can reveal complexities otherwise unsuspected in verbal artworks; this work thus constitutes a revaluation of otherwise relatively unvalued native American oral traditions. Ethnopoetics has a function in revealing skill and complexity which might otherwise go unnoticed. Placing value on formal complexity, and formulating a theory of how it works, is part of the ethnopoetic project which in the present book is applied to English verse.

6.2   Conventional evidence for the line-group boundaries

In the sections which follow I look at conventional ways in which line-groups are evidenced (making extensive use of Häublein 1978:45–81). I emphasise that this is not a typological project: my aim is not to establish a list of conditionals relating to form which might be titled 'literary knowledge' and which corresponds to Culler's (1973) notion of 'literary competence'. There is no such list.

The difference between 'conventional' and 'emergent' for conditionals is a difference in how much evidence there is for the conditional; if a conditional works well for many texts then it is conventional, and if it works just for this text then it is emergent (perhaps to become conventional at some later stage). But the conventional conditionals are not necessarily remembered as part of some special list; they can just as easily be reinvented and reformulated each time as can the emergent conditionals. Every conditional is just as strong as it is taken to be, and has just the formulation given to it at any moment.

Linguistic boundaries and line-group boundaries

Like the line, the stanza boundary tends to coincide with a syntactic boundary, which I suggested as the basis for conditional (6) in the previous section:

> (6) If this is a line-group boundary then it will coincide with a syntactic boundary.

This is basic to Puttenham's definition of the line-group ('staffe'):

if we consider well the forme of this Poeticall staffe, we shall finde it to be a certaine number of verses allowed to go together and ioyne without any intermission, and doe or should finish vp all the sentences of the same with a full period, vnlesse it be some special cases, & there to stay till another staffe follow of like sort: (George Puttenham (1589:68))

Häublein (1978) argues that another kind of linguistic boundary involves particular speech acts at line-group boundaries: the first line of a stanza can begin with a question or exclamation or interjection or expletive; questions are also characteristic stanza-concluding devices. Similarly there can be a change of speakers or a shift to quoted speech. In Breton's poem, discussed above, the shift from ¶B to ¶C is introduced by 'See what her true shepherd says' (implying that ¶C is the shepherd speaking), and the shift from ¶C to ¶D is introduced by 'The sweet subject of my song', again marking this as the beginning of a new speech act, the song, within the larger text.

The possibility that these discourse-level boundaries coincide with line-group boundaries is seen also in the characteristic use of certain connectives at line-group boundaries. Thus for example 'but' is fairly common at the beginning of a verse paragraph. George Wither's 'When I With a Serious Musing . . .' (1635;F:247) is thirty lines in two verse paragraphs, the second of which begins with the only 'but' in the poem. Thomas Carew's 'Reader When These Dumb Stones . . .' (1640;F:339) is thirty-four lines in two printed paragraphs in which 'but' is used twice, once at the beginning of the second verse paragraph. Milton's 'To the Ocean . . .' from *Comus* (1637;F:19) is in three verse paragraphs, the second of which begins with the only 'but' in the poem (and the third begins with a trochaic inversion). While 'but' is not used uniquely at the beginnings of verse paragraphs, it is used with sufficient frequency to permit a weak conditional:

> (13) If this line begins with 'but' then it is the first line in a line-group.

'But' is not the only connective which can play this role. Both 'but' and 'and' play a role in George Gascoigne's 'The Green Knight's Farewell to Fancy' (1575;J:209), a poem laid out in ten six-line stanzas. Here there is evidence that the stanzas are further grouped into larger sections based on the placement of the connectives 'but' and 'and'. The first stanza ends:

> But since I find thy fickleness, *Fancy* (quoth he) *farewell*.

The second stanza ends with a line similarly structured:

> And since I find myself deceived, *Fancy* (quoth he) *farewell*.

The final lines of the first nine stanzas begin as follows, each then ending on: '... *Fancy* (quoth he) *farewell*'.

But since (1) – And since (2) –
But since (3) – But since (4) – And since (5) –
But since (6) – But since (7) – But since (8) – And such (9)

Thus the poem builds units of two, three and four stanzas, each sequence ending in a stanza which changes the pattern (to 'And such'). The tenth stanza then ends with the following two lines, which contract the but–and sequence into the two lines and alter the ending, thus bringing the poem to a halt:

> But since I must accept my fortunes as they fell,
> I say God send me better speed, and *Fancy Now Farewell*.

The coincidence of discourse-level boundaries with line-group boundaries also relates to the characteristic semantic coherence of the line-group. As we will see later in this chapter, connectives such as 'but', 'so' and 'and' have a particularly important role in evidencing lineation and line-grouping in oral narratives.

The fact that the line is often a semantically coherent unit can be explained by the fact it is also often a syntactically coherent unit. In contrast the characteristic semantic coherence of line-groups is best explained in pragmatic terms; the parts of the line-group are interpreted as together having a coherent meaning. In this case, evidence for form (i.e. for the stanza as a unit) is taken as evidence for meaning. The conditional could be either a boundary conditional such as (4), or a 'coherence' conditional such as (14):

> (4) If this line introduces a new kind of content then it is at the beginning of a line-group.
> (14) If these lines form a line-group then they are a distinct unit of meaning.

However, there are some stanzas which do not seem to have a semantic unity. Häublein sees this as a fault in Ralegh's 'Farewell False Love . . .' where 'the stanzaic units disappear completely in a welter of details' (1978:62), because for most of the poem each line consists of one or two noun phrases put together in a list. These are the first two stanzas:

> Farewell false love, the oracle of lies,
> A mortal foe and enimie to rest:
> An envious boye, from whom all cares arise,
> A bastard vile, a beast with rage possest:
>   A way of error, a temple full of treason,
>   In all effects contrarie unto reason.
>
> A poysoned serpent covered all with flowers,
> Mother of sighes, and murtherer of repose,
> A sea of sorows from whence are drawen such showers
> As moysture lend to everie griefe that growes,
>   A schole of guile, a net of deepe deceit,
>   A gilded hooke, that holds a poysoned bayte.
>
> Sir Walter Ralegh, 'Farewell False Love', 1588 (Latham 1951:7)

It is difficult to dispute Häublein's claim that the stanzas are not distinct in meaning; in terms of meaning, the text might be interpreted as not in line-groups at all but as a continuous sequence of lines. To be set against this are various kinds of evidence for stanzas, which includes layout, punctuation (until the last stanza the only full stops are at the ends of stanzas) and rhyme (stanzas end on couplets). Thus there is evidence for division into stanzas, to be set against the evidence (against stanzas) coming from the lack of semantic distinctness. Instead of taking conditional (14) to be so strong as to undermine the text (which is Häublein's view) we might instead read the text as deliberately ambiguous in form. Ralegh tends to construct formally ambiguous texts, and supporting evidence that formal ambiguity is important in this poem comes from a complication in the internal structure of the final stanza. The final stanza ends with this couplet:

> False love, desire, and beauty frail adieu!
> Dead is the root whence all these fancies grew.

Here, there are three aspects of the penultimate line which suggest that it should be the final line: it repeats the key phrase 'false love', previously seen in the first line; it ends with 'adieu'; and it ends with an exclamation mark (previous stanzas have had only commas at the ends of stanza-internal lines). Thus this line implies that it is final, an implicature which is counteracted by the fact that there is then another line which follows it.

Layout and other visual evidence

Layout is strong evidence for the line-group, as manifested in indentation (or some other typographical modification) at the beginning of verse paragraphs and empty lines between stanzas.

(1) If this line is indented then it is at the beginning of a line-group.
(15) If this line is preceded by a blank line then it is at the beginning of a line-group.

Both conditionals characteristically hold strongly. Like the line, it is really only in the twentieth century (after Mallarmé) that ways have been found of significantly weakening the force of visual evidence, such that even on the page the division into line-groups is less strongly evidenced (see Rothenberg and Joris 1995).

Sometimes layout works as visual evidence for line-groups because the stanza is used as a coherent visual object to represent something external to the poem. This is the case in seventeenth-century English pattern poetry, where the stanza represents a shape. And it is also the case in abecedarian structures such as that seen in the Hiberno-Latin hymn 'Altus Prosatur', which has twenty-three stanzas, each of which begins with a word whose first letter is a letter of the Latin alphabet, giving a sequence a, b, c throughout the text (Clancy and Márkus 1995:40).

Visual evidence can sometimes be the only consistent source of line-grouping, with no supporting evidence. The mediaeval English poems *Cleanness* and *Patience* exist in one manuscript only; they have a double oblique stroke in the left-hand margin at the beginning of every fourth line, which has been interpreted as evidence for quatrains by some modern editors but not others (Andrew and Waldron 1996:49). The visual evidence is consistent, but other evidence is not. Thus there is a tendency for *Cleanness* to have major syntactic boundaries every four lines: this is true at the end of lines 4, 8, 11, 16, 20, 24, 28, 32 but then becomes less clear, and there are other major syntactic boundaries at the ends of other lines. Perhaps the scribe of the original manuscript interpreted the line as having emergent stanzaic organisation, and put marks in the margin to strengthen the evidence.

A note on sequence and evidence from layout

In a performance of a text, line-groups are ordered; whether on the page or spoken, one line-group follows another. The order of line-groups would thus appear to be a formal explicature of the text; by interpretive use (resemblance) the order of line-groups can be taken as representing the order of the contents of each of the line-groups.

line-group A precedes line-group B
                        by resemblance
contents of line-group A precede contents of line-group B

An ordering of contents might for example be an ordering of actions or events, or emotional states, or stages of a life. This is not true for all poems; it is not true of at least the first two stanzas (possibly all three) of the following (complete) poem, where the contents can be interpreted as unordered, even though there is an ordering of stanzas:

Tichborne's Elegy
Written with his own hand in the Tower before his execution

My prime of youth is but a frost of cares,
  My feast of joy is but a dish of pain,
My crop of corn is but a field of tares,
    And all my good is but vain hope of gain.
    The day is past, and yet I saw no sun,
    And now I live, and now my life is done.

My tale was heard and yet it was not told,
  My fruit is fallen and yet my leaves are green;
My youth is spent and yet I am not old,
    I saw the world and yet I was not seen.
      My thread is cut and yet it is not spun,
      And now I live, and now my life is done.

I sought my death and found it in my womb,
  I looked for life and saw it was a shade;
I trod the earth and knew it was my tomb,
    And now I die, and now I was but made.
      My glass is full, and now my glass is run,
      And now I live, and now my life is done.

Chidiock Tichborne 1586 (J:393)

There is some reason to think that at least the final couplet belongs at the end because it has an increased amount of repetition in comparison to the previous two couplets. Otherwise, despite Tichborne's use of various 'stage of life' terms, there is no obvious ordering of contents. This might mean that the interpretation of interpretive resemblance between stanza order and contents order takes place at a risk; the conclusion of ordered content which it implies might or might not be confirmed by other interpretations derived from the text.

However, Häublein (1978:99) makes an interesting suggestion which might lead to a different conclusion (drawing on suggestions by Johnson 1972). Citing texts including Tichborne's he proposes a 'principle of stanzaic mobility', which 'involves a lack of logical progression, inter-stanzaic *stasis* and extreme stanzaic self-sufficiency'. He shows that sixteenth- to eighteenth-century poets, songwriters and critics were aware of the mobility of stanzas in some poems;

after 1800 it becomes less characteristic. He quotes Samuel Johnson (on Pope's *Essay on Criticism*):

Almost every poem, consisting of precepts, is so far arbitrary and immethodical, that many of the paragraphs may change places with no apparent inconvenience; for of two or more positions, depending upon some remote and general principle, there is seldom any cogent reason why one should precede the other. (Samuel Johnson, *Life of Pope*, 1781 (Hill 1968:III,99))

Häublein suggests that texts have stanzaic mobility as a formal characteristic when their stanzas can be reordered without apparently having any effect (e.g. on the meaning). Though Häublein does not make the connection, there is an analogy here with Labov and Waletzky's (1967) way of identifying a non-narrative clause, which can be reordered without affecting the order of events. He argues that stanza order involves more than just layout on the page, or temporal sequence in performance; it also involves various kinds of link between stanzas which tell the reader that one stanza must follow another. Links can be weak or strong; strong links include, for example, enjambment between stanzas (as in Tennyson's *In Memoriam*). Where links are weak, the stanzas are more mobile; where they are strong, the stanzas are less mobile. Thus the ordering of stanzas is tendential and based on various kinds of evidence, and not just on layout or temporal sequence. This suggests that it is not an explicature of the text that the stanzas are in a certain order. The explicature is thus 'Stanza A is printed above stanza B' and the thought 'Stanza A is ordered before stanza B' is an implicature, based on the explicature but also taking the strength of links between the stanzas into account.

Metre

In traditional codifications a named 'metre' is quite often a description of a whole line-group rather than a description of just a line; this is true for the Welsh metres such as *englyn penfyr* (p. 52) and for the sapphic metre (p. 126), both of which fix the varying metrical structures of a sequence of lines rather than a single line. In some cases, we might take the metrical grid to encompass the line-group (as discussed in the previous chapter), while in other cases we might take the line-group to be a heterometric sequence, with each line in a different metre. In either case, the metrical structure of the sequence of lines can tell us where the line-group begins and ends.

There is another way in which metrical structure can evidence line-group boundaries, which is that metrical irregularities can appear at the beginning or the end of the line-group. We saw this earlier, and I formulated a conditional:

(9) If this line begins with a trochaic inversion then it is at the beginning of a
    line-group.

Gray's 'Elegy Written in a Country Churchyard' is laid out in quatrains. The first trochaic inversion involving a polysyllable in the poem is on the word 'Haply', in the following quatrain. Trochaic inversion here marks a line-group.

> Haply some hoary-headed Swain may say,   97
> 'Oft have we seen him at the peep of dawn
> 'Brushing with hasty steps the dews away
> 'To meet the sun upon the upland lawn.   100
>
> Thomas Gray, 'Elegy Written in a Country Churchyard', 1751 (L:37)

Line 97 has the first trochaic inversion, and line 98 initiates the long quotation which concludes the poem. Thus there is a division of the text into parts at this point, with the end of the first part cued by the line-initial trochaic inversion. (It is worth noting that this is the first trochaic inversion involving a polysyllable, though there are earlier ones which involve monosyllables; as I suggest on p. 38, Gray tends to distinguish between polysyllabic and monosyllabic inversions.)

Altered line length can be a significant source of evidence for line-grouping; it is quite common for the final line in a stanza to be longer or shorter than the preceding, and we saw examples of this in the texts discussed in chapter 6, section 1, and formulated as these conditionals:

> (2)   If this line ends on a short foot then it is at the beginning or end of a line-group.
> (11) If this line begins on a short foot then it is at the beginning or end of a line-group.

In the Greek sapphic, the last of three lines is longest, while in Horace's revision of the sapphic, the last of four lines is the shortest. Less commonly, the first line in a stanza is longer or shorter, as in Welsh *englyn penfyr*, which has a ten-syllable line followed by two seven-syllable lines. In English the most systematic manifestation of this is for an iambic pentameter stanza to end on a hexameter line. The most influential text in this regard is Spenser's *The Faerie Queene*, which has eight iambic pentameter lines and a ninth iambic hexameter line. Spenser's stanza is directly copied, and adapted, as for example in Charles Newton's 'Stanzas' (1797;L:822), or Chatterton's 'Aella', which have stanzas in five iambic pentameter lines and a concluding hexameter, or Wordsworth's 'Resolution and Independence', which has stanzas in seven lines of which the seventh is hexameter, or Shelley's 'Stanzas Written in Dejection, near Naples' which are eight iambic tetrameter lines and one iambic hexameter line.

Hexameters can also be used as evidence of a boundary at the end of a verse paragraph, which suggests a conditional such as the following:

> (16) If this line is a hexameter then the next line begins a new line-group.

Joseph Addison's 'A Letter from Italy, to the Right Honourable Charles Lord Halifax' (1704,L:41) is 168 lines of iambic pentameter in three printed verse paragraphs of unequal length; each of the verse paragraphs ends on a hexameter line. Thomas Holcroft's 'To Haydn' (1794,L:685) is twenty-six lines of iambic pentameter in three printed verse paragraphs, two of which end in hexameters. Sometimes the hexameter offers evidence for a line-group boundary where there is no evidence from layout. Thus Sarah Fyge Egerton's 'The Emulation' (1703,L:37) is a thirty-nine-line text in iambic pentameter printed as a single verse paragraph. However, there is evidence for a division into two line-groups in the deployment of the single hexameter line 26, which comes at the end of the section describing the 'old' and is followed by the section describing the 'new'; thus here a grouping of lines is evidenced by a combination of meaning and the hexameter. Anne Finch's 'A Nocturnal Reverie' (1713,L:106) is a fifty-line text printed as a single paragraph with a single hexameter line as line 46, followed by four lines. Evidence that the final four lines constitute a line-group comes partly from the hexameter and partly from the fact that line 47 is the first line to mention 'me' (previously the experiencer has been 'we'). Like most kinds of conditionals relating to a line-group boundary, conditional (16) can only hold somewhat weakly. John Winstanley's 'Fanney's Removal in 1714' (1714,L:132) is an eighty-one-line text in iambic pentameter, divided by layout into verse paragraphs, one of which ends on a hexameter line. But there are two other hexameter lines in the poem and apparently no other evidence to take these as ending line-groups internal to the printed paragraphs. It is possible that where there is also evidence from layout, conditional (16) is weakened, but in a text without other visual evidence for line-grouping such as those by Egerton and Finch, (16) is a stronger conditional.

Different aspects of metre can be used to communicate line-grouping, as in the following complete poem:

Low-anchored cloud,	
Newfoundland air,	
Fountain-head and source of rivers,	3
Dew-cloth, dream drapery,	
And napkin spread by fays;	
Drifting meadow of the air,	6
Where bloom the daisied banks and violets,	
And in whose fenny labyrinth	
The bittern booms and heron wades;	9
Spirit of lakes and seas and rivers,	
Bear only perfumes and the scent	
Of healing herbs to just men's fields!	12

Henry David Thoreau, 'Low-anchored Cloud', 1849 (S:142)

This unrhymed variable-length poem presents evidence that it is divided into two sestets each divided into two triplets. Evidence for this division comes from various sources; in the first half of the poem, lines 3 and 6 are distinctive (i.e. finishing off each triplet) while in the second half of the poem lines 7 and 10 are distinctive (i.e. initiating each triplet). The lines vary in length between two and five iambic feet in the sequence 224 334 544 444: the only five-foot line initiates the second sestet, while in the first sestet the four-foot lines end each triplet. These four-foot lines also begin with missing syllables. The only trochaic inversion, 'Spirit', initiates the final triplet. There are two lines with extrametricality on the word 'rivers', the first ending the first triplet and the second initiating the final triplet. In the second half of the poem, within each triplet the first line is end-stopped and the second line enjambs into the second. Thus various kinds of evidence conspire to suggest a division into four triplets.

Rhyme schemes

Rhyme schemes can constitute evidence for the line-group. If there is a complex pattern, the line-group is evidenced when all rhymes are completed. A couplet can constitute evidence for the end of a longer group, as represented by the already-used conditional (7):

> (7) The last two lines of a text form a distinct line-group.

Like all conditionals, this sometimes holds and sometimes does not; the last two lines of a poem are not always a distinct line-group, but if there is other evidence for this grouping, then (7) contributes to (strengthens) the overall evidence for the group.

Rhyme schemes characteristically hold between sub-groups of lines, sometimes within a larger grouping. Häublein (1978:35) comments on the way in which certain rhyme schemes allow for different ways of dividing the stanza into smaller line-groups. The cinquain ABABB suggests either two alternate rhymes and one concluding line, or a tercet plus couplet:

AB AB B   or   ABA BB

And the Spenserian stanza can be sub-analysed either as two quatrains with the final hexameter separated off, or as a quatrain and a final couplet bracketing a tercet:

ABAB BCBC C   or   ABAB BCB CC

In this way, certain uses of rhyme are a source of chronic ambiguity in the implication of sub-groups of lines within a stanza.

Milton's *Lycidas* (1638) is an iambic pentameter text in verse paragraphs, with an irregular rhyme scheme; only at the end of the text does a regular scheme emerge. Thus the final two verse paragraphs (from 'Weep no more . . .' to the end) have the following rhyme scheme:

irregular	couplets emerge	regular sequence
ABABBACCDEDEFFGFG	HH II	JK JK JK LL

The regular sequence with which the poem ends is an eight-line verse paragraph, ending on a couplet; Heath-Stubbs (1969:37) reads this as an *ottava rima* sequence.

Herman Melville makes distinctive use of rhyme; in several poems, lines do not in general rhyme, but each stanza has one rhyme involving the final line and one other (usually the second line in the stanza). Thus 'A Utilitarian's View of the Monitor's Flight' is in six-line stanzas with rhyme –A– – – –A; 'Stonewall Jackson (Mortally wounded . . .)' is in six-line stanzas with rhyme –A–A–A. The more complex version of this strategy is seen in 'The College Colonel', where the final line in each stanza rhymes with the second line and, if the stanza is longer than four lines, with other lines as well. The stanzas of 'Stonewall Jackson (Ascribed to a Virginian)' have final lines which do not rhyme within the stanza; instead the final word in the final lines is 'war' in the first and last stanzas, and 'star' in the other stanzas; something similar is seen in 'Afterward' where the word 'Golden' ends the first and last stanzas.

Summary

In this and the previous section we have seen that there are many weak conditionals which can be formulated to deduce the conclusion that line-groups exist. The kinds of evidence for line-grouping in metrical verse include:

(a) Layout (indentation and blank separating lines) constitutes strong evidence for line-grouping just as it does for lineation.

(b) The coincidence of linguistic boundaries and line-group boundaries, particularly higher-level boundaries such as discourse units, initiated by connectives.

(c) Shifts in content at line-group boundaries and the semantic coherence of the line-group.

(d) Changes in metre, metrical variations (hexameter in a pentameter sequence, short initial or final feet, extrametricality) or metrical irregularities (such as trochaic inversion).

(e) Rhyme schemes.

(f) Repetition and parallelism. The beginnings of line-groups may be similar, begin or end on the same words, etc.

Most kinds of evidence are weak, in that they are not strictly found only at line-group boundaries; only evidence from layout is strong because it is consistently found at line-group boundaries. Complexities can emerge when different line-groups are evidenced in different ways, particularly when – as in stichic texts with concealed quatrains, etc. – the two kinds of formal organisation do not align, but instead contradict one another.

6.3   Line-groups, counting and grids

In chapter 1 I introduced a mechanism for counting by building a bracketed grid. Metricality fundamentally involves counting, but the counting mechanism builds a structure which can then be exploited by other aspects of the line. This explains why metrical lines characteristically have regular placement of stressed syllables, or rhyme, or word boundaries, depending on the tradition and the metre. The grid made available by a counting mechanism is a differentiated (periodic) structure to which other characteristics of the line can be attached.

In this section I ask whether the counting of lines into a line-group might also involve the construction of a grid. If line-groups are counted by building a bracketed grid then this explains why line-groups have other characteristics such as systematically varying line-lengths and systematically organised rhyme patterns. I suggest that these are systematically made possible by attaching them to the periodic grid required to count the lines into the stanza. In contrast, in texts which are not counted out in this way (i.e. stichic texts, not organised into stanzas) we are much less likely to find varying line lengths and complex rhyme patterns. Thus I propose to extend to line organisation within the stanza the mechanism used for metrical organisation within the line; there is a precedent for this in Hayes and MacEachern (1998) though taking a very different (Optimality Theory) approach.

I will use the same kinds of rule as proposed for metrical lines. Each line projects as an asterisk on gridline 0. Iterative rules build a grid. Other aspects of the stanza can be attached by condition. Consider for example the two-line-group; suitable rules and the grids they build might be (a) or (b).

Table 6.1 *Two-line-group (a)*

	bracket	foot size	direction	head
line 0	(	binary	L>R	right

```
  L L        (i.e. L = line)
 (* *(   0
     *    1
```

Table 6.2 *Two-line-group (b)*

	bracket	foot size	direction	head
line 0	(	binary	L>R	left

```
  L L
(* *(   0
  *     1
```

These line-group grids could be structured as extensions of the metrical grids; each metrical grid ends on one asterisk and this asterisk could represent the line as a whole in the stanza grid. We could attach various conditions, primarily relating to rhyme and to any metrical differences between the lines. We could get AA rhyme (i.e. if this was a rhyming couplet) by a condition such as:

A line rhymes with a line to which it is adjacent at gridline 0.

At gridline 0 the two lines are undifferentiated by the grid, but at gridline 1 the lines differ because one projects and the other does not. Counting by grid differentiates the counted elements; this differentiation can be seen in differences between the lines which perhaps arise precisely because the lines are counted by grid. Asymmetrical two-line-groups include English poulter's measure (6+7 foot line-pair), the Greek elegiac couplet (hexameter + 'pentameter' line-pair) or Welsh *Toddaid* (10+9 syllable line-pair). I suggest a general condition, along the following lines:

A longer line projects to gridline 1.

Thus the poulter's measure will project as in line-group (a) and the *Toddaid* and elegiac couplet will project as in line-group (b). In principle, we could equally have written the condition as 'A shorter line projects to gridline 1'. But there is an analogy between the asymmetries in the line-group and the asymmetries in the metrical line; greater prominence in the metrical line tends to mean further projection in the grid. While this is not a universal requirement (we saw that in Sanskrit classical metres, short and presumably less prominent syllables can project further than long syllables) it nevertheless is a broad correlation. Similarly, it may be that asymmetries involving line length might usefully be captured by making the longer line project further, always allowing for the possibility of letting the shorter line project further.

Once we reach three-line-groups, we have many possible ways of building a grid. This is one option:

Table 6.3 *Three-line-group (a)*

	bracket	foot size	direction	head
line 0	(	ternary	L>R	right

```
  L L L
(* * *(   0
      *   1
```

The grid for three-line-group (a) could project from a rhyming triplet (AAA rhyme) or from Welsh *Englyn Unodl Crwca* (7+7+16 syllables), where the longest line would project to gridline 1. Alternatively, we might project the head to the left to get a grid which would project from Welsh *Englyn Unodl Union* (16+7+7 syllables), where again the longest line would project to gridline 1.

An alternative would be to build the three-line-group by constructing binary feet at gridline 0.

Table 6.4 *Three-line-group (b)*

	bracket	foot size	direction	head	final foot
line 0	)	binary	R>L	right	unary
line 1	)	binary	R>L	right	

```
    L  L L
   *) * *)   0
)  *    *)   1
        *    2
```

This structure could be used to project from tercets, three-line-groups rhyming ABA then BCB then CDC etc. The condition would be:

Rhyme holds between two lines which project as adjacent asterisks at gridline 1. The line which projects to gridline 2 rhymes with the line projecting to gridline 0 in the previous line-group.

Alternatively, we might have the rules and structure, changing the position of the gridline 0 foot.

Table 6.5 *Three-line-group (c)*

	bracket	foot size	direction	head	final foot
line 0	)	binary	R>L	left	unary
line 1	)	binary	R>L	right	

```
  L  L L
  *) * *)   0
  )* *   )  1
       *    2
```

This could be used to project the 5+7+5 mora pattern of the Japanese haiku where the longest line projects to gridline 2. It is easy to make grids count to any number, and by itself this proves nothing about how the line-group is counted. However, the fact that line-groups are often asymmetrical is in part explained by the possibility that they are counted by building a grid.

Four-line-groups might be built from binary or ternary feet. This is one way of building them from binary feet:

Table 6.6 *Four-line-group (a)*

	bracket	foot size	direction	head
line 0	)	binary	R>L	left
line 1	)	binary	R>L	right

```
  L L L L
  )**) * *)   0
  )*   *   )  1
       *      2
```

We could attach various conditions to this, which relate to length of lines and to rhyme:

Condition	Pattern
The longest line projects to gridline 1.	4+3+4+3 foot line (English 'common metre')
The longest line projects to gridline 2.	3+3+4+3 foot line (English 'short metre') 9+9+10+9 syllable line (Welsh *Gwawdodyn*)
Rhyme holds between lines which are foot-adjacent at gridline 0.	AABB rhyme
Rhyme holds between lines which are foot-adjacent at gridline 1 and between other lines.	ABAB rhyme

| Rhyme holds between lines which do not project to gridline 1. | –A–A rhyme |
| Rhyme holds between lines which do not project to gridline 2. | AA–A rhyme (*Rubaiyat* rhyme scheme) |

While this type of grid can have various conditions attached to it, there are some types of line-group which are best dealt with by a different type of grid, such as the following:

Table 6.7 *Four-line-group (b)*

	bracket	foot size	direction	head	final foot
line 0	)	ternary	R>L	right	unary
line 1	)	binary	R>L	right	

```
  L  L L L
 *) * * *)  0
 ) *     *)  1
         *   2
```

Condition: Rhyme holds between lines which are foot-adjacent at gridline 1 and between other lines.

This suits Tennyson's *In Memoriam* stanza with its rhyme pattern of ABBA.

Five-line-groups are not common in English, and the patterns found show mainly ABABB and ABAAB rhymes. I suggest the following rules and grids, which differ only in the placement of the gridline 0 head:

Table 6.8 *Five-line-group (a)*

	bracket	foot size	direction	head	final foot
line 0	)	ternary	R>L	right	binary
line 1	)	binary	R>L	right	

```
  A B A A B   (rhyme scheme)
  L L L L L
 * *)* * *)     0
 )  *    *)     1
         *      2
```

Condition: Rhyme holds between lines which are foot-adjacent at gridline 1 and between other lines.

Table 6.9 *Five-line-group (b)*

	bracket	foot size	direction	head	final foot
line 0	)	ternary	R>L	left	binary
line 1	)	binary	R>L	right	

```
A B A B B   (rhyme scheme)
L L L L L
* *)* * *)      0
)*   *    )      1
     *          2
```

Condition: Rhyme holds between lines which are foot-adjacent at gridline 1 and between other lines.

Six-line-groups in English include the tail rhyme stanza rhyming AABCCB, often with lengths 443443, which can be dealt with by ternary feet:

```
A A B C C B
L L L L L L
(* * *(* * *(   0
(    *     *(   1
          *    2
```

The Burns stanza, with rhyme AAABAB and lengths 444242, can be dealt with by building three binary feet; here lines projecting just to gridline 1 are two-foot lines which rhyme.

```
A A A B A B
L L L L L L
(* *(* *(* *(   0
(   *   *   *(   1
    *           2
```

The third common type of six-line stanza, the *Venus and Adonis* stanza, has ABABCC rhyme; the special status of the ending can be achieved by shifting the grid head to the end. Now heads projecting to gridline 2 rhyme only with the adjacent syllable; otherwise heads projecting to gridline 1 rhyme with each other and non-heads rhyme with each other.

```
A B A B C C
L L L L L L
(* *(* *(* *(   0
(   *   *   *(   1
          *    2
```

Compound grids

For groups of seven and more lines, I suggest that the line-group is built by combining two separate grids. This fits well with the internal structures of these line-groups, as I now show.

The only common seven-line stanza is Chaucer's *Troilus* stanza rhyming ABABBCC. I suggest we see this as projecting first the grid for five-line-group (b) and then the grid for a two-line-group, so that it is structured as ABABB+CC. There are several types of eight-line stanza, which I propose to analyse as follows:

a   *ottava rima* stanza ABABABCC   = ABABAB + CC
b   ABABCDCD   = ABAB + CDCD
c   ABBACDDC   = ABBA + CDDC
d   ABABCDCD   = ABAB + CCDD
e   Provençal *ballade* ABABBCBC   = ABAB + BCBC

While there is no problem in principle with building a grid to count up to eight, of these rhyme schemes only (b) would be easy to state over such a grid. Breaking the line-group into two sections in this manner makes the internal shifts in rhyme scheme easy to handle. This approach fits with the intuition of critics. Häublein (1978:29) comments about eight-line stanzas that they have a precarious unity, and are likely to split into two quatrains. Puttenham (1589:93) suggests that eight- and ten-line stanzas need to have rhyme between the first and second halves 'lest otherwise the staffe should fall asunder and seeme two staues'.

The only common nine-line stanza is the Spenserian stanza with a rhyme pattern of ABABBCBCC (and the last line is a hexameter). Again, this can be split into two grids, as follows:

```
A B A B B   C B C C   (rhyme scheme)
L L L L L   L L L L
(* *(* *(*  (* *(* *(        0
(  *  * *(  (  *   *(        1
     *           *          2
```

Conditions: (Grid A left, Grid B right)
          Grid A: lines adjacent at gridline 1 rhyme; other lines rhyme
          Grid B: line projecting to gridline 2 rhymes with line projecting to gridline 2 in Grid A; other lines rhyme.

Häublein comments that stanzas longer than nine lines are rare in English, and tend to be invented for particular poems. He also comments that such stanzas tend to be heterometric. Finally, consider the sonnet, which is a group of fourteen lines, but undoubtedly best handled by splitting into sub-grids (4+4+6 in the Italian, where the octave itself is generally rather clearly split; 4+4+4+2 in the English).

Is there evidence that lines are counted by building a grid?

On the page there is fairly direct visual evidence for the number of lines in a stanza; the height of the stanza directly relates to the number of lines (which is not as true for the length of a line and the number of syllables), and there are indentation techniques used to make the structure and hence size of a stanza visually clear. Thus there is not obviously a need to appeal to some special generative mechanism, with the ontological and cognitive cost this entails, in order to count lines into a line-group.

However, I have spent some time on showing how lines might be counted into grids in order to answer a question which might not otherwise even have been asked. The question is: why do lines often differ in length within a stanza and why do lines usually rhyme in complex patterns within a stanza? The answer to this question is that these are exploitations of the way the lines are counted into the stanza. A quatrain with an ABAB-rhyme 4343-foot pattern shows a periodic pattern because it exploits the periodic binary grid required to count up to four. These kinds of complex systematic structure seem to be characteristic of stanzas rather than stichic texts (i.e. texts not divided into stanzas). If stanzas are counted by building grids then we can explain why. Stanza organisation is like metricality, involving specialised mechanisms but thereby opening up kinds of complexity otherwise unavailable.

6.4   Lineation and line-grouping in oral narratives

It has been claimed, particularly by Dell Hymes (1981) and Dennis Tedlock (1978, 1983) that oral narratives in some narrative traditions can be analysed as verse. The narratives in question are not metrical, and do not involve canonic parallelism or other highly ostensive methods for communicating that they are divided into lines. Instead, division into lines, and into line-groups is evidenced by a combination of formal and semantic characteristics of the text (for a summary see Fabb 1997:193–220). These are thus implicit verse traditions (not overtly recognised as verse), as opposed to the explicit verse traditions discussed elsewhere in this book. In this section I look at the possibility that lines and line-groups are implied in oral narratives.

Evidence for lineation and line-grouping is particularly convincing for North American narrative traditions. Literary traditions exploit different kinds of form, and it is not necessarily the case that all narrative traditions have lineation and line-grouping. Even within the same tradition some narratives might be verse, others not, and others might have an intermediate status between verse and prose with lineation as an emergent formal characteristic of the text. In this section I will suggest that there is evidence for lineation and line-grouping in English oral narratives; I will use as an example the following narrative.

There were one of the Sydenham maids, and her got herself betrothed to Sir Francis Drake. But afore they could be married, he had to go away on a voyage, and how long it'd be afore he could come back, no-one knew, and he didn't trust her father. So they took their troth-plight, the two of them, afore Drake sailed away. Well, he sailed away, for three long years, and Sir George Sydenham, he found another suitor for his daughter, a much richer one. Well, no matter what the maid do say, marriage were announced, and she were half afraid of Sir Francis Drake, but she were more afraid of her father. So she gave in.

Well now, Sir Francis Drake, he did some very strange things – he did sit on Plymouth Hoe, a-whittling of a stick, and all the chips that fell into the sea, they did turn into ships, to go fight the Spanish Armada. Now, although he'd been gone three years, he knew what was happening, so at the very door of the church, he dropped a red-hot cannonball in front of the bridal party. Oh! Give 'em a fright, did – and when he come home at last, 'twas to find his bride and her dear father waiting for him with smiles. As for t'other bridegroom, he'd a taken hisself across the length and breadth of England. But I expect Sir Francis Drake knew where he was too!

(Told by a member of Watchet Women's Institute, 1950. (Briggs and Tongue 1964:94, reproduced in Briggs 1970:39). Spelling Standardised.)

This is a representation of an oral narrative. Some of the specifically oral characteristics are lost, and so cannot be used in our analysis (e.g. intonation is used to indicate narrative structure in some traditions (Woodbury 1987) but here we cannot make reference to it). The representation divides the narrative into two major groups (i.e. two paragraphs); I will show that there is good evidence for this basic division from other aspects of the text.

In many traditions, including explicit verse traditions, the line tends to correspond to the sentence. In chapter 5 I suggested that this might be formalised for English verse as a weak conditional:

(17) If this is the end of a sentence then it is the end of a line.

For this oral narrative I propose to make the notion of 'sentence' more precise by redefining the relevant constituent as a syntactic constituent with its own verb, which usually means either a root or subordinate sentence.

(18) If this is the first word in a syntactic constituent which has its own verb then it is the beginning of a line.

This conditional will derive a set of conclusions about the narrative which divide it into the following sequence of thirty-three lines. If we apply this conditional to any text, we thereby conclude that it is in lines (i.e. verse). I explain the line-groupings (left-hand column) next.

¶A	There were one of the Sydenham maids,	1
	and her got herself betrothed to Sir Francis Drake.	2

¶B	But afore they could be married,	3
	he had to go away on a voyage,	4
	and how long it'd be	5
	afore he could come back,	6
	no-one knew,	7
	and he didn't trust her father.	8
¶C	So they took their troth-plight, the two of them,	9
	afore Drake sailed away.	10
¶D	Well, he sailed away, for three long years,	11
	and Sir George Sydenham, he found another suitor for his daughter, a much richer one.	12
¶E	Well, no matter what the maid do say,	13
	marriage were announced,	14
	and she were half afraid of Sir Francis Drake,	15
	but she were more afraid of her father.	16
¶F	So she gave in.	17
¶G	Well now, Sir Francis Drake, he did some very strange things –	18
	he did sit on Plymouth Hoe,	19
	a-whittling of a stick,	20
	and all the chips that fell into the sea,	21
	they did turn into ships,	22
	to go fight the Spanish Armada.	23
¶H	Now, although he'd been gone three years,	24
	he knew what was happening,	25
¶I	so at the very door of the church, he dropped a red-hot cannonball in front of the bridal party.	26
	Oh! Give 'em a fright, did –	27
¶J	and when he come home at last,	28
	'twas to find	29
	his bride and her dear father waiting for him with smiles.	30
¶K	As for t'other bridegroom, he'd a taken hisself across the length and breadth of England.	31
¶L	But I expect	32
	Sir Francis Drake knew where he was too!	33

By itself this tells us nothing; any text can be divided into sections based on one verb per section. It will need confirmation from elsewhere. The division into lines receives some local strengthening from a conditional involving parallelism. In some narrative traditions, parallelism plays a significant role in evidencing the line and the line-group. We might formulate a conditional (19):

> (19) If this section of text is parallel to a preceding or following section of text then it is a line.

Parallelism is a kind of interpretive resemblance; as a relation between two sections of text it is not a fact but an inference. Parallelism can be inferred (weakly) between lines 10 and 11 and (more strongly) between 15 and 16. This strengthens the conclusion that at least these sections of the text are lines.

Now I propose to divide the text into line-groups. As is often the case, selected connectives demarcate the line-groups fairly systematically. I propose the following conditional:

> (20) If this line begins with a connective 'but', 'so', 'well' or 'now' then it is the first line in a line-group.

This is related to a connective used in the analysis of line-groups in explicit verse:

> (13) If this line begins with 'but' then it is the first line in a line-group.

Note that 'and' is not included in (20) though it is a discourse connective; in this narrative it does not seem to contribute systematically to line-grouping. Applying this conditional to the text, we derive all the line-groups given above except for ¶J and ¶K (for which there is other evidence). These connectives are only used at the beginnings of line-groups, but they are not used at the beginning of every line-group. This kind of tendential relation between linguistic and literary form is characteristic of implied rather than generative or determinate form, and is good evidence that line-grouping is an implicature of the text rather than an observer-independent fact of the text.

The evidence for lines and line-grouping considered so far is basically evidence from linguistic form. However, content plays an important role in implying narrative form. Smith (1968) distinguishes two kinds of structure in a literary text: formal structure and thematic structure. Formal structure arises by text-internal repetition, and is the primary focus of the present book. Thematic structure is the deployment of patterned and stereotyped meaning in the text, and thus includes various kinds of conventional expression, topoi, motifs, character-functions (Propp 1968), etc. In metrical verse, which I have concentrated on for the most part, there is plenty to say about formal structure without ever really needing to refer to thematic structure. The same can not be said of narrative structure, where thematic structure has a much more dominant role, and where Smith's 'formal structure' tends neither to be as complex nor as codified and explicit as in metrical verse. Formal structure and thematic structure are more closely linked in narratives: the close association between the line and the sentence in narrative is because the line is a coherent meaning group (i.e. we do not really find 'enjambment' in a narrative). The same is true of line-groups. Thus we might exploit a conditional used earlier in this chapter, but with a much more central role in defining the line-group in oral narrative:

> (14) If these lines form a line-group then they are a distinct unit of meaning.

Being 'a distinct unit of meaning' is itself something which has to be decided; a section of text can be interpreted as distinct on the basis of various kinds of evidence. (14) can provide evidence for making ¶J a line-group because it describes the return home; this is a distinct unit of meaning in that it involves a new arrangement of participants, time and place. Similarly (14) provides evidence for making ¶K a line-group because it describes the distinct action of the bridegroom. Conditionals like (14) are fairly weak, because of the weakness of the notion of 'distinct unit of meaning'; however, they are likely to derive conclusions which in part coincide with the conclusions from (20) and thus these line-groups have their status strengthened.

This division into line-groups strengthens the evidence for division into lines. This is because all the connectives involved appear at the beginnings of lines (some connectives can also be sentence-internal in principle); thus there is a coincidence of line-group boundary and line boundary which strengthens the evidence for both types of form. Nevertheless, the evidence for lines and the evidence for line-groups is still quite weak. A very large number of texts might be divided into lines and line-groups by the conditionals listed so far. Thus we need to find more evidence that this lineation is really there. The evidence comes from counting the lines into the line-groups. This is what we find:

A	B	C	D	E	F	line-group
2	6	2	2	4	1	number of lines

	G	H	I	J	K	L	line-group
	6	2	2	3	1	2	number of lines

Comparing the two lines, aligned like this, there is a pattern. This suggests that the text is not just organised into sentences, some of which begin with connectives. Instead we have units organised into larger units in a pattern repeated across the text. The sizes of lines in parallel groups are almost exactly the same (only ¶E and ¶J differ). Thus there are two groups-of-groups or 'metagroups' (as reflected also in Ruth Tongue's transcription into two paragraphs). This finding strengthens the evidence for lines and for line-groups by conditionals such as (5), used earlier, and (21) which is clearly related to (19):

> (5) If this is a line-group then it will be of the same length as another line-group in the same poem.

(21) If this section of text is parallel to a preceding or following section of text then it is a metagroup.

Further evidence for the metagroup boundary comes from two sources. The second metagroup (beginning line 18) begins 'well now', which has two connectives from conditional (20) and thus might be taken as even stronger evidence than usual for a boundary; or alternatively as evidence for a stronger boundary (i.e. a metagroup boundary). And the line which concludes the first metagroup (line 17) is one of the shortest lines in the entire narrative, and thus I suggest exploits a conditional like (22):

(22) If this line-group is very short, it is at the end of a metagroup.

As we saw in the discussion of metrical verse, there are conditionals (2 and 11) which put short lines at the boundaries of line-groups; (19) seems to operate by the same principle of length difference at a boundary. Like most conditionals, it is weak; lines 7, 29 and 32 are also very short, which means that they weakly evidence the end of a metagroup as well, but no other conditional leads to the same result, so the conclusion that these are also metagroup boundaries remains vanishingly weak.

One of the consequences of this parallelism is that the first two lines and the last two lines fall out of the pattern. Evidence that this is correct comes from two more conditionals, which express general expectations about narrative structure:

(23) If this is the first line-group in a narrative it will describe the pre-existing circumstances at the beginning of the sequence of events.

(24) If this is the final line-group in a narrative it will describe events taking place after the end of the narrative proper.

(23) gives us what Labov and Waletzky (1967) call the 'orientation' of the story, and (24) the 'coda' of the story. Like other kinds of narrative form, the decision that a particular part of text is orientation and another part is coda is an inferential decision, based on available evidence and derived with a certain degree of strength. (There is often some ambiguity, with both orientation and coda being interpretable as separate from the story or as part of the story.) Conditional (7) can also be used here to further strengthen the evidence for the final line-group; it is a little unexpected to find a narrative ending on a couplet just as in many metrical verse texts, but this is what seems to be happening here:

(7) The last two lines of a text form a distinct line-group.

Note furthermore that both first and last line-groups include the phrase 'Sir Francis Drake'; this is also used at the beginning of the second major section (line 18) and only once otherwise, which suggests that this phrase is also deployed in a way which evidences the component structure of the narrative.

There are many advantages for texts to imply that they are divided into lines and line-groups. In narratives, these implicatures of form seem to function as ways of developing meanings which might not otherwise be communicated by an unorganised text. The strongly communicated central division of this narrative and the parallelism between the two halves can lead to an interpretation of the second half of the narrative as a reworking of the first half. The theme of knowledge is restated (line 7 and line 25); the theme of 'giving in' is restated in the parallel sections ¶F and ¶K; section ¶J inverts the parallel section ¶E (the father will or will not let his daughter marry Drake). And most significantly of all, perhaps, the long section ¶G can be taken to explain section ¶B. The reason for Drake's having to go away is never overtly explained, but if we read ¶G as Drake having to save his sexual potency in order to fight the Armada (he fights by 'whittling his stick' into the sea to make ships) then this explains why he cannot yet get married. This encourages a further reading of the story as in the first half relating to a human Drake who cannot act and 'does not know' and in the second half to a wizard Drake who is all action and knowledge (Briggs 1970:40 says that Drake was held to be a wizard). There are rich interpretive possibilities here, which are opened up precisely by first inferring for the narrative this organisation into lines and line-groups. The role of form here in opening up interpretation perhaps recalls Empson's (1953:28) comment on metrical verse that 'A metrical scheme imposes a sort of intensity of interpretation upon the grammar, which makes it fruitful even when there is no 'song'.'

This analysis thus shows that a division of an oral narrative into lines and line-groups can hold fairly strongly, and that this division has a role in organising the meaning of the narrative. The relation between linguistic form (sentence structure, use of connectives) and literary form (i.e. division into lines and line-groups) is fairly close, at least in this narrative, but it is not fully consistent. This is what we would expect if lineation and line-grouping are implicatures of the text.

Other kinds of implied form in narratives

I suggested that line-group ¶A might be identified as 'orientation' and line-group ¶L as 'coda'. Labov and Waletzky (1967) suggest that narratives can be divided into ordered functionally defined sub-sections, with the core of the narrative consisting of a complication followed by a resolution; it may be bracketed by orientation and coda. I suggest that these kinds of form hold by being implied; various kinds of evidence tell us for example that a particular section of the narrative is the complication or the resolution. Conclusions about the identities of these subsections might be strong or weak, and can be contradictory or ambiguous.

Consider for example the resolution. 'Being a complication' and 'being a resolution' are inferred characteristics of a text; they depend on what the hearer thinks the text is about. But the identification of a section of the text as the resolution is also achieved by formal means. Labov and Waletzky show that the arrival of the resolution in a narrative is heralded by various kinds of markedness, including quotation of direct speech, repetition, and so on; in particular there is commonly an intervention by the speaker into the narrative, evaluating the narrative, just before the resolution occurs. In the Drake narrative, line 27, 'Oh! Give 'em a fright, did – ', is the first explicit intervention into the narrative by the author, and includes the first exclamation in the narrative. This suggests that a conditional along the following lines is in operation:

> (25) If this line-group is an authorial intervention then the next line-group is
> the resolution.

This conditional weakly implies that the following line-group is the resolution. This is a weak implicature because formal markedness and authorial interventions do not guarantee that the resolution is about to come, and Labov (1972) allows authorial evaluations of this kind to be scattered through the narrative and not only before the end (see also Peterson and McCabe 1997). But (25) may strengthen a conclusion already reached on the basis of other inferences.

Another kind of narrative form claimed by Labov and Waletzky is between narrative clauses and other kinds of clause (narrative clauses are sometimes called storyline clauses; for a summary see Fabb 1997:165–77). For Labov and Waletzky, the identification of a clause as a narrative clause is a determinate fact about the text, just as much as identifying a word as a noun or verb is a determinate fact about the text. The basic criterion is that two clauses are narrative clauses if their sequence is itself meaningful: if two narrative clauses are reordered then the sequence of events they describe is also reordered. Thus narrative clauses are in a sequence which exactly represents the sequence of events.

There are several reasons for thinking that Labov and Waletzky's formulation is too strict, and that 'being a narrative clause' is not a determinate observer-independent kind of form. First, it has been argued that narrative clauses can be re-sequenced (for example in flashbacks, or in clause-topicalisation techniques of news reporting) without altering the order of the events (Bell 1995, but for a contrary view, Schokkenbroek 1999). This might depend on the genre, as Labov (1997:411) acknowledges. Second, there is another way of defining what a narrative clause is, which depends not on order but on other linguistic characteristics of the clause, which involves a tendential relation between linguistic form and 'being a narrative clause' (sometimes rephrased as 'being a storyline clause' but this is the same basic notion). Hopper and Thompson (1980) suggest that narrative clauses tend to have a high number of 'transitivity features' (such as having an agent, an affected patient, describing a real event, and so on), but that there is no absolute requirement that narrative clauses be highly transitive; instead it is a tendency. In languages with free placement of the verb (i.e. not English, but perhaps Old English), narrative clauses are likely to have the verb at the beginning or end rather than the middle of the sentence if the clause is a narrative clause (Longacre 1995), but again this is a tendency rather than a rigid rule. By these criteria, being a narrative clause is a matter of degree, and we might expect to get intermediate cases, clauses which show a mixture of narrative and non-narrative status. (It is worth noting that Labov and Waletzky's original proposal allows for an intermediate case between narrative and non-narrative clauses, a kind of clause which can be moved a little without affecting the narrative, but which cannot be moved too far.)

Given the approach to literary form promoted in this book, there are several ways that we can retain Labov and Waletzky's notion of narrative clause, fit it together with Hopper and Thompson's notion of the storyline clause, and allow for some flexibility of definition. First, we must ask how the sequence of narrative clauses expresses a sequence of events. I suggest that this must be an interpretive relation, operating by interpretive resemblance between the two sequences:

(26) Narrative clause A precedes narrative clause B.
             by resemblance
(27) Event described by narrative clause A precedes event described by narrative clause B.

Already, we have some flexibility, because resemblance can be strong or weak. In genres such as narratives of personal experience, where precedence of clauses almost guarantees precedence of events, this resemblance is held to be strong, such that the conclusion that there is a precedence of events is strong. In genres like news reporting, where the demands of information structure mean that there is sometimes an inverse relation between order of sentences and order of events, the interpretive relation is held to be weak.

The second possibility relates to the identification of a clause as a narrative clause. For Labov and Waletzky the 'precedence test' tells us whether a clause is or is not a narrative clause. We can retain this test, but instead focus on the notion of 'precedence' and the sequence of clauses. In discussing stanzaic sequence earlier, I suggested that the sequence of stanzas might appear to be an explicature of the text but that in fact it is an implicature of the text; the only explicature is the actual vertical order on the page or temporal order in speech. This vertical order is interpreted by resemblance as implying a certain sequence of contents. The same might be true for the characterisation of narrative clauses; temporal order (which is an explicature) may be out-competed by other kinds of evidence in determining which clauses are taken to 'precede' other clauses. Thus while precedence might tell us which the narrative clauses are, precedence is not itself a determinate relation between two clauses. Thus 'being a narrative clause' will hold only as strongly as precedence holds. This, again, might be made genre-dependent.

Finally 'being a story' or 'being a narrative' is probably best thought of as a kind of implied generic form (like 'being a sonnet'). One of Rubin's (1995) criticisms of linguistic approaches to narrative which involve the use of 'story grammars' to generate stories (and by implication specialised kinds of narrative cognition) is that they falsely assume a categorial distinction between story and non-story. In the approach suggested here, none of the special characteristics of narratives involve specialised types of cognition; 'this is a narrative clause' is just an inference which might be formulated alongside other inferences such as 'this is a narrative'.

Do narratives have generated form?

In this book I have proposed that literary texts have three kinds of form: form which is generated, form which is explicit and form which is implied. Of these three kinds of form, the most 'ontologically expensive' is generated form because it requires a small but dedicated cognitive system to create it. The only kind of generated form which seems well justified is generated metrical form, projecting from a linguistic representation of the line. There is little reason to think that narrative form in general is generated. This is primarily because most kinds of narrative form hold to a certain extent and are not fully regulated, not categorially present or absent.

There have been attempts to argue that a whole narrative is like a whole sentence, and has the same kind of form as a sentence. If this were true, it might suggest that narratives have generated form, because sentences certainly have generated form. Thus we might write a 'story grammar' which generates a narrative just as grammatical rules generate a sentence (see Rubin 1995:30, who evaluates but in the end rejects such an approach). But in practice, the similarity between a narrative and a sentence holds by analogy rather than rigorously, with notions such as 'subject' and 'predicate' reinterpreted metaphorically as components of narrative. Most telling is the fact that the generated form of a sentence is basically hierarchical rather than linear, such that what differentiates a sentence subject from a sentence object is that the subject is higher in the structure than the object, not that it precedes it. In syntax the linear ordering of component parts is important, but is subordinated to the asymmetrical hierarchical relation between them (Kayne 1994). Syntactic structures are basically asymmetric hierarchical structures. There is indeed hierarchy in a narrative, so that for example an episode might contain sub-episodes. But as Labov and Waletzky (1967) showed, the key relations are linear: one sentence follows another, one episode follows another. Rubin (1995:191) has a further criticism even of the relatively flat hierarchical structures claimed for narratives: hierarchical structures are not well suited to expressing the linear relation between narrative units, and are not well suited to expressing the procedural kind of memory characteristic of oral traditions. Thus the apparent similarity between narratives and sentences is superficial, providing no basis for a generative rule system or 'story grammar' which can create a narrative.

There is one possible area in which generative rules might play a role in narrative. As the analysis of the Drake story shows, counting seems to be important in oral narratives. Lines are counted into line-groups, and line-groups are counted into groups-of-groups. Hymes (1992:93) suggests that common patterns involve counts of two and four units, or counts of three and five units; he calls these 'pattern numbers' and shows that they are characteristic of whole literary traditions. It is worth asking whether this kind of counting involves a grid. I have argued that in order to count syllables into a line, and possibly lines into a line-group in metrical verse, a counting-grid is the best option. But for narratives this is not obviously the case. First, the numbers involved are generally low, usually up to about five (episodes, lines, characters etc.). Second, the pattern numbers can be understood as mimicking other counted-out things which are manifested elsewhere in the culture; the Yupik pattern of five (4+1) may mimic the hand, while the Lakota pattern of four may mimic the four directions of the wind. (Butterworth (1999:33) discusses other ways in which ritual can be the basis of a counting system which operates basically by mimicry.)

However, there are two reasons which justify at least continued speculation that grids might be used to count narrative elements. First, the common patterns of three divided into 2+1 (e.g. two unsuccessful attempts to do something followed by one successful attempt) could be seen as based on a simple grid with a single ternary foot, where one of the three elements is designated as the head:

unsuccessful   unsuccessful   successful
(*   *   *   (0
                                *   1

Second, if narrative elements are counted by building grids it explains why patterns of five can usually be broken down into 3+2, and patterns of four can usually be broken down into 2+2. This suggests that counting is basically binary or ternary. By themselves these kinds of evidence for using a grid are insufficient, but they suggest that we should leave open the possibility that grids are used for counting for a wider range of texts than just metrical verse.

6.5   Summary

In this chapter I have suggested that line-groups are analogous to metrical lines in two ways. First, the line-group as a unit of text, like the line as a unit of text, is a kind of implied form, holding of the text only as the content of a thought about the text. Layout is just another kind of evidence for line-grouping and does not finally determine line-grouping as a fact of the text. The second analogy between the line-group and the metrical line is in the suggestion that both might have their internal structures counted out by a similar mechanism, which builds a differentiated grid. Just as the stress maximum rule takes a 'free ride' on the binary grid built to count iambic pentameter, so rhyme schemes such as ABAB take a 'free ride' on the binary grid built to count a quatrain. In the final section of the chapter I looked at a kind of text otherwise unexplored in this book: the oral narrative. There is a tradition of treating oral narrative as having a tendency towards lineation and line-grouping. I showed that the tendential aspects of this are compatible with the general account of lineation and line-grouping as kinds of implied form. While this book has concentrated until now exclusively on metrical verse, the proposal that literary form is almost always implied form should extend beyond metrical verse to oral narratives which have verse-like structures.

7   Complexity

My goal in this book has been to establish what literary form is, and how it holds of a text or a performance of the text. I have proposed two fundamentally different ways in which literary form holds. The generated metrical form holds of the text by virtue of being generated by rule from a linguistic representation of the text. In contrast, the explicit literary form and the implied literary form hold of a text by virtue of being the content of thoughts about the text. The explicit form is a thought about the superficial facts of the performance such as the thought that 'there are fourteen words with no words to their right'; the implied form is derived by inference, either by interpretive use (resemblance between two thoughts) or by modus ponens ('if . . . then' deductions based on conditionals).

These different kinds of literary form exist only because literary form holds between a person and a performance of a text, and is not a context- and user-independent and inherent fact of the text itself. This psychological status for form leads to the split between generated metrical form on the one hand and explicit and implied form on the other. More significantly, it means that since most literary form is implied form, therefore most literary form takes on the complexities, indeterminacies, ambiguities and contradictions which are characteristic of inferential processes. While specific texts are composed in ways which accentuate these difficulties, the difficulties are present wherever there is literary form. Literary form is by its nature complex and multiple.

Throughout this book I have suggested that the multiplicity of literary form is experienced as aesthetic. In some cases, the multiplicity is a mass of weak implicatures, which Sperber and Wilson suggest constitute a 'poetic effect' and are hence experienced as aesthetic. In other cases, the multiplicity involves indeterminacy and choice; dividing a text into lines, establishing which syllables project and which metre holds, often involve choices between a large number of possibilities. This choice, I suggest, is again experienced as aesthetic. The third kind of multiplicity is the contradictoriness and incompatibility between different conclusions about the literary form of the text. Following Empson and others, I suggest again that this contradictoriness is experienced as aesthetic.

My strategy has been to separate form off from other aspects of the text, and look at it independently. As a strategy, this is characteristic of generative linguistics, which works by isolating problems and dealing with them separately rather than attempting a single holistic account. This correlates with the modular nature of how we process language. I have attempted to describe the aesthetic experience of form while separating form off from other aspects of the text and its performance. Thus I have claimed that being in some state of cognitive complexity counts as being in a state of aesthetic experience. But this cannot be the full story, because we would not want to claim that all kinds of experience of complexity, multiplicity and contradiction are aesthetic experiences. If literary form is experienced as aesthetic then it somehow relates to other aspects of the literary experience. I now suggest two further factors which may explain why literary formal complexity is experienced as aesthetic. The first is meaning, and the second is the particularity of a text's performance. (In this context, see also MacMahon's (2001) Relevance-Theoretic account of 'unstable authorial attitudes'.) I suggest that in both cases formal complexity is experienced as aesthetic because it is itself in contradiction with these other aspects of the text. These are kinds of 'tension'.

By making literary form the content of thoughts about a text, I have in effect claimed that literary form is just another kind of meaning. A text communicates thoughts about the world which it represents but it also communicates thoughts about itself. There are undoubtedly local relations between thoughts about form and thoughts about meaning; these are the kinds of formal symbolism which are common in literary texts, including for example the relation between enjambment and meanings of flow or flight (pp. 149, 162). These relations involve emergent conditionals, and are part of specific inferences. It is easy to understand how these relations hold between literary form and literary meaning because in both cases we are dealing with thoughts, and we know how one thought can lead to another. By themselves these local relations are not enough to explain how meaning pushes formal complexity into aesthetic experience. Instead I suggest that there is a basic tension between the two kinds of meaning implied by a text; on the one hand, a text tells us about some reality external to the text itself, the world of its author or its fictional characters. On the other hand, the text tells us about itself; it not only tells us things which on the whole are completely unconnected to the world it represents (in Browning's sonnet cited at the beginning of this book, there is no general relation between lineation and rhyme on the one hand, and the relation between writer and addressee on the other). Not only does it tell us all these other things – about rhyme, lineation, metre, genre – it also tells us these things in ways which can be difficult to grasp, indeterminate and contradictory. Thus while form might locally relate to meaning, the persistence and persistent complexity of form in general works against meaning. I suggest that this is one of the reasons that literary texts have form whose complexity is experienced in a particular way. More than any other kind of form, literary form demands our attention at the same time as our attention is also demanded by literary content. This is a tension between form and meaning.

There is another tension between form and performance. This is what Foucault calls the distinction between structure (form) and event (performance), with the event as 'the domain of absolute contingency' and structure as the attempt to rationally grasp absolute contingency (Rabinow 1986:113). It is also the distinction between the density of the text itself and the articulation of any representation (e.g. transcription) of the text (Goodman 1976). There is always a gap between the formal explicature which is stated in an abstract vocabulary and the performed text itself, which is only particularities. Thus we have another basic contradiction between the performed text which in itself has no form at all, and the thoughts about the text which give the text its form. But this gap is not just a gap between not having form and having form; it is a gap between not having form and having kinds of form which are complex, indeterminate, ambiguous and contradictory. Thus the multiplicity of literary form is in tension with the formlessness of the performance itself.

Literary form is complex because it is a matter of how the text is thought, and because it is not a fact about any instance of the text. This complexity is further complicated by the fact that form is developed from performances which by their 'absolute contingency' are in themselves formless. And the formal complexity is complicated by its coexistence with a collection of 'external' meanings (the content of the text) with which it has no general relation. Verbal art is experienced as aesthetic because it exploits to the full every option for making verbal behaviour difficult.

Bibliography

Allott, Miriam and Super, Robert H. (ed.) 1986, *Matthew Arnold*. Oxford: Oxford University Press.

Andrew, Malcolm and Waldron, Ronald (eds.) 1996, *The Poems of the Pearl Manuscript*. Exeter: University of Exeter Press.

Arnold, E. Vernon 1905, *Vedic Metre in its Historical Development*. Cambridge: Cambridge University Press.

Atkins, H. G. 1942, 'Holding Down the Trochees'. *Modern Language Review* 37: 356–8.

Attridge, Derek 1974, *Well-weighed Syllables: Elizabethan Verse in Classical Metres*. Cambridge: Cambridge University Press.

1982, *The Rhythms of English Poetry*. London: Longman.

Austin, T. R. 1984, *Language Crafted. A Linguistic Theory of Poetic Syntax*. Bloomington: Indiana University Press.

Bamberg, Michael G. W. 1997, *Oral Versions of Personal Experience: Three Decades of Narrative Analysis*. *Journal of Narrative and Life History*, volume 7, special issue. London: Lawrence Erlbaum.

Banti, G. and Giannattasio, F. 1996, 'Music and Metre in Somali Poetry'. In Hayward, R. J. and Lewis, I. M. (eds.), *Voice and Power. The Culture of Language in North-East Africa*, pp. 83–128. London: School of Oriental and African Studies.

Bauman, Richard 1975, 'Verbal Art as Performance'. *American Anthropologist* 77: 290–311.

Bell, Alan 1995, 'News Time'. *Text & Society* 3(4):305–28.

Bridges, Robert 1921, *Milton's Prosody*. Oxford: Clarendon Press.

Briggs, K. M. (ed.) 1970, *A Dictionary of British Folk Tales in the English Language. Part B: Folk Legends*. Volume II. London: Routledge.

Briggs, K. M. and Tongue, R. L. 1966, *Folktales of England*. London: Routledge.

Brogan, T. V. F. 1981, *English Versification, 1570–1980: A Reference Guide*. Baltimore: Johns Hopkins University Press.

1999, *English Versification, 1570–1980: A Reference Guide. Hypertext Version*. http://ham.t.u-shizuoka-ken.ac.jp/versif/Versification.html. Based on Brogan 1981, *English Versification*.

Browning, Elizabeth Barrett 1889, *The Poetical Works of Elizabeth Barrett Browning*. 6 volumes. London: Smith Elder & Co.

Butterworth, Brian 1999, *The Mathematical Brain*. London: Macmillan.

Bysshe, Edward 1705, *The Art of English Poetry*. 2nd edition, London. Reprinted by Garland, New York, 1971.

Campion, Thomas 1602, *Observations on the Art of English Poesie*. In Smith 1904, *Elizabethan Critical Essays*, II:327–55.

Chomsky, Noam 1957, *Syntactic Structures*. The Hague: Mouton.

Chomsky, Noam and Halle, Morris 1968, *The Sound Pattern of English*. New York: Harper & Row.

Clancy, Thomas Owen and Márkus, Gilbert 1995, *Iona. The Earliest Poetry of a Celtic Monastery*. Edinburgh: Edinburgh University Press.

Clough, A. H. (Mrs) (ed.) 1869, *The Poems and Prose Remains of Arthur Hugh Clough*. 2 volumes. London: Macmillan.

Coulson, M. 1992, *Sanskrit. An Introduction to the Classical Language (Teach Yourself Sanskrit)*. 2nd edition. London: Hodder & Stoughton.

Culler, Jonathan 1973, *Structuralist Poetics: Structuralism, Linguistics and the Study of Literature*. London: Routledge and Kegan Paul.

Cureton, Richard 1992, *Rhythmic Phrasing in English Verse*. London: Longman.

Daniel, Samuel 1603, *A Defence of Rhyme*. In Smith 1904, *Elizabethan Critical Essays*, II:356–84.

Darbishire, Helen (ed.) 1952, *The Poetical Works of John Milton*. 2 volumes. Oxford: Oxford University Press.

Davis, Herbert (ed.) 1966, *Pope. Poetical Works*. London: Oxford University Press.

Devine, A. M. and Stephens, L. D. 1984, *Language and Metre. Resolution, Porson's Bridge, and Their Prosodic Basis*. Chico, CA: Scolar's Press.

Dixon, R. M. W. 1972, *The Dyirbal Language of North Queensland*. Cambridge: Cambridge University Press.

Dixon, R. M. W. and Koch, G. 1996, *Dyirbal Song Poetry. The Oral Literature of an Australian Rainforest people*. St Lucia: University of Queensland Press.

Duncan, Thomas G. (ed.) 1995, *Mediaeval English Lyrics 1200–1400*. Harmondsworth: Penguin.

Empson, William 1953, *Seven Types of Ambiguity*. 3rd edition. London: Chatto and Windus.

Fabb, Nigel 1997, *Linguistics and Literature: Language in the Verbal Arts of the World*. Oxford: Blackwell.

1999, 'Verse Constituency and the Locality of Alliteration'. *Lingua* 108: 223–45.

2001, 'Weak Monosyllables in Iambic Verse and the Communication of Metrical Form'. *Lingua* 111(11): 771–90.

2002, 'The Metres of "Dover Beach"'. *Language and Literature* 11(2):111–129.

Fabb, Nigel and Halle, Morris 2001, 'The Delimitation of Feet in Metrical Verse', paper given at the Linguistic Society of America, January 2001.

(in preparation), *A Treatise on Meter*.

Fieler, Frank B. (ed.) 1968, *Barnabe Googe. Eglogs, Epytaphes, and Sonettes*. Gainesville, FL: Scolars Facsimiles and Reprints.

FitzGerald, Edward 1954, *Rubáiyát of Omar Khayyám*. Maine, George F. (ed.). London: Collins.

Fitzgerald, Colleen 1998, 'The Meter of Tohono O'odham Songs'. *International Journal of American Linguistics* 64(1):1–36.

Fodor, J. 1975, *The Language of Thought*. New York: Thomas Y. Crowell.

1983, *The Modularity of Mind*. Cambridge, MA: MIT Press.

Fowler, Alastair (ed.) 1991, *The New Oxford Book of Seventeenth Century Verse*. Oxford: Oxford University Press.

Fox, J. J. (ed.) 1988, *To Speak in Pairs. Essays on the Ritual Languages of Eastern Indonesia*. Cambridge: Cambridge University Press.

Freeman, Donald C. (ed.) 1970, *Linguistics and Literary Style*. New York: Holt, Rinehart and Winston.

Fuller, J. (ed.) 2000, *The Oxford Book of Sonnets*. Oxford: Oxford University Press.

Gascoigne, George 1575, *Certayne Notes of Instruction*. In Smith 1904, *Elizabeth Critical Essays*, I:46–57.

Gaskill, H. 1996, *The Poems of Ossian and Related Works*. Edinburgh: Edinburgh University Press.

Golston, C. 1998, 'Constraint-based Metrics'. *Natural Language and Linguistic Theory* 16:718–70.

Goodman, N. 1976, *Languages of Art: An Approach to the Theory of Symbols*. Indianapolis, IN: Hackett.

Halle, Morris 1987, 'A Biblical Pattern Poem'. In Fabb, Nigel, Attridge, Derek, Durant, Alan and MacCabe, Colin (eds.), *The Linguistics of Writing*, pp. 252–64. Manchester: Manchester University Press.

1992, 'On Metric Verse in the Psalms'. Unpublished typescript.

2001, 'On Stress and Meter and on English Iambics in Particular'. Unpublished typescript.

Halle, Morris and Idsardi, William 1995, In Goldsmith, J. (ed.) *The Handbook of Phonological Theory*, pp. 403–43. Oxford: Blackwell.

Halle, Morris and Keyser, Samuel Jay 1966, 'Chaucer and the Study of Prosody'. *College English* 28:187–219.

1971, *English Stress. Its Form, Its Growth and Its Role in Verse*. New York: Harper and Row.

1999, 'On Meter in General and on Robert Frost's Loose Iambics in Particular'. In Muraki, M. and Iwamoto, E. (eds.), *Linguistics: In Search of the Human Mind. A festschrift for Kazuko Inoue*, pp. 130–53. Tokyo: Kaitakusha.

Halle, Morris and Vergnaud, J-R. 1987, *An Essay on Stress*. Cambridge MA: MIT Press.

Hanson, K. and Kiparsky, Paul 1996, 'A Parametric Theory of Poetic Meter.' *Language* 72(2):287–335.

Hartley, Anthony 1965, *Mallarmé*. Harmondsworth: Penguin.

Häublein, Eric 1978, *The Stanza*. London: Methuen.

Hayden, John O. (ed.) 1977, *William Wordsworth. The Poems*. 2 volumes. Harmondsworth: Penguin.

Hayes, Bruce 1983, 'A Grid-based Theory of English Meter'. *Linguistic Inquiry* 14(3): 395–420.

1988, 'Metrics and Phonological Theory'. In Newmeyer, F. (ed.), *Linguistics: the Cambridge Survey*, II: 220–49. Cambridge: Cambridge University Press.

1989, 'The Prosodic Hierarchy in Meter'. In Kiparsky, Paul and Youmans, G. (eds.) 1989, *Phonetics and Phonology 1: Rhythm and Meter*, pp. 201–60. San Diego, CA: Academic Press.

2000, 'Faithfulness and Componentiality in Metrics'. Unpublished typescript, UCLA.

Hayes, Bruce and MacEachern, Margaret 1998, 'Quatrain Form in English Folk Verse'. *Language* 74:473–507.

Heath-Stubbs, John 1969, *The Ode*. Oxford: Oxford University Press.

Hewitt, H. Marmaduke and Beach, George 1891, *A Manual of our Mother Tongue*. Volume II. London: W. H. Allen & Co.

Hill, George Birkbeck (ed.) 1905, *Samuel Johnson. Lives of the English Poets*. 3 volumes. Oxford: Clarendon Press.

Hobbes, Thomas 1650, *Answer to Davenants Preface to Gondibert*. In Spingarn, *Critical Essays of the Seventeenth Century*, II:54–67.

Hodges, John C. (ed.) 1964, *William Congreve. Letters & Documents*. London: Macmillan.

Hollander, John 1975, *Vision and Resonance. Two Senses of Poetic Form*. New York: Oxford University Press.

Holtman, A. 1996, 'A Generative Theory of Rhyme: an Optimality Approach'. PhD thesis, Utrecht University.

Hopper, P. J. and Thompson, S. A. 1980, 'Transitivity in Grammar and Discourse'. *Language* 56(1):251–99.

Housman, A. E. 1933, *The Name and Nature of Poetry*. Cambridge: Cambridge University Press.

Hudak, Thomas John 1990, *The Indigenization of Pali Meters in Thai Poetry*. Athens: Ohio University Center for International Studies.

Hymes, Dell 1981, *'In vain I tried to tell you'. Essays in Native American Ethnopoetics*. Philadelphia: University of Pennsylvania Press.

   1992, 'Use all there is to use'. In Swann, B. (ed.), *On the Translation of Native American literatures*, pp. 83–124. Washington: Smithsonian Institution Press.

Idsardi, W. 1992, 'The computation of stress'. PhD dissertation, MIT.

Ing, Catherine 1951, *Elizabethan Lyrics. A Study in the Development of English Metres and Their Relation to Poetic Effect*. London: Chatto and Windus.

Jakobson, Roman 1960, 'Closing Statement: Linguistics and Poetics'. In Sebeok, T. (ed.), *Style in Language*, pp. 350–77. Cambridge MA: MIT Press.

   1966, 'Slavic Epic Verse. Studies in Comparative Metrics'. In Jakobson, R., *Selected Writings IV. Slavic Epic Studies*, pp. 414–63. The Hague: Mouton.

   1987, 'Grammatical Parallelism and its Russian Facet'. In Pomorska, K. and Rudy, S. (eds.), *Roman Jakobson. Language in Literature*, pp. 145–79. Cambridge MA: Harvard University Press.

Jay, Peter and Lewis, Caroline 1996, *Sappho through English Poetry*. London: Anvil Press Poetry.

Johnson, Paula 1972, *Form and Transformation in Music and Poetry of the English Renaissance*. New Haven: Yale University Press.

Jones, Emrys (ed.) 1964, *Henry Howard Earl of Surrey. Poems*. Oxford: Oxford University Press.

   1991, *The New Oxford Book of Sixteenth Century Verse*. Oxford: Oxford University Press.

Jump, John D. 1974, *The Ode*. London: Methuen.

Karlin, Daniel (ed.) 1997, *The Penguin Book of Victorian Verse*. Harmondsworth: Penguin.

Kayne, Richard S. 1994, *The Antisymmetry of Syntax*. Cambridge, MA: MIT Press.

Keith, A. B. 1920, *A History of Sanskrit Literature*. London: Oxford University Press.

Kennedy, Judith M. (ed.) 1989, *Barnabe Googe. Eclogues, Epitaphs, and Sonnets.* Toronto: University of Toronto Press.

King James VI 1584, *Ane Schort Treatise conteining some Reulis and Cautelis to be obseruit and eschewit in Scottis Poesie.* In Smith 1904, *Elizabethan Critical Essays,* I:208–25.

Kinsley, J. (ed.) 1958, *The Poems of John Dryden.* 4 volumes. Oxford: Clarendon Press.

Kiparsky, Paul 1968, 'Metrics and Morphophonemics in the Kalevala'. In Gribble, C. (ed.), *Studies Presented to Professor Roman Jakobson by his Students,* pp. 137–48. Cambridge, MA: Slavica. Anthologised in Freeman 1970, *Linguistics and Literary Style,* pp. 165–82.

1972, 'Metrics and Morphophonemics in the Rigveda'. In Brame, Michael (ed.), *Contributions to Generative Phonology,* pp. 171–200. Austin: University of Texas Press.

1975, 'Stress, Syntax, and Meter'. *Language* 51:567–616.

1977, 'The Rhythmic Structure of English Verse'. *Linguistic Inquiry* 8:189–247.

Kiparsky, Paul and Youmans, G. (eds.) 1989, *Phonetics and Phonology 1: Rhythm and Meter.* San Diego, CA: Academic Press.

Knott, E. 1957, *An Introduction to Irish Syllabic Poetry of the Period 1200–1600.* 2nd edition. Dublin: Dublin Institute for Advanced Studies.

Krupat, Arnold 1979, *The Voice in the Margin. Native American Literature and the Canon.* Berkeley: University of California Press.

Labov, William 1972, *Language in the Inner City. Studies in the Black English Vernacular.* Philadelphia: University of Pennsylvania Press.

1997, 'Some Further Steps in Narrative Analysis.' In Bamberg 1997, *Oral Versions of Personal Experience,* pp. 395–415.

Labov, William and Waletzky, J. 1967, 'Narrative Analysis: Oral Versions of Personal Experience'. In Helm, J. (ed.), *Essays on the Verbal and Visual Arts. Proceedings of the 1966 Annual Spring Meeting of the American Ethnological Society,* pp. 12–44. Seattle: University of Washington Press. Reprinted in Bamberg 1997, *Oral Versions of Personal Experience,* pp. 3–38.

Laing, M. 1805, *The Poems of Ossian, &c. Containing the Poetical Works of James Macpherson, Esq. in Prose and Rhyme: with Notes and Illustrations by Malcolm Laing, Esq.* 2 volumes. Edinburgh: Archibald Constable and Co.

Latham, Agnes M. C. (ed.) 1951, *The Poems of Sir Walter Ralegh.* London: Routledge and Kegan Paul.

Lemon, Lee T. and Reis, Marion J. (eds.) 1965, *Russian Formalist Criticism. Four Essays.* Lincoln: University of Nebraska Press.

Lennard, John 1991, *But I Digress. The Exploitation of Parentheses in English Printed Verse.* Oxford: Clarendon Press.

Levin, Samuel R. 1971, 'The Conventions of Poetry.' In Chatman, Seymour (ed.), *Literary Style: A Symposium,* pp. 177–93. London: Oxford University Press.

Longacre, R. E. 1995, 'Left Shifts in Strongly VSO Languages'. In Downing, P. and Noonan, M. (eds.), *Word Order in Discourse,* pp. 331–54. Amsterdam: John Benjamins.

Lonsdale, Roger (ed.) 1977, *Gray and Collins. Poetical Works.* Oxford: Oxford University Press.

1987, *The New Oxford Book of Eighteenth Century Verse.* Oxford: Oxford University Press.

MacMahon, Barbara 1995, 'The Freudian Slip Revisited: a Case of Mistaken Identity in *Finnegans Wake*'. *Language & Communication* 15(4):289–328.

2001, 'Relevance Theory and the Use of Voice in Poetry'. *Belgian Journal of Linguistics* 15 (forthcoming).

Macpherson, James 1760, *Fragments of Ancient Poetry*. 2nd edition. Facsimile edition, Edinburgh: James Thin, 1970.

Marotti, Arthur F. 1995, *Manuscript, Print, and the English Renaissance Lyric*. Ithaca, NY: Cornell University Press.

Mason, John 1749, *An Essay on the Power of Numbers*. Printed by James Waugh for M. Cooper, reprinted Menston, Yorkshire: Scolar Press, 1967.

Maxwell, J. C. (ed.) 1986, *Wordsworth, The Prelude: a Parallel Text*. Harmondsworth: Penguin.

McGann, J. (ed.) 1981, *Lord Byron. The Poetical Works*. 6 volumes. Oxford: Clarendon Press.

Morris–Jones, J. 1980, *Cerdd Dafod*. Cardiff: Gwasg Prifysgol Cymru.

Mulhauser, F. L. (ed.) 1974, *The Poems of Arthur Hugh Clough*. Oxford: Clarendon Press.

Mullick, Ila 1974, *The Poetry of Thomas Randolph*. Bombay: Nirmala Sadanand Publishers.

Neijt, Anneke 1993, 'Stress Shift in Dutch Hexameters'. in Drijkoningen, F. and Hengeveld, K. (eds.), *Linguistics in the Netherlands 1993*, pp. 93–104. Amsterdam: John Benjamins.

Nespor, M. and Vogel, I. 1986, *Prosodic Phonology*. Dordrecht: Foris.

Newbolt, Henry 1912, 'A New Study of English Poetry'. *English Review* 10: 657–72.

Newton, Robert P. 1975, 'Trochaic and Iambic'. *Language and Style* 8: 127–56.

Oliphant, E. H. C. 1932, 'Sonnet Structure: An Analysis'. *Philological Quarterly* 11: 135–48.

Orgel, Stephen (ed.) 1971, *Christopher Marlowe. The Complete Poems and Translations*. London: Penguin.

Peterson, Carole and McCabe, Alyssa 1997, 'Extending Labov and Waletzky'. In Bamberg 1997, *Oral Versions of Personal Experience*, pp. 251–8.

Pettigrew, John (ed.) 1981, *Robert Browning. The Poems*. 2 volumes. Harmondsworth: Penguin.

Pilkington, Adrian 1992, 'Poetic Effects'. *Lingua* 87:29–51.

2000, *Poetic Effects. A Relevance Theory Perspective*. Amsterdam: John Benjamins.

Poppe, N. 1958, 'Der Parallelismus in der epischen Dichtung der Mongolen'. *Ural-Altaische Jahrbücher* 30:195–228.

Prince, A. 1989, 'Metrical Forms'. In Kiparsky, Paul and Youmans, G. (eds.), *Phonetics and Phonology 1. Rhythm and Meter*, pp. 45–80. San Diego, CA: Academic Press.

Propp, V. 1968, *Morphology of the Folktale*. 2nd edition. Austin: University of Texas Press.

Puttenham, George 1589, *The Arte of English Poesie*. In Smith 1904, *Elizabethan Critical Essays*, II: 1–193.

Rabinow, Paul (ed.) 1986, *The Foucault Reader*. Harmondsworth: Penguin.

Rarick, Louise 1974, 'Ten-Syllable Lines in English Poetry'. *Neuphilologische Mitteilungen* 75:66–73.

Raven, D. S. 1965, *Latin Metre*. London: Faber & Faber.

Rice, C. 1996, 'Generative Metrics'. *GLOT International* 2(7):3–7.

Rice, John 1765, *An Introduction to the Art of Reading with Energy and Propriety*. London: Tonson, J. and R., reprinted Menston, Yorkshire: Scholar Press, 1969.

Ricks, C. (ed.) 1969, *The Poems of Tennyson*. London: Longman.

Roper, D. (ed.) 1995, *The Poems of Emily Brontë*. Oxford: Clarendon Press.

Rothenberg, Jerome and Joris, Pierre 1995, *Poems for the Millennium*. 2 volumes. Berkeley: University of California Press.

Rowlands, Eurys 1979, 'Cynghanedd, Metre, Prosody'. In Jarman, A. O. H and Hughes, G. R. (eds.) *A Guide to Welsh Literature Volume 2*, pp. 202–17. Llandybïe, Dyfed: Christopher Jones.

Rubin, David C. 1995, *Memory in Oral Traditions*. Oxford: Oxford University Press.

Russom, G. 1987, *Old English Meter and Linguistic Theory*. Cambridge: Cambridge University Press.

Schokkenbroek, Christina 1999, 'News Stories. Structure, time and evaluation'. *Time and Society* 8(1):59–98.

Sheridan, Thomas 1781, *A Rhetorical Grammar of the English Language*. Dublin, reprinted Menston, Yorkshire: Scolar Press, 1969.

Smith, Barbara Herrnstein 1968, *Poetic Closure. A Study of How Poems End*. Chicago: University of Chicago Press.

Smith, G. Gregory (ed.) 1904, *Elizabethan Critical Essays*. 2 volumes. Oxford: Oxford University Press.

Spengemann, William C., with Roberts, Jessica F. (eds.) 1996, *Nineteenth-Century American Poetry*. Harmondsworth: Penguin.

Sperber, Dan 1985, *On Anthropological Knowledge*. Cambridge: Cambridge University Press.

Sperber, Dan and Wilson, Deirdre 1986, 2nd edition 1995, *Relevance: Communication and Cognition*. Oxford: Blackwell.

Spiller, Michael R. G. 1992, *The Development of the Sonnet. An Introduction*. London: Routledge.

Spingarn, J. E. (ed.) 1957, *Critical Essays of the Seventeenth Century*. 3 volumes. Bloomington: Indiana University Press.

Sprat, Thomas 1668, *Account of the Life and Writings of Abraham Cowley*. In Spingarn, *Critical Essays of the Seventeenth Century*, II:119–46.

Stevenson, R. L. 1885, 'On Style in Literature: its Technical Elements'. *Contemporary Review* 47:548–61.

Stewart, George R., Jr. 1924, 'A Method Toward the Study of Dipodic Verse'. *PMLA* 39:979–89.

Tarlinskaja, Marina 1976, *English Verse. Theory and History*. The Hague: Mouton.

Taylor, Dennis 1988, *Hardy's Metres and Victorian Prosody. With a Metrical Appendix of Hardy's Stanza Forms*. Oxford: Oxford University Press.

Tedlock, D. 1978, *Finding the Center. Narrative Poetry of the Zuni Indians*. Lincoln: University of Nebraska Press.

   1983, *The Spoken Word and the Work of Interpretation*. Philadelphia: University of Pennsylvania Press.

Terhune, A. K. and Terhune, A. B. 1980, *The Letters of Edward Fitzgerald. Volume II 1851–1866*. Princeton: Princeton University Press.

Thompson, John 1961, *The Founding of English Metre*. London: Routledge and Kegan Paul.

Treip, Mindele 1970, *Milton's Punctuation and Changing English Usage 1582–1676*. London: Methuen.

Unger, Christoph 2001, 'On the Cognitive Role of Genre: a Relevance-Theoretic Perspective'. PhD Thesis, University of London.

Venturi, Robert 1977, *Complexity and Contradiction in Architecture*. London: Architectural Press.

Walker, John 1781, *Elements of Elocution. Being the Substance of a Course of Lectures on the Art of Reading*. London.

    1785, *A Rhetorical Grammar, or Course of Lessons in Elocution*. London, facsimile edition, Menston, Yorkshire: Scolar Press, 1971.

Watts, Isaac 1721, *The Art of Reading and Writing English*. London: Clark, John, Matthews, Em. and Ford, Richard, reprinted Menston, Yorkshire: Scolar Press, 1972.

Webbe, William 1585, *A Discourse of English Poetrie*. In Smith 1904, *Elizabethan Critical Essays*, I:226–302.

Webster, Noah 1789, *Dissertations on the English Language*. Boston: Isiah Thomas & Co., facsimile edition, Menston, Yorkshire: Scolar Press, 1967.

Wilcox, Stewart C. 1950, 'The Prosodic Structure of "Ode to the West Wind"'. *Notes & Queries* 195:77–8.

Williams, G. 1953, *An Introduction to Welsh Poetry. From the Beginnings to the Sixteenth Century*. London: Faber.

Williams, Harold (ed.) 1958, *The Poems of Jonathan Swift*. 3 volumes. Oxford: Clarendon Press.

Williams, Raymond 1976, *Keywords: A Vocabulary of Culture and Society*. London: Fontana.

Wilson, Deirdre and Sperber, Dan 1992, 'On Verbal Irony'. *Lingua* 87:53–76.

Wimsatt, W. K. Jr. and Monroe, C. Beardsley 1959, 'The Concept of Meter: An Exercise in Abstraction'. *PMLA* 74: 585–98.

Woodbury, A. C. 1987, 'Rhetorical Structure in a Central Alaskan Yupik Eskimo Traditional Narrative'. In Sherzer, J. and Woodbury, A. C. (eds.), *Native American Discourse. Poetics and Rhetoric*, pp. 176–239. Cambridge: Cambridge University Press.

Wright, David (ed.) 1968, *The Penguin Book of English Romantic Verse*. Harmondsworth: Penguin.

Youmans, G. 1988, 'Iambic Pentameter: Statistics or Generative Grammar?' *Language and Style* 19:388–404.

    1989, 'Milton's Meter'. In Kiparsky, Paul and Youmans, G. (eds.), *Phonetics and Phonology 1: Rhythm and Meter*, pp. 341–79. San Diego, CA: Academic Press.

Subject index